The Sunflower

T0294421

THE
SUNFLOWER

Conforming the Will of Man to the Will of God

by
St John of Tobolsk

Translated from the Russian
by Nicholas Kotar

Edited by Holy Trinity Monastery

Holy Trinity Publications
The Printshop of St Job of Pochaev
Holy Trinity Monastery
Jordanville, New York
2018

Printed with the blessing of His Eminence,
Metropolitan Hilarion First Hierarch
of the Russian Orthodox Church Outside of Russia

The Sunflower: Conforming the Will of Man to the
Will of God © 2018 Holy Trinity Monastery

Translated from the Russian edition published
by The Printshop of the Kiev Caves Dormition Lavra, 1890

PRINTSHOP OF
SAINT JOB OF POCHAEV

An imprint of

HOLY TRINITY PUBLICATIONS
Holy Trinity Monastery
Jordanville, New York 13361-0036
www.holytrinitypublications.com

ISBN: 978-0-88465-460-5 (paperback)
ISBN: 978-0-88465-469-8 (ePub)
ISBN: 978-0-88465-470-4 (Mobipocket)

Library of Congress Control Number 2018942654

Cover Design: James Bozeman

Scripture passages taken from the New King James Version.
Copyright © 1982 by Thomas Nelson, Inc. Used by permission.
Psalms taken from A Psalter for Prayer, trans. David James
(Jordanville, N.Y.: Holy Trinity Publications, 2011).
Old Testament and Deuterocanonical passages taken
from the Orthodox Study Bible.
Copyright © 2008 by Thomas Nelson, Inc. Used by permission.

CONTENTS

EDITOR'S PREFACE

Why does God, whom we know to be all-good, permit suffering and trials in our life, the lives of those we love, and indeed that of the whole creation? This is certainly not a new question: relatively early in the very first book of the Bible the Lord God speaks to His servant Abraham of His intention to judge the cities of Sodom and Gomorrah for their gross wickedness. Abraham intercedes before God for the cities and asks, "Shall not the Judge of all the earth do right?" (Gen 18:25). For Abraham this is both a question and a confession of his faith in God.

The book you have in your hand grapples with this question in a practical manner. It addresses how we should live as faithful believers, and thus it is far from an abstract intellectual discussion. It is truly theology—that is, the knowledge of God acquired by bringing our life into conformity to His will. The Saviour Himself taught His disciples during His sojourn on earth "I have come down from heaven, not to do My own will, but the will of Him who sent Me" (John 6:38). This volume likewise exhorts us to bring our will in line with the will of God or as the Apostle Paul states it: "Let this mind be in you which was also in Christ Jesus…" (Phil 2:5).

It seems appropriate to offer a brief synopsis of the historical journey of this work to the form in which it is presented here. This journey in some way mirrors that of the more widely known work *Unseen Warfare*, written by the Roman Catholic priest Lorenzo Scupoli and first published in Venice in 1589 with the title *The Spiritual Combat*. Some two centuries later it was translated into Greek and edited for the benefit of Orthodox Christian readers by St Nicodemus of the Holy Mountain who also added to and otherwise amended the original text of Scupoli. Almost a century after this, the sainted Russian Orthodox Bishop Theophan the Recluse translated St Nicodemus's text into Russian and further adapted the text for his own time and place.

ix

In not dissimilar fashion this English language work we have entitled *The Sunflower* has evolved from an early seventeenth-century book entitled *Heliotropium* authored by Jeremias Drexelius (1581–1638), a German Roman Catholic Jesuit priest and convert from Lutheranism. At the beginning of the following century it was published in a somewhat amended form, but still in Latin, by St John of Tobolsk (1651–1715), the Orthodox Archbishop of Chernigov and ancestor according to the flesh of the more widely known St John of Shanghai and San Francisco. One year prior to his death the saint was able to publish the first Slavonic language edition. In 1890 an edition was published in Russian by the print shop of the Kiev Dormition Lavra, the same monastery where St John of Tobolsk had received his monastic tonsure.

The English language edition presented here for the first time was translated from the 1890 Kiev text by Dn Nicholas Kotar and then further amended by the editorial team of the Holy Trinity Monastery. These amendments were made to correct inaccuracies in the citation of scriptural texts and certain other historical details. The 1890 edition was also adapted to make the text more suitable for our own time and place, and to avoid anything that might be thought to lead to "the confusion of the faithful," as a contemporary Greek priest once put it. While we have tried with the greatest care to provide full citations for the scriptural quotations throughout the text, we have not been able to do the same for those from the Fathers. If God so wills, and time permits, we hope that this defect might be remedied in a subsequent edition.

Holy Trinity Monastery, Paschaltide 2018

PART 1

DISCERNING THE WILL OF GOD

 CHAPTER 1

Discerning the Will of God and Conforming to It

I

The beginning of all wisdom, given to us by the most exalted Divine Wisdom, our Lord Jesus Christ, is our faithful fashioning of ourselves—in all actions and words—to the will of God. Our Saviour taught us this truth during His earthly life by word and deed and by preaching and parable. His own life was a model of the Christian life, the only life worthy of emulation.

In order to explain this need to conform our will to His, the Holy Fathers offer two fundamental truths:

1. Our success in the Christian life depends entirely on how well we submit our will to the will of God. The more complete our submission to the divine will, the more fruitful and successful our spiritual life will be. Everyone knows that a Christian's perfection is founded on love for God and fellow man. All the books of the Holy Scriptures are filled with proof of this: "'You shall love the Lord your God with all your heart, with all your soul, and with all your mind'. This is the first and great commandment. And the second is like it: 'You shall love your neighbor as yourself'. On these two commandments hang all the Law and the Prophets" (Matthew 22:37–40). "And now abide faith, hope, love, these three; but the greatest of these is love" (1 Corinthians 13:13). "But above all these things put on love, which is the bond of perfection" (Colossians 3:14).

In a word, the fulfillment of God's Law depends entirely on our love for God and for every human being. Love must be the foundation of all our actions. This is the fashioning of the will of man to the will of God. Whatever God wants, I want as well. Whatever God does not want, I do not want either. There is nothing more powerful than such love! This is the opinion of Blessed Jerome[1] and other wise Fathers.

2. Nothing (except sin) occurs without God's will. Chance (*fortuna,* ἡ τυχή)—whether good or evil—is not something real. It is merely the dreamy reverie of pagans, who imagine, in their ignorance, a certain divinity named Fortune, who has alleged power to bring happiness or misfortune in the lives of people or even entire nations. Blessed Augustine, mocking the ignorance of the pagans, asked them, "For what reason is your goddess Fortune sometimes good, sometimes evil? Maybe she stops being a goddess when she is angry, turning instead into a hateful demon?"[2] Christian wisdom completely rejects such a divinity. Good and evil, life and death, poverty and wealth—all these depend exclusively on the Lord. This is obvious and is self-evident in the Holy Scriptures.

II

Everything in the world, even that which appears to be evil (except sin), occurs by the will of God. Theologians explain this in the following manner. The beginning of all evil is sin. Each sin consists of (1) a cause (*causa,* αἰτία) and (2) its necessary consequences, which God corrects by warnings, chastisements, and eventually death. The cause of sin is the self-will of a proud sinner; punishment for sin in general, being a bitter consequence of sin's cause, occurs by the will of God solely for sin's correction (chastisement) or elimination (death).

Thus, if we remove the cause of sin (self-will) from our understanding of sin, we will clearly see that not even one of its bitter or evil consequences occurs without God's permission. Both the bitterness of personal sin and natural disasters—hunger, drought, storms at sea, and other events that do not occur directly as a result of man's sin—all occur by the will of God. All human misfortunes and sorrows stem from God's will for the accomplishment of the righteous aims of divine providence; only sin is hateful to God (just as evil is hateful to good or lies are hateful to truth); however, God allows sin, lest He destroy humanity's free will. Therefore, this will of God that allows sin is also called divine economy or divine providence. Everything that we normally call evil (except sin, which is evil par excellence) occurs by the will of God.

This is a fundamental principle that must not be forgotten; for it is very wise, necessary, and pious to understand that every evil, sorrow, or misfortune is a salvific punishment sent by God for our improvement. However, it is not God who is the cause of the fault (i.e., our sin) that inexorably brings His just punishment in its wake. From this, we can make the following conclusion:

Since everything in the world occurs by God's command and will, it is our duty to accept everything that God sends to us without complaint, thereby fully submitting to His will. By doing this, we will conform our will to His divine will, never ascribing anything in the world to blind chance, as did the ancient pagans. Darkened by polytheism, they ascribed human prosperity either to special divinities or to blind chance. Their misfortune they ascribed to the ignorance and evil intentions of other people. These ignorant reveries of the ancients are entirely inappropriate for Christians and should be rejected outright. It is inexcusable to think in this way: this or that happened because this or that person came to hate me, or harmed me with slander or aspersions; everything would have been different if this or that person was well disposed toward me or if this or that person had spoken on my behalf. Such complaints are useless, unwise, and unhelpful. On the contrary, it is much better to accept all misfortunes with the words "This is the Lord's will." As we have already mentioned, everything—good and evil—occurs by the will of God.

III

Many delude themselves when they think that only natural disasters (floods, earthquakes, failed harvests, sinkholes, rising prices, harmful atmospheric conditions, epidemics, sudden death) occur by the will of God, since for the most part such misfortunes have no immediate relation to sins. Such delusional people imagine that the unfortunate consequences of human malfeasance (angry words, mockery, fraud, forgery, theft, robbery, insults by word or action, physical harm inflicted on others) occur without God's permission or will. Only human anger and fallen human will, they say, cause such evil. Therefore, not only in ancient times but even today we often hear complaints such as these: "The lack of food and other necessities of life are a result not of God's will but of greed among the people." Such complaints are typical of people who do not know and do not fear God. Such complaints are unworthy of a Christian and should be cast out into utter darkness.

Here is an example. A man who desires to deprive his neighbor of all property creeps up to a house in secret, unnoticed by anyone. He places flammable materials under the house, lights them, and creeps away just as secretly. Soon the house is on fire; the flame grows; the fires leap on the wind to ignite nearby buildings. People rush from all over to help put out the fire and protect adjacent buildings from damage. The arsonist is among the people ostensibly helping to put out the fire, but he has a different intention. Taking advantage of the confusion, he steals various things from the houses, apparently to save them from the fire. When in reality/actuality, he keeps them for himself.

All these actions of the arsonist, though they are the direct cause of the destruction of the victim's house and property, are no different from any natural disaster (if we do not consider the evil intention of the arsonist, but look at the damage in and of itself). They are from God in the same way as lightning that strikes a man or burns down a house, or a tornado that carries away a farmer's collected hay. In a sense, the arsonist is merely another form of a natural disaster. He can neither enter the house, nor leave it, nor light the house on fire without God's permission.

However, the arsonist's will is evil, his intention sinful. The reason for this evil is not God, but the free will of the arsonist. This is his sin, even if God allowed him to accomplish his evil intention, for of course God could have prevented the arsonist if it were His will. The Lord did not stop the arsonist, but allowed the evil to happen, according to His righteous judgment. The reasons why God allows such things to happen will be more fully considered in subsequent sections.

IV

As for accidental physical injuries, they also have the same cause as deliberate physical injury inflicted by a criminal. Both are allowed by God, as we will see from the following example.

Let us imagine that someone injures his leg. He cannot walk properly; although he tries to walk, it is difficult for him. He has a natural desire to walk, but he cannot, not because he desired to inflict an injury on himself, but because this injury was an accident. However, the comparison between accidental injury and physical assault cannot be carried further than this. The essential difference between them is that the accidental injury occurs exclusively by God's permission, whereas a premeditated assault is not the work of God's will (for it is the creation of a perverted self-will, typical of a fallen reasoning creature, something that God merely allows, but does not will). God does not merely prohibit sinful action, but He also does not help us do what our fallen will demands, neither does He sanction our departure from the way of righteousness and His Law.

God is not the source of our moral fall—the Fall is the only true evil in the world—and by definition cannot be. "His eye is too pure to see evil, and You are not able to look upon affliction" (Habakkuk 1:13). "Thou hast loved righteousness, and hated iniquity" (Psalm 44:8). Therefore, it is undoubtedly true that all calamities that result from secondary causes—whether human or not—occur by the will of God. They are sent down by His mighty right hand, His foresight, and His providence.

Beloved reader, it is God Who directs His hand to your chastisement. God prompts the tongue of the one who ridicules or slanders you. God gave the devil authority to overthrow you. God Himself, by the word of Prophet Isaiah, confirms this, saying, "For I am the Lord God. There is no God besides Me, and you have not known Me ... I am He who prepared light and made darkness, who makes peace and creates troublesome things. I am the Lord God who does all these things" (Isaiah 45:5, 7). The Prophet Amos expresses it even more vividly: "If evil should be in a city, has not the Lord brought it?" (Amos 3:6). It is as if he were saying, "There is not a single calamity that can occur without God's will, even if the evil intention of men provides the inspiration, means, and strength to accomplish it."

Thus God, desiring to punish King David for his sins of adultery with Bathsheba and Uriah's murder, allowed Absalom's incestuous union with his stepmother. God said, through the Prophet Nathan, "Behold, I will raise up adversity against you from your own house, and I will take your wives before your eyes, and give them to your neighbor [Absalom] and he shall lie with your wives in the sunlight. For you did it secretly, but I will do this before all Israel in the sunlight" (2 Kingdoms 12:11–12).

Blessed Augustine expressed the same thought beautifully, saying, "Thus God corrects the righteous through the unrighteous." At the same time, God's justice often uses unrighteous kings and evil princes as instruments to teach the righteous patience and to punish the evil for their crimes and transgressions. We see many such examples in ancient times, when God revealed His will through the evil-intentioned strivings and actions of unrighteous people, with the purpose of accomplishing His righteous judgments over those who are guilty before Him. As a loving father punishes his children with a switch for misbehaving—but later, seeing their improvement, caresses them and throws the switch into the fire—God punishes people who pervert their morality through fallen acts and falseness. Here is an example.

God, through the Prophet Isaiah, threatened the depraved nation of Israel with destruction and the utter desolation of Palestine by the Assyrians, saying,

Woe to the Assyrians! The rod of My anger and wrath are in their hands. I will send My wrath against a lawless nation; and I will order My people to seize spoils and plunder, to trample down their cities, and turn them into dust. However, he does not think in the same way, nor does he consider the same thing in his soul; but his heart will change, so as to utterly destroy many nations. (Isaiah 10:5–7)

Here God clearly shows that the Assyrians perform His will, though they do not know it. God calls them the instruments of wrath and the rod of His anger against the lawlessness of the Israelites. Therefore, He ascribes the punishment to Himself: "I send them," God says, "to take spoils from Israel and to humble those who do not submit to Me, those who raise themselves up in their own estimation. They have rejected their faith in the One God, and they have preferred the pagan idols with their mad and cruel rites and sacrifices."

As for the King of Assyria, his own thoughts (while fulfilling the will of God) are quite different. He is sure that he is doing all this according to his own will, and he will not listen to reason, but will rush forward to kill and annihilate the nations, but in the end his actions serve the will of God. However, when the war against Assyria has the needed effect and inspires the repentance of Israel, then woe to that rod, woe to the Assyrian, for all of them, like a useless switch, will be thrown into the fire. We must assess in the same light all righteous chastisement allowed by God for our sins.

The Roman Emperor Titus, while walking around the walls during the siege of Jerusalem, saw pits full of dead and mutilated bodies. He sighed heavily and, raising his hands and eyes to heaven, said, "Merciful God! This is not my doing!"[3]

V

Some people might ask, "If it is true that all calamities come by the will of God, then is it not pointless to oppose it?" Is it not wrong to take medicines for sickness? Why should we raise armies against an invading force? Why do we not willingly give him the keys to our fortresses, why do we not eagerly welcome him into our homeland for our own destruction? Why do we not emulate the Blessed Lupus of Troyes,[4] who welcomed Attila the Hun with the following words: "I greet you Attila, scourge of God!"?

In answer, the Apostle Paul says, "[Do] not think [of such things] more highly than [you] ought to think, but think soberly" (Romans 12:3). In other words, do not reason drawing upon the categories of the fallen world, but rather with humble understanding being always cognizant of the higher order of divine providence. In this spirit of sobriety, let us try to resolve these seeming contradictions. It is obvious that wars and other such calamities occur with the will of God. However, this does not mean that we must not arm ourselves against enemies or not take medicine to heal our illnesses, considering such things to be contrary to the will of God. Scholastic theologians distinguish two types of divine will—*voluntas signi*, or the will of God according to His sign, and *voluntas benepaciti*, or the will of God according to His good pleasure. The first is not important for our discussion; we have already spoken enough of it. However, while *voluntas benepaciti* continues in this world, we cannot fully know in advance God's intention for us; we will only fully understand it afterward.

Let us try to explain this using the example of physical illness. No matter what the direct natural cause of the illness, there is no doubt that the sickness occurs by the will of God. However, the sick man has no idea how long God intends the sickness to continue, and so it is not contrary to God's will to use whatever means necessary to heal the sickness. If, after various medicines, he remains ill, then he can be sure that it is God's will that he patiently endure a prolonged and serious illness.

Let every sick person humbly consider his disease in such a light. Let him remember that is it pleasing to God to keep him in his bed of sickness. Still, the sick man does not know whether or not it is God's good intention for this particular sickness to be fatal; therefore, he can seek any means of healing or relief or consolation without it being considered sinful. To prove the blamelessness of seeking medical help: if God does not will to restore the sick man to health, He can easily prevent any medicines from being effective.

Enemies and wars should be considered in a similar light. God allowed enemies to conquer Israel many times in order to prevent that nation's disorderly conduct and forgetfulness of their God. As long as the Israelites accepted God's hand in these invasions, they fought their invaders off. However, when Jeremiah told them that it was God's will for them to submit to Nebuchadnezzar, they refused, and were sorely punished for it.[5] Similarly, if a fire cannot be put out—despite all the efforts of the firemen—then it is obvious that God has judged that this house must burn, but not arbitrarily. Rather, God allows such calamities to test the patience of His friends and to punish His enemies. All other misfortunes and misadventures can be judged likewise.

On the other hand, the permissibility of self-preservation is proven also with examples from everyday life. When a father wants to see his son's success in the art of swordplay, he gives him a wooden sword and tells him to attack. This is not a case of the son assaulting his father, but a sparring between equals. In the same way, whoever tries to put out the fire or defeat his enemy or heal a sickness does not oppose the will of God chastising us for our sins, but merely sets himself against the cause of his misfortune (i.e., sin), which is abhorrent to God. A house could be burned by a hateful or greedy man, for example. All such causes are sinful and reprehensible, and fighting them is never a sin. Similarly, treating illnesses does not oppose the will of God, but rather opposes human suffering, for there is hardly any disease that is not the direct result of lack of restraint (e.g., overeating, drunkenness, untidiness). Consequently, the physician opposes not God, but the causes of sickness.

Equally so, whoever fights an invader with weapons opposes not God, but those who unjustly invade his homeland. In all similar cases, protecting oneself and one's own is even required, unless it is revealed that such self-defense is not pleasing to God.

VI

Is it so strange that divine providence uses evil people as instruments to fulfill God's holy will? Even the demons fulfill the will of God. According to St Gregory the Great,[6] this is done by the miraculous design of God's mercy. The same weapon that the hateful enemy uses to destroy us is used by our merciful Creator for our correction, in order to bring us back to life.

The following is written concerning King Saul: "But the Spirit of the Lord departed from Saul, and a distressing spirit from the LORD troubled him" (1 Kingdoms 16:14, LXX). How can we make sense of this phrase: "an evil spirit from the Lord"? If it is an evil spirit, it is not a spirit of God, whereas if it is God's spirit, it is not evil. However, these passages are self-explanatory. This spirit is called evil because the perverted desire of Saul's heart tormented and choked him. It is called God's spirit because God allowed the spirit to enter him as a punishment for Saul's sins.

In order to understand difficult passages such as these in the Holy Scriptures, we offer Blessed Augustine's explanation of the Biblical phrase "those that are true of heart" (Psalm 31:11). What is this "truth of the heart"? Blessed Augustine wrote, "Those that are true of heart are those who do not oppose God." Beloved reader, consider thoroughly the meaning of this expression "true of heart." However, in order to do this, it is necessary to know the difference between a true and an evil heart. Any person who suffers innocently, yet bears his sufferings patiently—whether they be mockery, sorrows, labors, reproaches—because he believes that this is pleasing to God, is like Job, who uttered nothing unwise about God, knowing that God was not ignorant of what occurs in the world. Such a person knows that God punishes some people; while He forgives others and shows them mercy. Such a person is true of heart.

On the contrary, those of an obstinate, perverted, and ignorant heart are those who react to any loss or misfortune with these words: "We suffer unjustly, and this is God's fault, since it is His will that we suffer." Or, if they do not dare to openly ascribe injustice to God, they nonetheless do not believe in divine providence, and so deprive God of His rule over the cosmos. God is incapable of doing wrong, they say,

> But it is still unfair that I suffer, no one knows how much! I know that I am sinful, but to tell you the truth there are people much worse than I, and yet they enjoy life while I suffer. It is not fair that those who are worse than I live in fullness of joy and pleasure, while I, though I do not sin or sin only a little bit, live in terrible sorrow and am subject to constant attacks. This is an obvious injustice; I know well that God cannot be unjust, yet injustice exists in the world. Therefore, I conclude that God does not direct the works of men, and His providence does not rule over us.

Those who are "untruthful of heart," who have perverted hearts, may make any of the three false assumptions:

1. There is no God.
2. If there is a God, He is unjust, since injustice in the world is pleasing to Him, and He allows everything.
3. God does not direct the course of human events and has no care or solicitude for people's fates.

These three assumptions are false and are the greatest injustice against God. Whoever thanks God in all situations—whether in joys or misfortunes—has a true heart. Like Job, such a person says, "The Lord gave, and the Lord has taken away. Blessed be the name of the Lord."[7]

Beloved readers, notice that I have never yet said, "This misfortune is the devil's fault." No, everything that happens to you—whether good or evil—you ascribe to your God, knowing that the devil can do nothing if the Most High God, who has authority over life and death, did not allow him in some way to harass you for your correction. God punishes the unrighteous (the godless, those who transgress openly against their conscience, those who openly reject the truth, and so on). He chastises His children who have sinned, and you should not hope to be left without this chastisement, unless you want to be deprived of all heavenly inheritance: "For whom the Lord loves He chastens, and scourges every son whom He receives" (Hebrews 12:6).

Is this always the case? Did you expect you would be able to hide yourself from His punishment? Truly, God chastises everyone; no one is spared the rod. Let it be known that even the Only-Begotten Son of God, who never committed sin, did not spare Himself punishment, though He needed no correction.

According to Blessed Augustine, neither the devil nor any human being can accomplish any evil without God allowing it. In order to explain this, we will answer the following questions in the next chapter: What does God allow? In what manner does He allow it? For what reason does God allow evil?

 CHAPTER 2

Why Does God Allow Evil?

Many erroneously confuse God's permission with human inaction. Human inaction (and/or sanction) leads to a great many evils, physical and moral, especially when the condoner could have warned others of these evils or even prevented them outright.

If we consider God allowing evil to be the same thing, we make a grave error. For example, if I attack another person, considering my adversary to be a villain and the cause of all my misfortunes, or if I raise my voice or even my hand against him, I can delude myself into thinking that the all-knowing God is not looking at me, and though He has the opportunity to prevent my misfortunes, He allows them instead. In order to correct this criminal thought, we must consider God's permission of evil in three aspects: (1) what God allows; (2) why God allows it; (3) is God's will actively involved in the process?

In order to better understand this problem, we must distinguish two kinds of evils that God allows. The first kind is general misfortune, which includes insults, difficulties, sickness, mockery, dishonor, impoverishment, imprisonment, ailment, exile, and death. Strictly speaking, all these evils cannot be called "evil," but only bitter medicines sent to us by God for our spiritual healing.

The second category of evil, which is the only kind that is actually "evil," is our sinfulness (transgressions against God's commandments). God allows the first category of evils by His will either as punishment for the ungodly or as chastisement for sons and daughters. However, we cannot say that God *desires* the second kind of evil. God does not desire sin; He merely suffers it. Everything that exists in the world exists only by the desire and word of God, by whose will "all things were made … and without Him nothing was made that was made" (John 1:3). But sin is not something real; it is only a phantasm, an "anti-reality." It is a shadow of reality; it is nothing. Sin exists merely in word, the result of created, rational beings refusing to submit to God. Therefore, sin first occurred and continues to occur against God's will. It is not of God, though God may allow it.

The reason God allows sin is hidden in the mystery of the perfection and the sinlessness of God's direction of the world (His providence), a mystery that will remain unknown until the time of its revelation. God knows all futures in every detail, and He can easily prevent sin (so hateful to Him); however, He allows it, desiring to create good from evil, truth from lies, for the admonition and correction of people, to let them see the consequences of sin both for the sinner and for society.

Thus, we see the important distinction between "what God allows" and "what man allows." Either man cannot prevent evil at its inception by human means, or he allows it to occur through his own perversion. God, on the contrary, has the authority to prevent evil to cut off the fulfillment of an evil intention. God also has the will to allow this or that evil to occur.

A question arises: why did God allow sin to be committed in the first place? Or, in other words: what incites God to allow people to sin?

I

God's limitless goodness would have never allowed any evil to occur on earth if He could not create the greatest good from it, and if actions committed in anger could not work toward people's salvation. God allowed envy to flourish among Joseph's brothers, but for what good purpose? Was it not to save from starvation not merely Joseph's family but all of Egypt? God allowed unrighteous Saul to persecute meek David in all possible ways, but was this not for the benefit of David and the entire Kingdom of Israel?[8] Of course it was, and not only for them but for the whole human race, for through David came Christ our Saviour.

God allowed the unfairly slandered Daniel to be cast into a pit of angry lions.[9] For what? In order to raise him and his friends to the highest rungs of power and glory. But why must I limit myself with the countless examples from the Old Testament, when God even allowed the envious chief priests, Pharisees, and elders of the Jews to condemn the only-begotten Son of God, Jesus Christ, to death.[10] This permission of ultimate evil resulted in the greatest of all possible goods—the salvation of the human race. Thus, every permitted evil reveals the richness of God's glory and His goodness to every person and to all of mankind. Thus, He reveals His goodness, mercy, power, authority, fore-knowledge, and providence. Thus, His most exalted wisdom and righteousness illumine us through mysterious ways, inspiring many watchful people to a life of virtue and an increase of fruitful labors that are rewarded many times over both in this life and in the next.

O, how wondrous and majestic is the revelation of God's providence in His everyday permission of evil! It is not difficult to create good from good; but it is extremely unusual to turn evil into good. There is a Russian saying: "on a calm sea anyone can man the wheel." It is not great wisdom to direct a ship to land when there is a fair wind and a following sea, when the ship is fast and the sailors know their work well, and when land is already in sight. It is an entirely different matter when the sea is stormy, the ship is damaged, the waves loudly pound the deck, and water fills the interior of the ship; or when the night is dark, pirates have surrounded the ship, and there are only a few poorly armed sailors. In such a case, it takes a captain of uncommon courage to escape danger. The captain proves his wisdom and experience through action.

We see something similar in God's direction of the world. What seems at first glance to be God permitting evil is revealed to be God leading us to the best possible end by His unutterable wisdom and righteousness. By allowing criminal acts and misfortunes, God sometimes turns even the ungodly into His closest friends. God's providence directs everything to the best possible end, and so the evil intentions of an unrighteous man can turn to his eventual benefit and honor. Personal attacks and insults often strengthen us. The worst kinds of crimes confirm many in piety and virtue, turning them away from perdition. Therefore, many people who seem completely lost end up saved.

Joseph's chains and prison led to his honors and exalted position. The envy of his brothers gave him more than the goodwill of the entire world. Saul's anger gave David the crown of kingship. The lion's den led Daniel to even greater glory and honor, more than any earthly king. Christ entered paradise from the Cross together with the repentant thief, then ascended from the Mount of Olives to the heavens and sat on the right hand of God the Father.[11]

If God did not allow people to sin and if He did not correct the sinners and through that correction create good from evil, then we would hardly be able to recognize the righteousness of God that punishes the wicked and rewards the virtuous. But by allowing evil to occur, God helps us understand the need to recognize His providence. We realize how miraculous the paths of God are; that He is able to create countless good from the greatest of evils. Boethius (ca. 480–524 A.D.) had the following wise observation: "The order of God's dominion always achieves His goals, for if something goes awry from God's path, then it will merely take a different road to reach the intended goal, lest something seem unwise in the dictates of Providence."

It is difficult for man to understand the great and countless actions of our unlimited and all-powerful God with his limited mind, or to express them with his weak word. However, it is enough for us to be convinced that God is the creator and the provider of all that is. He directs everything by the best of ways to accomplish the greatest good. Therefore, if we prudently contemplate the many various phenomena of nature and human society, we will see nothing evil in essence, and nothing unwise in the order of the Most High's direction of the world.

II

In the beginning of this chapter, we asked the reader to consider God's will from three perspectives: (1) the will of God that allows evil, (2) the reason for God's permission of evil, and (3) His will that cooperates with that which is allowed. Let us explore the third perspective now.

The Pre-eternal God, even before the ages, foreordained everything that He would accomplish within time. He not only foresaw and knew the best of reasons for allowing evil's entry into the world, but He also had an ever-free will to either permit or actively cooperate in an action that He permitted. Theologians have expressed this truth vividly and clearly thus: God is the provider of all that truly is and exists (i.e., everything that is not delusive). Nothing in the world happens or comes to life without the aid of the first and Most High Cause (the will of the Triune God).

Therefore, if everything that God allows is foreordained by Him from before the ages as fair and proper, and if God Himself willed to appear invisibly to help accomplish the external aspects of the permitted phenomenon, then why do we utter sorrowful and empty imprecations at God and man alike? Why do we often slander and even reject God's providence and the fairest of God's reasons for allowing this or that unfortunate event? Would it not be easier to humbly ascribe all that is unpleasant or painful to God's will and His desire for our improvement?

We must know, first of all, that God allows everything for good reasons. Second, God's intention to allow this or that misfortune is always essentially good. It is completely useless to struggle against this intention. We are obliged to step back and correct ourselves by repenting before God for our sins. Whether the actions allowed by God are accomplished by an evil or a good will, they serve God in either case. No matter what the intention of the perpetrator, in the end everything is accomplished for the best.

Truly, all the saints ascribed everything that occurred in their lives—both pleasant and unpleasant—to the will and action of God, because they never paid any attention to the sins of others, but interpreted all the actions of other people as either God's gift or a punishment permitted by God for their sins. The saints reasoned thus: "the all-good God would never have allowed anything evil if He did not know that from this evil He would create countless great benefits for us." Blessed Augustine said, "God considered it best to transform evil into good instead of not allowing evil in the first place. This is because God, who is all-good, would never have allowed evil if He was not so all-powerful and good to make good from evil."

St Theophilus said, "Mystically God intervenes in our delusions and sins, not to praise them or to cooperate with them, but to hold them in abomination, to hate them, and to correct them. God produces much good from evil, as though transforming fire into water." And further, he writes,

> Every person who abuses us (in whatever manner) combines in himself, as it were, two aspects of action—one is conscious, the other not. By conscious action he desires to attack us with the intention of dishonoring our person or depriving us of our property, and so on (even if he does not always succeed in his intention). If he succeeds by God's permission, he becomes the unconscious instrument of God's hand that punishes or corrects our actions. Thus, he unwillingly serves God.

The following historical figures were such unconscious servants of God: Nebuchadnezzar, Attila the Hun, Totila the Ostrogoth, Tamerlaine, and other scourges of God, including Vespatian and Titus, who, for the sake of the glory and spread of the Roman empire, tried to annihilate all Jews, though they were not successful.

III

Allow me to ask you, beloved brother Christian, you who so often fill the very heavens and earth with your sorrowful complaining. Tell me, what bothers you most—the evil intent of the one who persecutes you, or merely his ability to harm you? Or it is the one and the other together? You answer: "I am bothered by both equally." In response, I will tell you that neither an evil intention nor the accomplishment of that intention can result in any harm to you. An evil intention is toothless without the ability to bring the intention to fruition, while that ability depends entirely on God's permission, that is, on God's will that is always just and holy. You know well that all authority is given by God, so why then are you sorrowful? Why do you complain about that person who insulted you, if he did nothing more than what God allowed him to do? After all, he would not have been able to do anything without God's will.

You answer, "But that person has dishonored me!"

Dishonored? For your sins God punishes you, teaches you to be longsuffering, or desires to increase your reward for an unjust accusation. Why do you consider yourself dishonored?

"I hate that evil man and his evil will!"

But why do you always pay so much attention to the actions of other people? I advise you to direct your gaze to God and to your own conscience, which is your impartial inner eye. Even though human will is often evil and unrighteous, what can it do to you? In what ways does it succeed against you? You are upset that he managed to harm you, not that he wanted to harm you. But who made it possible for him to harm you? Did this not happen according to God's will? And if it is according to the will and authority of God, then it must be for a just and holy reason, worthy of praise, not grief. Consequently, either stop your whining, or direct your complaints at God's permission, and impress on your soul the fact that God would never allow any evil to harm you, if it did not serve for your own benefit. You are the only one who can harm yourself!

Who can do us any evil if we become zealots of virtue? Blessed Augustine said it beautifully,

> Do not fear your enemy, for he is only as strong as God allows him to be. Fear only the One Who can do whatever He wishes, and Who never does anything unjust. Whatever He does do, it is righteous, but if anything seems to us unfair, then—if there is no doubt that it occurred through God's will—we must believe that it is just and true.

You might ask: "If someone kills an innocent person, did he act justly or unjustly?"

There is no doubt that his action is culpable and worthy of punishment.

"Why did God," you continue, "allow such an unjust action?"

My beloved, I cannot tell you God's intention or the reason He allowed such a crime, since the wisdom of God is not fully comprehensible to the human mind. I only insist on both facts—(1) murder is unjust and (2) this murder would not have occurred had God not allowed it to occur, through His incomprehensible, yet righteous intention. In other words, the killer acted wrongly and his actions demand restitution; however, God's permission of the crime is righteous and wise, even if we do not yet understand His reasons fully.

Blessed Augustine examines the crucifixion of Christ through a similar lens:

Judas, the unlawful traitor of Christ and the persecutors of Christ are all transgressors against the law. They are all unrighteous; they are all sinners; they have all perished. However, the Father did not spare His Son (that is, He allowed Him to be killed), but gave Him up for the salvation of us all. (This is the mystical reason that God allowed His Only-begotten Son to be killed by oath-breakers, though it is still an incomprehensible reason.)

My beloved, if you are able, consider every similar situation, separating one aspect from the other (that is, the action of the evildoer from the permission of God), and only then try to understand it. Fulfill all the vows you made to the Lord (Psalm 75:12). Then determine what the evildoer did to you, and what the Righteous One did to you. The first wanted to commit a premeditated evil, knowing it to be evil. The second allowed the act to be accomplished, and this permission is just because the will of the evil one is not done, while the permission of the Righteous One is glorified. Do not be amazed that God allowed evil to be done; He allows it by His just judgment, he allows it in the best possible measure, quantity, and weight. There is no unrighteousness in Him. All you must do is completely submit yourself to Him, become one with Him.

There is only one successful way to remain calm when harassed. Whenever someone offends or insults you, pay no attention to his anger; instead, turn to the just God Who allowed your adversary to offend you, and do not answer his evil with more evil. God allowed it to happen for virtuous and just ends, even if they are not yet known to you. All the saints of God acted in this way. They never tried to find out who slandered them or for what purpose, but always directed their hearts to God, humbly admitting the righteousness of God's will. Therefore, they considered all insults as good deeds, and their persecutors as benefactors, saying, "Here are our true benefactors, for they do not flatter us. Those who praise and glorify us to our faces, those who flatter us and hinder our inner perfection, they are our enemies." Therefore, the saints always directed their mental gaze to God, and in all actions they relied completely on God's providence, always expecting good from God.

However, even though God permitted the evil act, the sinner's fault in no way deserves to be lessened. It doesn't matter that his unlawful action gave God an excuse to make a greater good out of his evil, for it is the richness of God's goodness that creates the good, not the sinner's intention. The sinner intended only evil, and so his fault remains. Thus, let us return to the arsonist I mentioned previously, who burned down his neighbor's house out of a desire to steal his belongings. If a decent and virtuous person, out of compassion for the poor man, builds him an incomparably better house on the spot of his burnt one, the arsonist cannot take the credit, nor is his guilt the less, even if the poor man came out the winner in the end.

The next chapter is a more thorough consideration of the hidden and unattainable judgments of God and His providence concerning mankind.

 Chapter 3

How to Recognize God's Will in His Inscrutable Judgments

During the course of our entire life, we must often repeat the words of the Prophet and King David: "Thy justice is as the mountains of God, Thy judgments are as the bottomless deep" (Psalm 35:7). What an abysmal depth, in truth! The two servants of Pharaoh in the Biblical story—the cupbearer and the baker—point to this depth, as it were. Both were servants of the same king, both lost his favor, both were arrested and imprisoned for their crimes, and both felt his wrath. He remembered both during a feast of his court, and he had the authority to forgive both (if this was pleasing to God's righteousness) or he could execute them both. However, he condemned one to death, while the other he favored and reinstated in his previous position. He ordered the baker to be hanged and left as food for the crows, while he ordered the cupbearer to resume his duties.[12] These are the judgments of God—some He sends from His face, others he grants to see His face, according to His great mercy. "For who can trace out His mighty words? Who will measure His majestic power with a number, and who will add to this measure while describing His mercies?" (Sirach 18:3–4)

I

Hidden and inscrutable are the judgments of God concerning Nebuchadnezzar, the King of Babylon, and concerning Pharaoh, who "did not know Joseph" (Exodus 1:8). Blessed Augustine said,

> The one (Nebuchadnezzar) was punished by God for his countless sins, and through this punishment was brought to

salvific and extremely beneficial repentance (improvement of himself). On the contrary, Pharaoh's heart was hardened, despite the plagues of God. He disdained them and perished in the Red Sea with all of his warriors. Both were human; both were pagan kings; both were punished.

Why then were their ends so different? One acknowledged the punishing hand of God, sighed before God in repentance, and corrected his behavior. The other did not submit to the will of God as revealed to him, remained sinfully obstinate, and perished.

Here is another example of the inscrutability of God's judgments. One of the greatest of the Kings of Judah was Asa, who did what was right in God's sight and strengthened his kingdom by destroying all idols in the land of Judah by exterminating the worship of idols, those abominations of the first kings of Judah. However, Asa, though a model king for thirty years, lost his original glory near the end of his reign, changing his behavior from the best to the worst. He imprisoned the Prophet Hanani who rebuked him for his misdeeds and executed many innocent people, and, finally, having fallen ill to a sickness of his feet, he did not turn to God in repentance for his sins or with a prayer for his healing. Instead, he turned to physicians and faith healers. Oh, how this change was for the worst! Oh, how different were his latter deeds from his former! He who was at first a righteous king became a self-assured disdainer of God's will, declared to him by God's prophet (cf. 2 Chronicles 15 and 16).

On the contrary, Manasseh, who was lawless and unrighteous throughout his life, and who led the nation of Judah to such wickedness that they became worse than the nations God destroyed before the sons of Israel, recognized in his misfortunes the heavy hand of God. He turned to God and repented of his wickedness and received forgiveness and mercy from God (2 Chronicles 33). O God! Truly Your judgments are unfathomable, a measureless depth!

II

Divine judgment concerning Saul and David, the first kings of the nation of Israel, could not be more different. They both were initially worthy of praise; they both committed serious sins that served as great temptations for their entire kingdom; they both were punished heavily by God. And yet, how differently did they respond to these punishments! Saul became hardened in his wickedness and died tragically. David turned the punishment into spiritual medicine for himself, and he became the beloved chosen one of God. It is not appropriate to ask why this happened or for what reason. Such questions are inspired by the spirit of hatred, leading many to perdition.

"Has God indeed said, 'You shall not eat from every tree of the garden?'" asked the most cunning of beasts (Genesis 3:1). Eve should have answered him thus: "We know that God commanded us not to eat from only one tree, the tree of the knowledge of good and evil. However, it is not for us to ask why He commanded this. It was pleasing to His holy will, and it is not right for us to doubt the reasons for His will." "For who has known the mind of the Lord? Or who has become His counselor? Or who has first given to Him and it shall be repaid to him? For of Him and through Him and to Him are all things" (Romans 11:34–36).

Some will doubtless insist that it is not forbidden to sometimes ask for the reason for this or that commandment. But whom shall you ask? Will you ask God, Who alone knows what is good or permissible? Imagine a servant demanding that his master give a reason for an order, or an employee asking his supervisor the reason for his latest assignment. The master would consider himself insulted by the question, and the supervisor would be justified in considering his employee insubordinate. How can you dare to attempt such brazenness before God? Other than His holy will, there is no other reason for God's providence.

How unexplainable and wondrous to consider the following: the Samaritans eagerly listened to the words of the Lord and begged Him to stay with them; the faithless Gergesenes, on the contrary, begged the Lord to leave them quickly. The faithless Jews were not instructed by any of the Lords' words, deeds, miracles, and signs, never coming to believe in the truth of His divine ministry. Your judgments, O Lord, are unfathomable!

The holy martyr Julian of Alexandria had an ailment that prevented him from walking and was carried by two servants to his trial. One of the servants was also a Christian, but he rejected both Christ and his master, and he perished in idolatry. The other, named Eunus, rejected neither God nor his master, remaining firm in his Christian faith. Both confessors of Christ were first placed on camels and led around the city of Alexandria in dishonor and shame, and then they were subjected to merciless beatings. Finally, they were thrown onto a burning pyre alive, where, joyfully confessing Christ, they gave up their souls to God. One of the soldiers, named Bessus, seeing their endurance and commiserating with these innocent martyrs, began to rebuke the people and their bloodlust. He was seized, taken to the judge and declared to be a Christian as well. The judge condemned him to death, and the executioner cut off his head. Thus, he received a martyr's crown, in place of the Christian servant who rejected his master.

St Athanasius of Alexandria, in his life of St Anthony the Great, describes the following event. Two monks decided to visit St Anthony in the desert. But they misjudged the difficulties of the journey, and they began to suffer from dehydration. One of them died, and the other was very near death. They were still several miles away from St Anthony, who sat in his monastery on a stone. He called two of his monks and said to them, "Run quickly into the desert and take a skin of water with you, for one of the two brothers has already died of thirst, while the other still lives, but suffers greatly. If you do not hurry, the other will die as well. God revealed this to me while I stood at prayer."

Having received his order, the monks immediately left, and having found the pilgrims, they buried the dead monk and refreshed the one still living with water and food, and then brought him to St Anthony.

While describing this event, St Athanasius makes the observation that someone might well ask—why did St Anthony not send his monks a little earlier to save the one who died? Such a question truly is not appropriate for a Christian, for this was not the work of St Anthony, but the judgment of God. God Himself uttered his righteous judgment over the one dying and the one already dead. He revealed His will to St Anthony to save the one and not the other.[13]

St Anthony the Great himself wondered at the hidden and inscrutable mysteries of God, and he called out to God in humility,

O Lord, my God! Sometimes it pleases You to give a long life to people who appear worthless and steeped in an abyss of sin, and sometimes You end the lives of people who are very useful of society far before their time. Some, who have sinned little, you punish heavily. Others live with no sorrows, happy, and through this become brazen to commit crimes. "Their injustice swelleth out like fat." (Psalm 72:7)

Then St Anthony heard a voice, "Pay attention to yourself, Anthony. That of which you ask is the judgment of God, and it is not for you to test or question it."[14]

"How glorious are Thy works, O Lord. Thy thoughts are very deep. These things an unwise man perceiveth not, and a fool doth not understand" (Psalm 91:6–7). Truly You are a mystical God, inscrutable to the mind of His creation.

In 1117, when—according to Rogerius of Apulia—all of Italy was struck by an earthquake, some inhabitants of Milan had gathered in a house to discuss issues of governance in the city. Suddenly, a voice was heard from the courtyard, calling one of those assembled out of the house. The man who was summoned had no idea who was calling him. Therefore, he hesitated at first, waiting for a recurrence of the call. Unexpectedly, some unknown man came up to the door and asked the man to quickly leave the house. No sooner had he walked out than the house collapsed, killing all those within.

Why was only one of them saved from death, while all the others died? The judgments of God are unfathomable! Who does not clearly see this based on these ancient miracles? Thus, the Angel of the Lord led Lot and his children out of Sodom, while all the others he left to the fire and brimstone.[15] In the same miraculous manner, many other people have been saved from disasters, even though they were together with many other people who died.

In 1597, a certain stubborn, intractable person lived on the so-called royal mountain in Sicily. He lived a dissolute life. A certain acquaintance of his, a pious monk, admonished him many times, telling him to improve his manner of living and to cease his odious, ungodly life and his debauchery with prostitutes. But the man continued in his obstinacy, self-will, and unbelief, refusing to be corrected. Some days passed after the monk's latest attempt to reform the man, and he died in the arms of a prostitute on her very bed, accidentally stabbed with a knife.

In the same place, another sinner also lived many years with a kept woman. Hearing of his friend's demise, he ceased his sinful cohabitation and became chaste, learning from the punishment and death of his friend. He bitterly repented his sins for the remaining sixty years of his life.

What can we say about all this except, "Thy judgments are as the bottomless deep; man and beast shalt Thou save, O Lord"(Psalm 35:7).

III

The Apostle Paul marveled at God's decree concerning Rebecca's twins Esau and Jacob, for though they were still in the womb, not yet having done anything good or evil that might predispose God toward either of them, God said,

> "Jacob I have loved, but Esau I have hated." What shall we say then? Is there unrighteousness with God? Certainly not! ... But indeed, O man, who are you to reply against God? Will the thing formed say to him who formed it, "Why have you made me like this?" Does not the potter have power over the clay, from the same lump to make one vessel for honor and another for dishonor? (Romans 9:13–14, 20–21)

Is the distinction between potter and clay any less than the distinction between God and man, a worthless worm? Who dares to say to God: why did You do this?

St Dorotheos (ca. 505–565 A.D.) mentions the following event. In a certain city port, a ship filled with prisoners arrived, bound for the slave markets. Many buyers gathered. In that city lived a certain rich, virtuous, and pious maiden. She was very happy that the time had come for her to buy a servant girl, whom she desired to instruct in morality and proper feminine behavior. She eagerly approached the slaver, who had two young girls, one of whom she bought for herself. As soon as she began to leave, another women—she was the owner of a brothel—approached and paid some pathetic amount for the other girl, whom she then took to herself to train as a prostitute. What an unequal fate for these two young girls!

Who will attempt to plumb the depth and mystery of these judgments of God? Both of these girls were innocent and young, both were sold, knowing nothing of the life awaiting them or their fate. Both were raised well, and both would have tended the fruit of their virtue during their lives, but only one was given to an instructor in a virtuous, Christian life. She took full advantage of this instruction and became a good Christian, an emulator of the angels. The other girl was sent to a school of odious debauchery, to an instructor of falsehood, temptation, and all possible abominations, and she also willingly followed the example of her teacher. She became the devil's currency, even though she may have followed a different path had she ended up with a better teacher. But Your judgments, O Lord, are a bottomless deep!

Except for a few differences, a similar situation occurred in St Gregory the Great's family. This most holy man had three aunts: Emiliana, Tarsilla, and Gordiana, all of whom dedicated their lives to Christ in a convent. Two of them, guarding their monastic vows, remained virgins until their death. The third, Gordiana, listened to no instruction and did not submit to her monastic authorities, ceased her communion with her holy sisters and returned to a secular life, drawn back by her sensuality. Your judgments, O Lord, are a bottomless deep!

"Behold, the Mighty One shall prevail by His strength. Who is so powerful as He? Who is he who examines His works? Or who can say, 'He has done unjustly'?" (Job 36:22–23) King David said, "I was humbled, and did not understand; I became as a beast before Thee" (Psalm 72:22). In other words, it is as if the king said, "I am not testing Your judgments, O God. I am nothing before You; I am like the beasts. It is my duty to listen to Your voice and to submit to my God, but not to assess Your works and decrees." It is not strange that David, who from childhood herded cattle and did not have a higher education, understood himself and judged himself so humbly by the goodness of his heart and by God's inspiration? But even the seraphim, the highest spirit-servants of God, do the same before God. For when the Word of the Lord declared to the heavens and the earth that the Jews had rejected God, then the seraphim (each of whom has six wings) closed their faces with two wings, closed their feet with two wings, and flew with the other two, revealing by this action that they could not rise up to the heights of the miraculous and inscrutable works of God with their minds, for no created being can understand the divine judgments of the almighty Creator. For them it is enough to know and to be convinced that the Thrice-Holy God is holy, and to confess to each other the unutterable perfection of our God, calling out to him, "Holy, holy, holy is the Lord of Hosts; the whole earth is full of His glory" (Isaiah 6:1–3).

God is thrice holy. He is holy in Himself, holy in His judgments, holy in His works. If the heavenly rational spirits humble themselves so, confessing the inscrutability of the divine mysteries, how much more should we, the weak dust of the earth (though we have received by the gift of God the breath of life and the word of reason), confess to God, crying out, "The Lord is righteous in all His ways, and holy in all His works" (Psalm 144:17). Blessed Augustine left us a great consolation in these words: "God can save some even without their good deeds, for He Himself is good; He can destroy no one, for He Himself is righteous."

IV

We often see amazing changes and catastrophes, unexpected events, in the world. Many such events are unpredictable enough for us to wonder about their consequences. Some events shock us with their unexpectedness, and we complain pointlessly, saying, "I never thought or guessed that something like this could happen." How ignorant we are in anticipating future events! Even some events in the present defy explanation. We simply cannot fathom their cause, except in one important aspect. That is, we can determine whether something happened because it was pleasing to God or because He allowed it to happen by His all-wise, inscrutable, but always righteous and good providence. For the Lord says, "My counsels are not as your counsels, neither are your ways My ways. But as heaven is distant from earth, so is My way distant from your ways, and your thoughts from My mind" (Isaiah 55:8–9).

St Gregory the Great said that searching out the secret reasons for God's judgments is nothing short of preferring our own sinful, proud opinions to His decrees. Our duty, our work, is to constantly—no matter what the unexpected circumstance—repeat the words of St Paul, "Oh, the depth of the riches both of the wisdom and knowledge of God! How unsearchable are His judgments and His ways past finding out" (Romans 11:33). In our earthly life, there is much we will never understand with our minds. It is enough for us to know, to become convinced, and to believe without doubt that God is never unjust, and on the last day of judgment, not a single person will be able to say anything to the Lord, except these words: "Righteous art Thou, O Lord, and true are Thy judgments" (Psalm 118:137).

At one time, King David, on seeing how the unrighteous prospered in the world and tempted some of the members of God's people, desired to understand God's reasons for this. He thought about it for a long time but could not come to a satisfactory conclusion, and humbly admitted, "I sought to understand, but it was too hard for me, until I went into the sanctuary of God" (Psalm 72:16–17). We must defer our complete understanding of those judgments that remain inscrutable to us in this life. Only in the future life shall we understand them and their final ends, as ordained by the most high wisdom of God.

Therefore, let us cease spreading the wings of our curious speculation concerning things that we cannot understand. The waves of the eternal ocean of the most high Reason, constantly turning and returning, rising and falling, exceed the quickness of the keenest minds, not only human minds, but even angelic. And how could we expect to plumb the depths of God's judgments? Who can understand God's providence? Who can say why that man was born in paganism, whereas this man in Christianity? Who can say why the good news of the Gospel came very late to many countries, and why so many thousands of people perished without receiving the chance to be saved by Christ's teaching, whereas in other countries the Gospel message was heard and assimilated quickly? Why is one kingdom full of heretics, another free of all defects of incorrect doctrine and full of true piety? Why does God postpone His punishment for sins for a time for some, whereas He punishes others immediately? Why are some innocent men convicted and executed, whereas the sins of others continue to have repercussions for their children and further descendants? Why did the Crusades, in which so many kings, princes, and counts put such great efforts into the freeing of Palestine and the Tomb of the Lord from the hands of the heathens, end up futile? Why did God give an opportunity for repentance to Adam, but not to Lucifer? Why did Jesus Christ have mercy on the fallen Apostle Peter, but not on Judas? Why does one die as a child, whereas another live to deep old age? Why does one who sinned only a little die without repentance, whereas another, who lived many years in debauchery, finally improves and receives an end worthy of a Christian? Why does one drown in riches and luxury, whereas another has not a piece of bread or a penny to his name?

Oh, you most restless and excessively curious mind! Why must you seek the answers to these questions? If you touch the fire of the divine judgments, you will melt from the heat. If you climb the unattainable mountain of divine foreknowledge and providence, you will fall. Like a moth or mosquito, you will fly in circles around the candle until it burns you. Thus, the human mind brazenly strives to pierce the secrets of the inconceivable divine fire. We, mortal men, cannot look directly at the works of the all-bright Sun, since our eyes are blind as a bat. The hidden mysteries of God are unattainable for us in this life.

"The works of the Lord are wondrous, and His works are hidden from men" (Sirach 11:4). Not a single human being ever dared to take the scroll written inside and on the back from Him who sits on the throne, except for the Lion of the tribe of Judah, the Root of David, the destroyer of death (this book is the book of divine judgments, the inside being His foreordaining, the outside, His providence for the cosmos, see Revelation 5). The pre-eternal, all-wise God has "ordered all things by measure, number, and weight" (Wisdom of Solomon 11:20).

So why do we, worthless ones, puff ourselves up with pride and brazenly seek to weigh the mass of fire, to measure the speed of wind, or to return yesterday to the present? It is enough for us to believe that the reason for all things is the will of God, and whoever seeks another power or authority does not know the essence of God. Every cause comes to be known in relation to another cause, and thus we have a series of causes that are all dependent on another. The cause that in its essence had no previous cause is the first cause, the reason for all other causes. But before God and His holy will nothing existed. Nothing came before God, and so the only cause of all causes is the pre-eternal One, the mighty and eternal God glorified in Trinity. What more do you seek? God allowed, God desired, God created everything. In the just and wise words of Salvian: "For us the most perfect truth must be the will of God. The highest wisdom must be a willing and calm acceptance of the decrees of divine will and providence."

CHAPTER 4

How to Determine God's Will in All Events and Actions

Different kinds of authorities are proper in different situations, such as a simple village home with many children, a school full of students, a country manor with a large family and servants, a monastery full of monks, or a military camp where several corps, battalions, and other units are stationed. However, in each of these situations, there is one and the same method to achieve proper order and well-being. That method is the submission of subordinates to their immediate superiors, instructors, or teachers. Such submission allows for the many different wills of subordinates to become united and harmonized under a single authority that organizes the various independent wills to perform their best possible action. A general leads badly if he cannot inspire complete submission in his subordinates, or if he cannot direct them to fulfill their responsibilities and obey his direct orders. On the contrary, everything will go well and reach its best possible result if the master of the house, the abbot, the teacher, or the general (and so on) leads all of his subordinates by his own wise word, example, order, or even just by the wave of his hand, in such a way that they know what is expected of them.

Just as a soldier is required to be always obedient to his commander, to follow his example, and to be ready to fulfill every one of his orders, so every true Christian must always, for his whole life, remain obedient to the hand and word of God. We must unquestioningly do everything that is pleasing to God, submitting to His holy will. May every one of us Christians have only one answer to God's summons: "Lo, I come; in the heading of the book it is written of me, that I should long to do Thy will, O my God; yea, Thy Law is within my heart" (Psalm 39:8–9). Let these words resonate in my memory, in my mind, in my will. May every one of us say, in emulation of our Saviour, "Your will, O God, is better for me than any other decree, and the fulfillment of Your will is the greatest good for me."

When Saul was struck down to earth by the incredible light from heaven and heard a voice saying, "Saul, Saul, why are you persecuting me?" he immediately asked, "Lord, what do You want me to do?" (Acts 9:4, 6). Let each of us repeat this question daily, whenever we are unsure about how to act in a given situation. "Lord, what do You command me to do? What is Your will in this case, O all-good Jesus? Reveal to me Your will in whatever way You choose, so that I may understand, whether by a kind word, by a wise counsel, or by any other revelation. I will eagerly follow Your good pleasure, given to me by You in prayer."

How can we know God's will in all situations? Let me indicate here several provisions by which the will of God is easily revealed. We will call them, for the sake of brevity, *commandments*.

THE FIRST COMMANDMENT

Everything that distracts us from God is contrary to the will of God. Everything that leads us to God is in agreement with the will of God. "For this is the will of God, your sanctification: that you should abstain from sexual immorality" (1 Thessalonians 4:3). This refers not only to sins of the flesh, but to any delusion that is contrary to God's Law. Whoever feels himself to be in such delusion must immediately say to himself, "This action that I consider, this friendship, this purchase, this way of life will not make me morally better, because it distracts me from God."

THE SECOND COMMANDMENT

The will of God is clearly and unequivocally defined for us by God's commandments and the canons of the Church. Therefore, we must assess any difficult situation by determining what the commandment of God and the tradition of the Church require of us. Furthermore, if there is nothing clearly stated for or against this particular event, we must try to determine whether we act in the spirit of the commandments and tradition.

When the rich young man asked Christ how to attain eternal life, Christ told him to follow the commandments, especially those that direct our relationships with other people.[16] "There is nothing better than the fear of the Lord; and there is nothing sweeter than to give heed to the Lord's commandments"

(Sirach 23:27). To the rich man who lived in comfort all his days and ended up in hell after death, Abraham was called to witness the will of God revealed through Moses and the prophets, saying (concerning the rich man's living brothers), "They have Moses and the Prophets; let them hear them" (Luke 16:29). The Apostle Paul further says, "Do not be conformed to this world, but be transformed by the renewing of your mind, that you may prove what is that good and acceptable and perfect will of God" (Romans 12:2). The "good will" of God is found in the ten commandments; the "acceptable will" is found in the commandments of the Gospel; the "perfect will" requires that everything commanded by God be fulfilled by us on earth just as it is accomplished in heaven by the angels.

THE THIRD COMMANDMENT

The Apostle Paul gives this commandment in his First Epistle to the Thessalonians (5:18–22). "In everything [both good and unpleasant] give thanks; for this is the will of God in Christ Jesus for you" (5:18). First of all, it is proper to note here that our gratitude to God for everything, no matter what happens to us, is extremely beneficial for us, especially in periods of worries and sorrows, and even more when we receive something good from Him. St John Chrysostom (ca. 349–407 A.D.) expressed himself beautifully, "Have you suffered some evil? If you do not wish for it to be painful, then thank God, and lo! the evil has already transformed into good. There is great wisdom in this."

The ancients taught their children a very useful custom. If a child were ever to burn its finger, he should immediately turn to God with the words, "I thank God!," a short but a very useful commandment. O Christian, whatever you may be suffering, whether you are burdened by misfortunes or sorrows, do not forget to exclaim, "I thank God!" Exclaim this one hundred times, one thousand times, without ceasing, "I thank God!" St Paul adds to this, "Do not quench the Spirit" (1 Thessalonians 5:19); make room inside yourself for the Holy Spirit. Often God reveals His will through mysterious signs by which we must be directed and in which we must believe only when the result of the inner direction is clearly to the glory of the One God.

St Paul continues, "Do not despise prophecies" (5:20). In other words, whoever desires to reconcile his own will with God's must never despise the Church's exegesis of Divine Scripture, as well as the prophetic writings of saintly and pious people. If one does not want to heed all of these writings, then one obviously does not want to know the will of God.

St Paul continues, "Test all things; hold fast what is good. Abstain from every form of evil" (5:21–22). As a currency inspector tests all coins for forgery, using the sound of the metal, the markings on the metal, and other signs (the real coin they keep, the false coin they throw away), so we must also test every one of our actions in the light of God's will. Everything truly coinciding with God's will we must retain, but everything within ourselves that has even a tinge of falsehood or sin we must despise and reject as contrary to God's will.

THE FOURTH COMMANDMENT

In order to know the will of God in any doubtful circumstance, we can also consult other sources. In addition to the commandments of God in Scripture and the canons of the Church, we can consult the writings and counsels of those who have truly lived (and still live) a Christian life, that is, our spiritual counselors and fathers. These men are the spiritual and worldly judges of our consciences. From the laypeople we can also include our physical parents, our teachers in school, as well as any true, lawful rulers of human society. Here is a historical example.

When Saul (who afterward became known as Paul) submitted himself totally to the will of God on the road to Damascus and asked God to tell him what to do, the Lord did not burden him with direct commands in excruciating details. Nor did He immediately send the Spirit of wisdom, but as a disciple, he sent him to the Apostle Ananias, saying, "Arise and go into the city, and you will be told what you must do" (Acts 9:6). Ananias was a trustworthy exegete of the will of God to Paul, just as St Peter was to Cornelius the centurion (Acts 10). In these Scriptural passages we see God's desire to reveal His will for mankind through other men. Therefore, we should not despise the good counsel of our spiritual elders: "Seek counsel from every sensible man, and do not treat any useful advice with contempt" (Tobit 4:18). If you follow this advice, you will not regret it. "For a man's soul sometimes tells him more than seven watchmen sitting high on a watchtower. And in all matters, pray to the Most High that He may direct your way in truth" (Sirach 37:14–15). "Persevere with a godly man who you know keeps the commandments, whose soul accords with your soul and will share in your suffering if you fall. Stand firm on the counsel of your heart, for no one is more faithful to you than it" (Sirach 37:12–13).

In order to resolve your doubt about how to act in accordance with God's will in any given circumstance, ask counsel and wisdom from your spiritual fathers and superiors, to whom you have entrusted your conscience and the entire moral activity of your life. Speaking more generally, you may ask counsel of any God-given authority, because their will (except the will to sin) is the will of God. Everything that a civil authority recommends (except for sin) we must accept as the words of God himself and must do it.

An example for emulation is St Paul himself. As he writes to the Galatians concerning his actions after his conversion to Christ, he says, "Then after fourteen years I went up again to Jerusalem with Barnabas" (2:1). For what reason did Paul delay his return to Jerusalem for so many years? "I went up by revelation, and communicated to them that gospel which I preach among the Gentiles, but privately to those who were of reputation [that is, the ruling Apostles], lest by any means I might run, or had run, in vain" (2:2). Here is a world-famous preacher who has been preaching the Gospel for fourteen years to the Gentiles, and yet he presents himself to the first among Apostles as one least among them, inviting them to be judges or even censors of his preaching. Therefore, everything in his teaching that the Apostles sanction and accept by general counsel, and everything that they add from their own preaching or anything they remove from his preaching, he would accept it all on faith and preach it to the Gentiles.

Most amazing of all is what Paul says concerning this journey to Jerusalem: "I went up by revelation." If he went by revelation to Jerusalem, then the same revelation could have easily told him everything that the Apostolic Council had decreed concerning the preaching of the Gospel. However, this revelation was not given to him, in order to show that God not only wishes to teach his chosen ones by direct revelation but also that God sometimes reveals His will through other people. Even the presentation of Paul's teaching to the judgment of the Apostles was not done because Paul doubted the orthodoxy of his teaching, but because other people, both the faithful and the doubting, needed this Apostolic sanction. All who have ever desired and striven to follow the will of God without sin acted in such a way to resolve doubts. They asked their elders and accepted their good and useful counsel. "Stand in the ways [i.e., pay attention to your works] and see, and ask about the eternal pathways of the Lord. See what the good way is and walk in it. Here you will find purification for your souls" (Jeremiah 6:16).

THE FIFTH COMMANDMENT

However, if the time and place are not conducive to asking counsel, then a person must resolve his doubts concerning the will of God on his own. In that case, he must prayerfully ask God how to act in accordance with His will. God will not reject his request in prayer, and He will resolve his doubts, often in unexpected ways. In such cases, a person must carefully examine the situation that bothers him from all possible angles in order to determine which choices are most likely to please to God, and which choices our sinful desires or passions prefer. Then, having examined everything without passionate attachment, a person must do what is more pleasing to God, even if his own will does not wish it, or his passions despise it. For the will of God never gives pleasure or joy to the passions, only labor and exhaustion.

In spite of this, we must follow the will of God, we must do what is pleasing to Him, not what is pleasing to our self-love and sinful flesh. Egotism, pride, and desires of the flesh are always shameful and lead to our fall; to counter them is always the safe choice: "If you turn away your foot from work because of the Sabbath, so as not to do your desires on the holy day ... then you shall trust in the Lord; and He will bring you to the good things of the land" (Isaiah 58:13–14).

Here are also several examples from personal experience. The best advice for a person with an upset stomach is not to eat anything that he really wants to eat (such as fresh watermelon, melon, cucumbers, mushrooms, alcoholic beverages, cold water, unripe fruits, or vegetables) because all this will not bring him any benefit, but will rather make his stomachache worse. These foods encourage overeating and encumber the digestive system, potentially harming not only a person with a sick stomach but even a healthy person (even though to partake of these in moderation can be quite pleasant).

Something similar occurs in our spiritual life. Most often we find pleasure in what sweetens our external senses. We find pleasure in what makes us sparkle; we like to show off everything that raises us in others' estimation. In short, we prefer everything worldly, temporary, anything that pleases our flesh. However, all this is harmful for our inner man. Whatever excessively captivates our will with the worldly and ephemeral also distracts our spirit from the divine and the eternal, making it hateful to God, because it distances us from Him and casts us into the abyss of evil: "Therefore put to death your members which are on the earth: fornication, uncleanness, passion, evil desire, and covetousness, which is idolatry. Because of these things the wrath of God is coming upon the sons of disobedience" (Colossians 3:5–6). "Do not walk after your own desire, but restrain your appetites" (Sirach 18:30). In your doubts, turn to God in prayer, and He will reveal His holy will to you in your actions.

Dear reader, you may be faced with a situation that seems morally neutral. For example, if you meet two beggars asking alms, both apparently equally destitute, and you, for whatever reason, cannot give them both an equal amount of money, then give to them unequally. Give one more, the other less, as you desire. You will not have sinned against God's will in this unequal gift. If a similarly neutral situation is more complicated and requires separate investigation and examination, then consult experts who can give you more information, and then ask God in prayer for His blessing on your good deed. If the decision concerns one of these morally neutral actions, and if it is completely unclear which path will please God more, it is better to wait and make no decision until you know, even slightly, that your actions and choices are not contrary to God's will. In all situations that lead to such doubt, it is very useful to listen to two excellent counselors—reason and conscience. If you allow both reason and conscience to diligently examine the question in doubt, then they will certainly find a fitting resolution on how to act and how to accomplish a given action with the blessing of God.

However, in some cases people with pure consciences become lost in the labyrinth of the many conflicts between the spiritual and the carnal man. In addition, the spiritual man sometimes finds himself in such confusion that he does not know what he must choose to do in order to avoid transgressing against God's will. This often happens even with those who preach in churches. Let this example serve for their comfort and instruction.

A certain homilist expounded and interpreted the word of God to his listeners, and he noticed that some of them, the majority in fact, had fallen asleep, while only a minority listened intently. This upset the homilist. However, he had a thought. "It is better," he thought, for them to fall asleep than to spend the time in useless conversation or gossip. If two or three do not sleep, that is enough to give me strength to continue my labor. "One good man is worth a thousand." Let any person faced with a difficult decision reason in the same way. It is enough for me if my two eyes—reason and conscience—remain awake. If only they will act according to God's will, then they will direct my own will to God's. As for the rest, I will not worry, and if in my weakness I do not satisfy the good will of God, I will at the very least have tried to please Him.

THE SIXTH COMMANDMENT

St Paul's prayerful words in Acts 9:6—"Lord, what do You want me to do?"— give us a good example of how to know the will of God. We also must repeat his prayerful request. In fact, it is habitual for all saints to address God thus constantly, especially before any actions that seemed fraught with spiritual risk. Always they pray God to reveal His will to them. "Lord, what do You want me to do?"

Moses and Aaron approached the Ark of the Covenant with the same prayerful request. Thus our ancestors did and still do. If the sky is suddenly covered with thick clouds and if thunder explodes like cannons with incessant flashes of lightning, they used to ring the bells in the bell tower to dissipate the clouds and to call everyone to fervent prayer to God for His mercy and help in their salvation. We must act likewise when we notice that the righteous sun of God's will departs from us and we are completely in the dark, unsure about our next action. We must, for our own benefit, raise our eyes to heaven and fervently knock on its doors, saying, "Lord, what do You want me to do?" This is what Apostle Paul did when he was suddenly blinded by a heavenly light; he fell down to the earth and heard the voice, "Saul, Saul, why are you persecuting Me?" In horror and trembling, he said, "Lord, what do You want me to do?" (Acts 9:3, 6).

It is useful to repeat this prayer often. But the most appropriate time to increase our repetition of this prayer is when we approach the communion of the divine and all-pure Mysteries of the Body and Blood of Christ with fear and trembling. Acknowledging our total unworthiness to receive them, we must beseech our Redeemer with our whole soul and heart, "Lord, what do You want me to do?"

The saints, inspired by God, advise us to constantly keep these words in our mind and on our lips: "Lord, I am unworthy, but I know this in my heart: let everything that is pleasing to You be pleasing to me as well. Whatever I promised, I will do and keep my promises." The constant commitment of oneself to God's will is a perfect deed, the most useful preparation for our unknown but inescapable hour of passage from this life to the next, where we will receive what we deserve based on our good or evil deeds in this life.

Aside: If anyone prays a long time for God to grant him something but does not receive what he asks, then let him know that the Merciful Heavenly Father is not rushing to fulfill the request, either because the request is not for his benefit, or in order to inspire the petitioner to pray more often and to learn patience for his greater reward.

There is not the slightest doubt that even the best father does not immediately grant the request of his son or daughter, in order to test their love for him and to teach them useful patience, which deserves a greater reward than lack of patience and a prideful ceasing of petition after the first rejection. How very appropriate, then, it is for us to act in the same way to our All-knowing Heavenly Father. If God answered our petitions immediately, as soon as we desired something, then we would completely stop praying to God, or we would pray very rarely and only when we needed to, if we could be bothered to do it at all.

It is much more useful for us to receive even small gifts from God only after long and frequent prayers, for ceaseless prayer is a great gift of God in itself, and it makes the petitioner worthy of greater mercy, consolation, and spiritual peace. Petitions that are repeated often, even though God seems not to hear them, have given great calm and silence to the hearts of many holy men.

When King David sinned with Bathsheba, the Prophet Nathan rebuked him for his sin and declared God's will concerning the death of the child conceived of that illicit union. King David prayed for a long time and fasted, shed tears, threw himself to the earth before God, begging him to deliver his young son from death. But when he heard that the child died, he immediately calmed himself. He changed his robes of mourning to festal robes and went to the house of God and worshiped Him (2 Kingdoms 12:14–23, LXX).

Even the God-Man Christ, having finished his third prayer in the garden of Gethsemane asking the Father to put aside the cup of suffering, calmly told his disciples, who were heavy with sleep: "'Rise, let us be going. See, My betrayer is at hand'" (Matthew 26:46).

This often happens: the unheard prayer brings comfort to the mind and heart, and we come to know that the will of God is not that our request be answered, but that we completely submit to His will.

When Samuel told Eli, the priest of the Hebrews, what a punishment God had ordained for his house and sons, Eli answered humbly, "He is the Lord. He will do what seems good to Him" (1 Kingdoms 3:18). It is as if he said,

> Your revelation of God's judgments is not pleasant to me, Samuel, but since it is clear to me that this is God's will, then I eagerly accept your words and know in them the will of God. My sons and I receive a just punishment for our deeds, condemned by the judgment of God, Whom no one has the right to contradict. May the Lord do everything that is pleasing to His will. We are his slaves; He is our Master. We are guilty of much sin; His work is to correct our sins by His just punishment.

When the Apostle Paul went to Jerusalem through Caesaria, many of the Caesarean Christians, knowing by prophecy that in Jerusalem he would suffer much sorrow and persecution from the Jews, wanted to convince him not to go there. However, Paul answered their tearful requests thus, "'What do you mean by weeping and breaking my heart? For I am ready not only to be bound, but also to die at Jerusalem for the name of the Lord Jesus'. So when he would not be persuaded, they ceased, saying, 'The will of the Lord be done'" (Acts 21:13–14). This is the one true means to consolation of soul if our prayer will not be answered. We must pray only for one thing: "The will of the Lord be done."

THE SEVENTH (AND LAST) COMMANDMENT

No one among the living can know the will of God better than he who truly and genuinely desires in all things to act according to God's will. Such a desire will truly serve as a guiding string in the labyrinth of life's choices, helping him avoid any inconveniences or delusions in understanding God's will. When a person who has such a zealous desire to act in accordance with God's will—or to always choose the path most pleasing to God—is faced with a difficult problem with several apparently valid solutions, he must pray immediately with his whole heart and soul. "Lord, if I knew conclusively what is pleasing to You, I would immediately do it. Therefore, I believe that You will invisibly guide my heart to the right choice."

Having poured out his heart before the All-seeing God, he can then act as he considers best, putting aside all doubt. He will not anger God by his action, because the loving Father never leaves His children to fall into delusion. If there is no good counselor who can give advice in a given situation, God sends His angel, as He sent an angel to Joseph in a dream when Joseph did not know how best to deal with Mary, his betrothed, after she was found to be with child.[17] Thus also did God send an angel to the three Magi who came to worship the God-Child in Bethlehem, in order to prevent them from returning to their country through Jerusalem.[18] Thus also did God send His angel to Abraham, to Hagar, and to many others to prevent them from making the wrong choices.[19] He sometimes also sends other people to instruct us to the right path.

In 324, Emperor Constantine the Great, having left Rome, began to build a new capital in Cilicia (on the Asian side of the Bosphorus Strait), but this did not please God, and in order to show Constantine a new place for the building of a new capital, God miraculously moved all the builders' tools and materials in a single night to the Thracian coastline of Europe, as we read in the Venerable Bede. Zonaras also adds that an eagle seized the building plans for the new capital in his beak and flew over the Bosphorus, leaving it near Byzantium.

In short, God never refuses to reveal His will in some way to those who whole-heartedly desire to know and fulfill it, for the Holy Spirit of Wisdom loves mankind. He never commits evil, since He is the true knower of our hearts, and as the One who encompasses all, He accepts our every word (if it is true), and He gives generously to all who call on Him (see Wisdom of Solomon 1:5–7). The Lord is near to all who truly seek Him, and He reveals His will to them through His miraculous and most sweet instruction: "He will fulfill the desire of them that fear Him, and He will hear their prayer, and save them" from any delusions or errors or dangers (Psalm 144:19).

 CHAPTER 5

How God's Will Is Revealed in Jesus Christ, and How We Can Conform Ourselves to It

St Cyprian (ca. 200–258 A.D.), that eloquent and God-pleasing hierarch of Carthage and hieromartyr, left us a short list of Christian virtues, desiring to indicate what God's will requires of His servants. This list was intended to be hung on the walls of churches, but above all to be inscribed in the hearts of Christians, as a model or mirror of proper Christian behavior and life. He considered it instructive to show everything that is pleasing to the will of God through the example of Christ's teaching and actions in the form of short axioms, each of which describes a particular virtue:

1. Humility in life (in being and action)
2. Unshakeable courage in faith
3. Modesty and discernment in our spoken words and other expressions of our thoughts and feelings
4. All actions must be righteous and true
5. Mercy must govern interactions with others
6. To constantly improve one's way of life
7. To never insult another
8. To patiently endure all insults
9. To live with everyone in peace
10. To love God with one's whole heart
11. To love God, for He is our Father
12. To fear God, for He is God
13. Never to compare Jesus Christ with anyone else (i.e., with no other reasoning, free beings, either human or angelic)
14. To unite with Him in love of heart

15. To be attentive to His glorious Cross, passion, and death. To worship Him with fear, repenting of our sins with hope that His Cross will redeem us

16. In conversations with others concerning the most holy name and dignity of Christ our Saviour, to be firm and constant in all that concerns the confession of our faith. To answer all questions concerning our faith firmly, with no trepidation, as the absolute truth. In the hour of our death, to have unshakeable courage, through which we will deserve the crown of Christ's confessors. This means that we must live as true sons and daughters of God, as co-inheritors of Christ, that is, to follow the commandment to fulfill in all things the will of the Heavenly Father.

I

Of all these suggestions, the ones that we must keep constantly in our minds and hearts are the seventh, eighth, ninth, and tenth. That is, we must never offend anyone; we must patiently endure all offenses; we must live in peace with our neighbors; and we must love God with our whole heart. We who are weak and foolish most often sin against these commandments. When the will of God sends us countless spiritual and material blessings, we accept them wholeheartedly. However, when God's will decrees—and nothing, except for sin, occurs without God's will—various punishments, insults, deprivations for us, and then we begin to complain. In other words, we do not accept God's will in these afflictions, and we reject them as though they are contrary to God's desires for us, ascribing them instead to human hatred or animosity or envy or other such sins of our neighbors. We fail to understand or remember that God allows even the sins of other people that do us evil to punish us for our correction. This is the greatest blindness and ignorance concerning the true significance of the misfortunes that God sends us.

Let us remember that in the entire expanse of earth and in all the height of heaven, nothing occurs outside of the First Cause, the will of God. Sin is the only exception to this rule; it began and continues to exist only from the evil spirit of falsehood that opposes God the Truth. The Word of God witnessed this directly and through the prophets and apostles. The Prophet Jeremiah cries out with tears, "Who is he who speaks and it comes to pass, When the Lord has not commanded it? Is it not from the mouth of the Most High that woe and well-being proceed? Why should a living man complain, a man for the punishment of his sins?" (Lamentations 3:33–35).

When the Jews who hatefully persecuted Christ insisted that God was their father, the Saviour answered,

> If God were your father, you would love Me, for I proceeded forth and came from God; nor have I come of Myself, but He sent Me ... You are of your father the devil, and the desires of your father you want to do. He was a murderer from the beginning, and does not stand in the truth, because there is no truth in him. When he speaks a lie, he speaks from his own resources, for he is a liar and the father of it. (John 8:42, 44, compare with 1 John 3:8)

"He who sins is of the devil, for the devil has sinned from the beginning. For this purpose the Son of God was manifested, that He might destroy the works of the devil."

O, how foolish and shameless is the person who insists that everything in the world (both good and evil) occurs without the cooperation or permission of God. Either St Cassian or Cassiodorus[20] expressed it clearly: we must believe that nothing in the world that either accomplishes a good deed through various means (many of them mysterious), or permits the doing of evil so that it can be turned to good for the one who has suffered, occurs without God's will.

Pagan antiquity invented Titans who united in order to battle the gods and tried to banish them from Olympus. Although such mythological tales are inappropriate for Christians—and we have long left them behind—they provide an instructive example. I speak to you who complain, grieve, and cry out in the midst of afflictions and misfortunes. You are like these Titans; they wanted to topple their gods from Olympus, and that is exactly what you are doing in your pride and insolence. You would like to seize God's scepter and deny the cosmos God's providence. All of created nature serves, submits, and obeys the laws of the most high Lawgiver, while the crown of creation, Man, alone opposes his Creator, alone revolts and wants to resist God. Why do we rage in futility?

God sends all unpleasant punishments and corrective measures—such as diseases, deprivations, and other calamities—for our improvement and for the preservation of the external order and the inner spiritual life in society. As a result of the sinfulness and wickedness of an entire community and in one place, the earth swallowed up an entire city, which happened by God's permission, in another place many thousands fell to the plague. All this happened by God's foreknowledge. In so many places we see thieving, wars, tyrants for rulers! All this occurs by God's permission.

However, let us leave this index of societal and natural disasters, and let us focus on personal misfortunes. Your enemy has stolen your property; another has attacked your honor; a third has offended and grieved you. All this was not merely by God's permission, but it was sent to you from Above. In this be completely assured, for God sends all things. Therefore, God's will not only requires that we never offend anyone or even act unfairly toward anyone (as though we were not capable of taking vengeance on our adversaries), but He also desires that we generously and patiently endure all offenses and preserve peace, even when others do not wish to live with us in peace.

In order to better understand the mysteries of God's will, let us further explain some aspects of it that we have already touched on in the first chapter.

II

Learned Scholastic theologians differentiate two aspects of divine will. One they call *voluntas signi* (the will expressed in obvious signs), the other, *voluntas benepaciti* (the will of God's unconditional goodness). The first includes everything that God decrees, forbids, allows, advises, and accomplishes or expresses in visible signs, such as the circumcision, the tablets of the Mosaic Law, and the establishment of the New Covenant through Jesus Christ. The second includes the constant mysterious action of divine providence to preserve, uphold, and perfect the order of cosmic life, revealed within that life either mystically or through the actions of the reasoning and free beings created by God. For example, it pleased God to give both angels and men eternal blessedness, but under the condition that both angels and men not act outside the boundary given by the commands of God by setting their own self-will and counsels in opposition to God's will. (Of course, the providence of God concerning irrational beasts is unconditional.)

This is how it pleased God to create Heaven and Earth with all the creatures that inhabit them. He gave them eternal, unchanging laws that govern the flow of cosmic life, including the natural laws directing the spin and movement of the planet and all phenomena associated with it. All these laws remain firm by His holy will, never changing. The Lord willed it so and only assigned to Himself the providence to oversee all events and actions in the moral and rational world. Thus, the actions of His most high rule over the world become slowly obvious throughout the course of human history.

No one can change this divine will; it is not subject to external laws or decrees. It remains unchangeable, all-wise, and holy in itself. God Himself confirms this through the mouth of the Prophet Isaiah: "Remember the former things of old, for I am God, and there is no other beside Me, declaring beforehand the latter events before they come to pass and are accomplished together. I say, 'All My counsel shall stand, and I will do whatever I will to do'" (Isaiah 46:9–10, KJV).

We are nothing more than beggars in rags, whether we like it or not, and we must accept everything God sends us with gratitude and patience. We are all subject to misfortunes and sorrows; some of us receive a pleasant and luxurious lot, while others walk a narrow and thorny path. God gives His patronage to all and He protects all equally. All of our work during life is by the sweat of our brow, and even more punishment and pain. We must train ourselves to be content with whatever God sends us and to work that calling to which we are assigned, never asking why. It is the greatest consolation to give ourselves up to God in everything, no matter what happens to us. Let us constantly keep in mind these words: "Thus it pleases God.[21] There is no one strong enough to oppose God's holy will."

Mordecai knew this and confessed this before God in his fervent prayer for the salvation of the Hebrew nation from Haman the Agagite, saying: "O Lord, Lord, almighty King, all things are under Your power, and there is no one to oppose You in Your desire to save Israel" (Esther 4:17b, LXX). Blessed Augustine beautifully expresses the same thought:

> Great and wondrous are the works of the Lord, provident and so wisely wrought that when the angels sinned—that is, did not act according to the command and will of God, but by their own will, and through this fell from communion with God—even their fall served for God as a means for them to fulfill His previously ordained will. For God turned their sin and their evil into the greatest benefit (that is, He confirmed the good will of the bright angels and reinvigorated fallen mankind through the redemption of the God-Man Jesus Christ).

Even though the wicked (i.e., those who do not believe in God and do not praise Him as is worthy) oppose God's providence and His most holy will, God transforms their evil self-will into good by His all-wise providence for the benefit of others, and maybe even for their own benefit.

Here we see how God "desires all men to be saved and to come to the knowledge of the truth" (1 Timothy 2:4) even if not everyone reaches such a level because some refuse to obey His commandments and even oppose them. Our Saviour warns them of the dire consequences of their choice:

Not everyone who says to Me, "Lord, Lord," shall enter the kingdom of heaven, but he who does the will of My Father in heaven. Many will say to Me in that day, "Lord, Lord, have we not prophesied in Your name, cast out demons in Your name, and done many wonders in Your name?" And then I will declare to them, "I never knew you; depart from Me, you who practice lawlessness!" (Matthew 7:21–23)

The one who understands this truly will always do God's will. So be it!

III

These words of Christ are true. True also is their logical conclusion. We can do nothing better for ourselves, or more salvific for our souls, than to completely submit to God's will, completely commit our will to God's, repeating the words of the priest Eli, "He is the Lord. He will do what seems good to Him" (1 Kingdoms 3:18, LXX), as well as Joab's words, "Today your servant knows that I have found favor in your sight, my lord king, because the king has fulfilled his servant's request" (2 Kingdoms 14:22, LXX), and the words of David, "If I find favor in the eyes of the Lord, He will bring me back and show me both it and its majesty. But if He says thus, 'I have no delight in you', behold, here I am, let Him do to me as seems good to Him" (2 Kingdoms 15:25–26, LXX), and the words of Judas Maccabeus, "But as God's will is in heaven, so He will do" (1 Maccabees 3:60, LXX).

Finally, pray to God, committing yourself completely to His will together with Christ the Saviour: "O My Father, if this cup cannot pass away from Me unless I drink it, Your will be done" (Matthew 26:42). The Son of God was so obedient, and so completely fulfilled the will of His Heavenly Father, that He said concerning Himself, "For I have come down from heaven, not to do My own will, but the will of Him who sent Me" (John 6:38). If this was required of the Son of God as a Man, then consider how much more appropriate it is for servants to submit to the Lord and Master of life and death, to completely follow His will, never opposing His lordship. Holy justice requires that what has always been pleasing to God should also be pleasing to every person.

When a soldier hears a bugle call or a drumroll announcing the march, he collects his things. When he hears the command to charge the enemy, he leaves everything that could encumber him behind, takes up his weapon, and is ready to listen to his commander with his whole heart, eyes, and ears, and to fulfill his every order to the letter. We must act in the same way, since we are in a lifelong warfare with the desires (passions) of the flesh, the allurements of the world, and the temptations of the proud spirits of darkness. We must obey our Commander, Teacher, and Master (Jesus Christ, our Saviour and Lord) in all things. We must emulate (as much as we are able) His example and His deeds, as described in the Gospels.

Let us, Christians, follow our Commander and Lord eagerly and unswervingly, committing ourselves completely to His holy will. No matter what happens to us on the path of life—whether sorrowful, uncomfortable, or difficult—let us bear everything patiently, without complaining, with good humor, knowing in advance that we will not only pick flowers on the road of life, but thorns as well. The good soldier does not hide from bullets or bayonets; on the contrary, he eagerly counts his wounds and boasts of them, never rebuking his commander, but becoming ever more tied to him with bonds of heart-felt love. Let us remember once and for all the call of our Saviour: "Follow me, and let the dead bury their own dead" (Matthew 8:22).

Whoever complains, cries, and sighs about the difficulties of doing what the will of God decrees for our temporary life, submitting to God only by necessity, is a fool. Who prefers coercion to willing obedience? Or should we just grumble and curse our own life if something uncomfortable or sorrowful or difficult occurs? Or should we be constantly horrified and complain about our lot with bitter wailing, when everyone, both good and evil, is subjected to the same pain? I speak of disease, death, exhaustion, and everything else that is unpleasant in life. We must endure universal human afflictions stemming from nature or society with equanimity. We are called to do this; we cannot avoid that which is beyond our power to change.

PART II

CONFORMING TO THE WILL OF GOD

 CHAPTER 6

On Completely Committing One's Life, Will, and Works to the Will of God

A certain famous theologian fervently and constantly prayed to God for eight years, asking Him to reveal a person capable of showing him a direct and true path to the acquisition of the heavenly kingdom. One day when this theologian was especially filled with a strong desire to find such a person and was incapable of thinking of anything else, he increased his prayers. Suddenly, he heard an invisible heavenly voice that said to him, "Go outside the doors of the church and you will find the person you seek."

The theologian, obedient to the mysterious voice, immediately went out and found a beggar in rags sitting at the doors of the church. His knees were covered with scabs and seeping with pus. The wise theologian approached him and said, "A good and fortunate morning to you, old man!"

The beggar answered, "I have never had an evil or unfortunate day in my life."

The theologian, desiring to correct his greeting, changed it. "May God send you all possible benefits!"

The poor man answered, "God has never sent me anything but good."

The theologian wondered if he had gone deaf. So he tried a different approach. "What is the matter with you, old man? I desire you to have abundance in all things."

The old man answered, "I have never lacked anything."

The theologian, thinking that the man might prove to be talkative, and desiring to test his knowledge, said, "I would like for all your desires in this life to be fulfilled. I hope God sends you everything you wish."

"I seek none of those things that you desire for me. Everything occurs according to my wishes if I make no plans for my life, but live solely by God's will."

The theologian said,

> May God preserve you, good man, for your lack of desire for a
> prosperous life. But I beg you, tell me, are you the only blessed beggar
> in the world? Were these words of Job spoken in vain? "For mortal
> man born of woman is short-lived and full of wrath." (Job 14:1) How
> are you alone delivered from all evil times and misfortunes? I do not
> understand your thoughts sufficiently.

Everything that I told you, master, I spoke in truth. When you desired that I have a good and prosperous morning, I answered that I never had an evil morning, because I am always content with the lot God gave me. I do not seek happiness and worldly success, and that gives me the greatest well-being. Ill fortune, prosperity, or calamities do no evil to anyone, except to those who either strongly desire them and run after them, or run away from them and fear their coming. I disdain money and do not make an idol of it. I only pray to the Heavenly Father, Who directs every person's life to the best, whether it be through joys or misfortunes. He knows completely whether joys or misfortunes are more salvific for a person. Therefore, I say that I have never experienced any misfortune, because everything in my life is as I wish. When I am hungry, I thank the all-seeing God for it. When I am burned by cold as by fire, or when rain or hail or snow pours down on me, I glorify God for it. If someone mocks me, strikes me, or insults me, I also thank God for it, for I am sure that this is allowed by God's will, and everything that God sends serves for my benefit and perfection. Thus, everything that God sends me or allows other people to do to me—whether pleasant or repugnant, whether sweet or bitter—I accept with equanimity. I accept everything as coming from the hand of the merciful Father, and I only desire that which God desires, and what it pleases Him to allow others to do to me. In this way, everything occurs by God's desire, which is also my own desire. Whoever considers worldly happiness as something important and significant should be pitied. Equally miserable is the one who seeks fulfillment in anything worldly. The only true and unshakable happiness and blessedness in this life is found by the one who sincerely, without doubt, commits himself to God's will and leads his life according to God's will, never opposing it. For the will of the Lord is the fullness of perfection and goodness; it never changes, and outside it there is no other better or more just will. It utters a righteous judgment concerning every person, and no one can justly say that His will contradicts itself. I apply myself and my mind completely to always desire only that which God wants of his rational creation in general and of me in particular. Therefore, I have never been troubled; for I gave my will completely into the hands of God, and now the desire of my heart is the same as God's desire and providence for me, and I thank God for His mercy, even if it seems bitter.

"Is this wisdom you speak to me?" countered the theologian. "But tell me further, I beg you. If God willed to cast you into hell, would you think the same way?"

The beggar answered,

Would God cast me into the abyss? Know this: I have two mighty hands with which I would grab God and not let go. One hand is humility, acquired by giving myself as a sacrifice to God; the other hand is love free of pretense for God, that pours forth from my deepest heart onto all my neighbors through my good deeds. With these hands I would grab God, and no matter where He would send me, I would take Him with me. Truly it would be better to be with God in hell than in heaven without Him.

This answer surprised the theologian exceedingly. Internally, he acknowledged that the path revealed to him by the old beggar would lead to God directly, with no delusion. Truly, this was the most perfect of all ways leading to God. The wise man wanted to discover even more wisdom hidden under the crude mantle of the beggar.

"Where have you come from?" he asked.

"I came from God."

"Where did you find God?"

"I found Him where I left all perishable things of this world."

"Where did you leave God?"

"I left Him in pure hearts and good will."

"Who are you, old man? To what social class do you belong?"

"Whoever I was, I am content with my lot and would not change it for the riches of all kings combined. Any person can be called a king if he wisely directs and rules over himself."

"Are you a king?" asked the wise man. "Where is your kingdom?"

"There," said the pauper, pointing up to heaven with his finger. "He is a king, whose kingdom is written in the book of fates."

Desiring to put an end to all questions, the wise man asked the beggar, "Who taught you all that you have told me, who put these words into your mind?"

I will reveal this to you, my lord. All my days I spend in silence, prayer, or in good and pious meditation, and more than anything I constantly hold in my mind and memory the need to seek out new ways to more completely unite myself to God through limitless submission to His holy will. Such total consecration of one's self to God can teach a zealous person much that is true, good, and holy, both in knowledge and in life experience.

The theologian had many more questions, but he had a firm hope that he would find another good time for them, and he parted from the beggar by saying, "Be healthy, old man!"

Then he left him, mulling all this over. He said to himself, "Truly I found the best teacher of the right way to God."

Blessed Augustine said, "Sometimes the unlearned appear before us and teach us about the coming kingdom of heaven; we, with our wisdom, do not seek it with enough zeal, instead becoming attached to things here in this life, becoming defiled with the filth of flesh and blood."

Jesus Christ speaks of this same opposition between spiritual humble-mindedness and worldly wisdom in His prayer to God the Father: "I thank You, Father, Lord of heaven and earth, that You have hidden these things from the wise and prudent and have revealed them to babes [that is, the pure in heart]. Even so, Father, for so it seemed good in Your sight" (Matthew 11:25–26). Truly, dirty rags sometimes hide the greatest wisdom. And who would have thought or believed that in such a simple, unlearned man could be found such exalted knowledge of the Divine Essence? Who would think to find in such unlettered simplicity such elevation of thought as the poor man's image of two mighty hands clinging to God, that is, one's complete self-offering to God and love for Him, expressed by the fulfillment of His commandments. With these hands—humility and love—truly God allows Himself to be seized by mankind, but from other hands He turns away.

CHAPTER 7

How Can Human Will Become Pleasing and Worthy of Union with God's Will?

After the Persian King Ataxerxes[22] acceded to the throne, he ordered that all the best and most beautiful maidens of the famous city of Susa join his court. In order to prepare them to meet the king properly, they were given a year to buy the proper clothing and jewelry and to cultivate the proper manners appropriate for people given such a high honor.

If so much time is required only to be found worthy of presenting oneself at the court of an earthly king, how much greater must our effort be to remain vigilant every minute of the day to our own will! Self-will is wild, egotistical, lacking in true spiritual nobility and the virtues necessary to make it beautiful. Little by little, one must cut off all aspects of self-will's wild ugliness; its irrational, bestial instincts; its self-contentment and egotism. Therefore, serving the eternal King of heaven even here on earth by living in purity, faith, and the love of the Gospels should be the entire purpose of our lives. We must fall before Him, our Saviour, in sincere prayer, acknowledging our unworthiness. We must firmly resolve to correct our sinful will and lead a pure life, cleansing our will with conscience and the communion of the Body and Blood of Christ, after repenting and promising not to continue along the thorny path of sin. Then we will be able also to serve Him in the eternal life, when unexpectedly, in the day or the night, He will require our presence at His righteous judgment to decide our eternal fate.

In order to more fully explain how to prepare our will for worthy union with God's will, I will indicate the means and the conditions (i.e., commandments) revealed in the word of God. We must follow these commandments to the letter if we hope to renew the soul in the original image and likeness of God. At the same time, we must avoid the insolence of trying to completely understand the profound mysteries of the limitless mind and wisdom of God with our limited minds.

The lawfulness and righteousness of these commandments of God consists not only in their divine origin but also simply in their inherent, obvious justice. When a lord or master accepts a new servant into his house, he agrees to terms with the servant in advance, offering his conditions. He might say, "If you are to live in my house, you will not invent foolish tales, you will not utter words offensive to God and to everything that the Church acknowledges as holy and sacred, you will not contradict the truth, you will not be drunk, you will not be idle. Instead, you will try to be faithful, diligent, obedient, and solicitous in performing your duties."

Every master has the right to offer his future employee such conditions and to demand that they be adhered to, or the servant will be thrown out of the house. Is the all-powerful, righteous, and all-wise God powerless, then, to insist on His own conditions for unity with His will when entering into a covenant with us?

Let us examine the most important aspects of human will that God desires and that please God when they correspond to His own will.

I

The heavenly Bridegroom of our souls, who exceeds all earthly purity, requires great spiritual purity of us as well. He wants no spot, defilement, or blight on our soul (see Ephesians 5:27). The human will that desires to become grafted to Him, like a branch to the vine, must first throw off all sinful impurity. Not only must the human will renounce avarice, come to hate the works of lust and any physical uncleanness, avoid being inflamed with anger, but even if it only feels a sinful inclination within itself, it must courageously humble and mortify such inclination. The human will must cast out even the memory of sin. Let the mind instead engage itself in serious reflections that aid the spiritual welfare of this life and the next.

But we are not here speaking of what should already be obvious to all. There is another kind of fall that either creeps up on us unnoticed or seizes the soul in a moment. We are speaking of envy, or the disquiet and sorrow in our soul when we see others enjoy wealth, happiness, or advantages that are denied to us. May our will never be guilty of this sin, may it be free from it, never subject to it or enthralled by it. The person who strives to emulate Christ must keep himself free from even a jot of this sin. When we see others' joy, we must not envy them, nor should we become angry with our own misfortune or lack of success. We should not complain or become angry in the midst of sorrows because any person who approaches God does not envy the happiness and wealth of others but prays to God instead:

> O Lord! It has pleased You to raise this man to high honors and wealth, while I remain in indignity and poverty. I do not oppose Your will in this, O my God, and I do not seek to know the reasons for it, for I know truly that it is reason enough that You will it. If You, O Lord, did not allow me to become poor and humiliated, then no human being, not matter how much they desire it, would be able to reduce me to such a condition. Only You have the power to do this, in a short time and without excess words, decreeing this state to be the best for me. I accept that You also allow other misfortunes: one person slanders me, another spreads rumors about me, a third attacks my honor, a fourth causes me all kinds of worries, even though I offended none of them, discomfited none of them. However, in all circumstances I find a sufficient, satisfactory answer: You allowed this, O Lord, You ordered it done. Let them be Shimei, and I will be David (2 Kingdoms 16:5–13, LXX), if this is pleasing to You, O my God!

The holy hierarch and martyr St Ignatius of Antioch (ca. 35–108 A.D.) said, "I am God's wheat and shall be ground by the teeth of wild animals, that I may become the pure bread of Christ." Thus God prepares us to become pure bread at the Lord's feast. Why do we complain about other people? They are millstones that grind us like wheat.

In order to purify our heart, we must plant the good seed of the word of God in our hearts, and we must let it find root. We must keep it firmly in our mind and memory, and prayerfully lift up our thoughts to God, saying, "Blessed be God for all ages! Lord, what do You order me to do? Let Your will be done in all things!" This is the first instruction and preparation for preserving one's will pure from sin in general, and especially from hatred and envy.

II

Secondly, God requires that our will is aligned with His. Everything He sends us, either good or not, whether sweet or bitter, we must accept as God's good will or as His punishment, with gratitude, with no complaining. In short, our will must be mighty in the faith that everything happens by God's will. Our will must endure hardships and sufferings eagerly with patience and kindness to others.

If we were completely sure that everything always occurs by God's will, then we would suffer less. Let us, then, run to God with heart-felt prayer during any misfortune or suffering, sincerely confessing our sins to Him and asking Him to help us to endure our sorrows. Let us pray in this manner, "Lord! Everything that I now suffer, I suffer by Your holy will; I am as sure of this as I am of my continued existence. Strengthen, O Lord, strengthen my will to courageously endure this burden that Your holy will has decreed for me."

If we doubt God's providence for us, or if we do not understand the real reason for our misfortunes, we can become despondent or at the very least sorrowful, even sometimes coming to doubt our salvation. O, how weak and vacillating we are in our faith in God's providence, not only concerning each one of us, but even of the smallest hair on our head, which does not fall without God's will! Jesus Christ Himself assured us of this, when he said, "Are not two sparrows sold for a copper coin? And not one of them falls to the ground apart from your Father's will. But the very hairs of your head are all numbered. Do not fear therefore; you are of more value than many sparrows" (Matthew 10:29–31, compare with Luke 12:6–7).

How great is His mercy! God Himself falls to earth with a sparrow; for truly the will of God is God Himself, acting constantly in every one of His creatures. He swims with the fish; He flies with the birds; He crawls with the snakes; He walks with the beasts. God does not leave a single one of His creatures without His providence concerning each of them. Even if a million birds are caught in a net, not a single one of them, not even the smallest one, will have been caught without God's will. Not a single bird falls to earth without the will of the Father in heaven. The same providence that cares for the smallest bird together with the eagle cares even more for the crown of His creation on earth, man. If no bird is caught in a net without God's will, then how can you, who have been created in the image of God and are destined to inherit the kingdom on high, wallow in your sorrow over your many deprivations, insults, sufferings, as if everything happened not according to God's will, but because of the evil intentions of people who hate you? In order to better understand that the providence of God extends not only to living beings, but even to inanimate creation, God said that all your hairs have been counted! When did a person ever correctly count the number of hairs on his own head? But God has counted them all, not only of one person, but of all people, and without His holy will not a single hair will fall out.

And yet, when something happens to us contrary to our desires, how often do we go outside of ourselves, lose all patience, accuse others of terrible things; today we blame this person for our problems, tomorrow another. As a stormy sea stirs up all of the impurities from its depths to the surface, our heart brings forth foul and blasphemous words of faithlessness, lack of patience in our sufferings. In our misfortunes, we fail to see our just punishment, doled out by the will of God for our benefit. Instead, we foolishly ascribe our problems to the hatred and enmity of other people or to some other imagined cause.

When our Saviour appeared to the disciples at the Sea of Tiberias after His resurrection, the sea was stormy and none of the disciples recognized Jesus, except for John, who told the others, "It is the Lord" (John 21:7). There are many among our brothers and sisters who are very weak in spirit and lack patience in their sorrows. When their sea of life is covered with the waves of various misfortunes and deprivations, they do not recognize the Helmsman who directs their ship invisibly during the course of their life. They do not recognize almighty God, Who uses different paths to lead each of us to salvation. In their blindness, they accuse those people whom they consider their enemies, and they rail at them, calling them evil, cunning, hypocritical, the source of all misfortunes. They say, "Those evil creatures have caused my affliction."

A person who is humble in mind and pure in heart thinks differently. He strengthens his will to courageously endure all possible misfortunes and afflictions by remembering that they come from the hand of God indicating, as with a finger, the correct path for improving his sins. He humbly calls out to God, "O merciful God! It is You who seeks my salvation, You who justly punishes me. It is You, O Lord! Blessed Be the Lord! Do with me everything that pleases You!"

III

The third quality of the human will that pleases God is generosity to one's neighbors, even when we ourselves have little, as well as a constant striving of the heart to God as the source of all good things. Such a quality of the human will is well expressed by a single phrase: *cheerful giver*. A person with such a wise and firm will to give cheerfully is worthy of great respect. In all his life's necessities (concerning his civil and familial duties), he is always moderate, he avoids luxury and flamboyance in food and clothing and in other external decoration. Such a person is content with what God sends him, and he thanks God, saying prayerfully within himself, "O my Lord, I am happy with whatever You give me in Your goodness. It is enough for my modest life, even if it seems little to a greedy mind. I thank You, O Lord, for the little You give me, for I consider myself to be unworthy even of the air I breathe." Such a person never envies his neighbors anything, even if they are more fortunate than he is. He desires everyone's success in every good work.

Such a cheerful giver, such a modest man, is beloved of God. No one ever hears him utter words of complaint or spite either against God or man. He will never say, "I barely managed to get this hard piece of bread for my family through heavy labor, while others have too much of everything, not working even a fraction of the time I work. Though they sow little, they harvest much."

The greatest part of our discontent and complaining comes from our limited understanding of God's providence and of His mysterious ways. Through His providence and mysterious ways God leads all of mankind—and each one of us individually—to the acquisition of the best possible temporal life, and even more to the acquisition of eternal blessedness, which "eye has not seen, nor ear heard, nor have entered into the heart of man the things which God has prepared for those who love Him" (1 Corinthians 2:9). Our heart, on account of its impurity, is more inclined to temporary good things than to eternal blessedness, and so our mind is usually limited to thoughts of the mutable and temporary, not the eternal and unchangeable. Since we do not think of the latter things, we cease to believe in God's existence and His most exalted direction of the cosmos.

The only true means to acquire happiness in this life and the next is to constantly direct our attention within—to our conscience, thoughts, words, and deeds—and to weigh these things without partiality. This will reveal to us the depth of our delusion in life and will show us the only path to salvation. This path is the complete commitment of our being, together with all the circumstances of our individual life, to the will of God. Let the sunflower be our preferred symbol of this turning toward God. Let us keep the image of the sunflower always in our minds.

Pliny wrote of the sunflower as nothing short of a miracle:

We have often noticed that the sunflower is a kind of wonder of nature. It constantly moves to face the sun, turning during the course of the day from the east to the west. At night, because of its exclusive love for the sun, it gathers together its petals and closes.

O Christian! Remember this once and for all: even on cloudy days the sun-flower continues to follow the sun in its focused love, even though it cannot see the sun. The Sun that illumines our life's path is the will of God. It does not always shine on us without clouds; often, clear days are followed by overcast days when rains, winds, and storms arise. No Christian is safe from these phenomena, these changes in spiritual weather. May our love for the Sun, the will of God, be as strong as the sunflower's, so that even in days of hardship and sorrow we will continue to sail unerringly along the sea of life, following the directions of the barometer and compass of God's will that leads us to the safe haven of eternity.

It is true that we will never reach complete calm and prosperity; everything on earth will never seem completely favorable. We will never be fully content with what God gives us. Even if we have excess in everything, it will always seem to us that we lack something. We will always be afraid, depressed, confused, lacking in faith, and busy every minute of the day with cares and various worries, sorrows, and useless sighs until we turn sincerely to God and commit ourselves and one another completely to the will of God, as the sunflower always seeks the sun. Let us diligently examine the visible signs of God's will in our daily life and try to conform our will to it. Let the will of God be for us a guiding star in life, and let this alone be stamped in our hearts forever.

Let us pray in the following words: "As it pleases God, let it also please me. Life or death, wealth or poverty depend only on the divine will, as it please the Lord. This is how it was, how it is, and how it always will be. Blessed be the name of the Lord!" (see Job 1:21).

Now our sun is covered with clouds, but it will dispel the darkness of our many sorrows sooner or later. Let us examine the history of the world. Very often dark times follow times of flourishing, and times of triumphant light replace the dark. In this way, let us prepare ourselves to know the will of God by carefully examining events in history, whose success or failure will indicate to us both God's good will and His disfavor (i.e., His punishment) to the righteous and to the wicked participants in these events. Through this, we will come to understand the experientially proven truth that each person must never act contrary to God's will in any work, even if this work is abhorrent to his own self-will.

A certain learned Jew (a scribe), who was in the crowd surrounding Jesus Christ, said to Him, "Teacher, I will follow You wherever You go" (Matthew 8:19). Let us also, in word and deed, follow every decree of God's will quickly and eagerly, no matter where He leads us.

IV

A human will that is pleasing to God is always longsuffering and steadfast. We ruin all our useful labors and undertakings by a lack of steadfastness and longsuffering. The nation of Israel, having lost their patience with Moses in the desert at Mount Sinai, turned to idols and made for themselves a golden calf, worshiping it as a god and falling down before it (Exodus 32:1–8). This is the kind of extreme action that comes from lack of constancy.

Two disciples (Cleopas and Luke) walked the road to Emmaus, speaking sorrowfully about the events surrounding the passion and death of Christ Jesus in Jerusalem. When the Lord came near them unnoticed, they did not recognize Him. He asked them:

> "What kind of conversation is this that you have with one another as you walk and are sad?" Then the one whose name was Cleopas answered and said to Him, "Are You the only stranger in Jerusalem, and have You not known the things which happened there in these days?... concerning Jesus of Nazareth, who was a Prophet mighty in deed and word before God and all the people, and how the chief priests and our rulers delivered Him to be condemned to death, and crucified Him. But we were hoping that it was He who was going to redeem Israel. Indeed, besides all this, today is the third day since these things happened." (Luke 24:17–22)

O blessed men! Did impatience and doubt creep even into your good hearts? Do you not realize that this third day, foretold by the Son of Man as the day of His victory of death, has not yet ended? Did your endurance not last three full days? O impatient ones! If this third day had already passed, if the fourth day or fifth day after His death had arrived, then it would have been permissible for you to foolishly doubt and lose hope in seeing Him resurrected from the dead. But the third day was only reaching its evening. Why must you be weak in faith and doubt the truth of His foretold resurrection?

Brothers, when it concerns our own desires, we are always very impatient, and if even the smallest delay occurs in the fulfillment of our desires, we cast all of our hope into an ocean of despair and impatience. But it is not this way with God: "The Lord is compassionate and merciful, longsuffering, and of great kindness" (Psalm 102:8). God does not desire to destroy a soul, instead taking into account the ones being banished from Him. He does not wish to send anyone away from Himself (for God is not quick to punish), and He gives us a long time to improve before He satisfies His own justice (as though He had to do it by necessity). He waits until the bitter end to utter the final condemnation over those who refuse to repent: "Depart from me, you cursed, into the everlasting fire prepared for the devil and his angels" (Matthew 25:41).

Brothers, we are weak in faith concerning all things. We lack firm, constant hope. If we ask for something two or three times and do not receive it, we immediately lose hope of ever being heard, becoming like those beggars who whisper outside a window once or twice, "Alms for the poor for the sake of Christ," and, not being heard by the master of the house or the inhabitants, leave, saying to themselves, "There is no one home." Knock, you sloths, knock! The door is opened to the one who knocks (see Matthew 7:8).

How often do we find ourselves in a situation that tests our longsuffering unbearably! Some seek a particular mercy for many years and all in vain. They never receive what they ask for because the desired inheritance is acquired by patience. The worker is not tired by his work, for he knows that the time for work passes quickly. But we, impatient ones, place limits to God's goodwill, counting the hours, and if the right hand of the Lord does not give us quick help or consolation in our moral or physical sufferings, then we begin to wail like children, "When, O Lord, will You help me? Why do You tarry to bring me the joy of Your aid? How long will You not heed my prayers, O Lord? If You don't arrange my welfare within a year, and if You won't listen to my constant prayer, then I will consider myself abandoned by You and I will cease praying."

In this sense, we are no different from the citizens of Bethulia, who during the siege of their city by Holofernes said to all the rulers and elders of the city:

> May God judge between you and us! For you have done us a great wrong by not making peace with the Assyrians. For now there is none to help us. And God has delivered us into the hands of them who laid us low in thirst and in great destruction. So call to them and surrender the whole city to be plunder to the army of Holofernes and all his forces. For it is better for us to be plunder to them, for we shall become their slaves, but our lives will be saved, and we will not have to watch our infants die before our eyes, and our wives and children breathing their last. We call all of heaven and earth to witness against you and entreat our God, the Lord of our fathers, who is punishing us according to our sins and the sins of our fathers, do according to these words spoken this very day. (Judith 7:24–28)

O impatient and weak-willed people! The despair enveloping you forced you to betray your own city to be sacked. You were condemned for your lack of faith by your own good priest Uzziah, who remonstrated you and begged you with tears, "Brothers, take courage, and let us endure yet five more days, in which the Lord our God will return His mercy to us. He will not utterly forsake us. But if these days come and go, and no help reaches us, I will do as you say" (Judith 7:30–31).

O beloved Uzziah, wonderful pastor and leader of your people! How low in your own estimation are people in general. It is as if you were saying to them, "Are you setting limits for God to give His help to you? You do this because you have lost your endurance and have completely consigned your longsuffering to oblivion."

Courageous Judith could not bear this weakness in her fellow citizens. When she heard of their decision, she called the elders of the city, including Uzziah, to herself, and said to them:

> Listen to me now, rulers of the people of Bethulia! Your words spoken today to the people are not right, nor is the oath you have sworn and pronounced between God and yourselves, promising to surrender the city to our adversaries unless the Lord turns and helps you in so many days. Now who are you to have put God to the test this day, setting yourselves up as God's equals among the sons of men? You are testing the Lord Almighty, but you will never come to know anything!... No, brothers! Do not provoke the Lord our God to anger. (Judith 8:11–14)

The elders answered this wise and courageous speech by agreeing with Judith's plan to save her city. They put themselves completely at her disposal, and they were not disappointed in her.

The example of Judith shows that only a long-suffering human will unite a person with God so tightly that the more calamities and sorrows loom over them, the more sure their hope becomes that God will help. In addition, such a person always cries out to God:

> Bear with me always in Your goodness and mercy, Lord. If I repeat my petition for ten, twenty, thirty years, or even longer, I will still not cease to ask, nor will I give You a deadline to answer my petition. Even if it becomes obvious that my petition will not be answered, even then my conviction in Your goodness and my faith in You teach me that You will

never leave me with nothing. If You do not give me what I ask, then You will reward me with something even greater.

The Prophet Habakkuk confirms this, "if he should tarry, wait for him, for he will surely come, and he will not tarry" (Habakkuk 2:3).

V

The fifth quality of a perfected human will that loves God is an ardent zeal in fulfilling the will of God. This person who truly loves God not only aligns his desires with God's, but he fulfills the desires of God with fiery zeal, while whatever displeases God he completely rejects. If anyone were to ask why he desires what God desires and rejects what God hates, he will say that the only reason is that God desires it or that God abhors it. God is the most exalted Love, an active Love, and whoever acts according to its laws abides in God (and in His Love), and God abides in Him (see John 4:16). Someone uttered this thought thus: "I love, because I love, and I love so that I may love, for love is always beloved."

According to Blessed Augustine, we must transform ourselves into love completely. As God desired to bring the cosmos into existence for the sake of His love, so we must turn ourselves into love for Him in gratitude, only for the sake of God and His holy will. The philosopher Epictetus[23] taught something similar:

What does it mean to commit yourself to God? This means that whatever God wants, His faithful creature wants as well. Whatever He does not want, His faithful creature does not want either.

However, this oneness of will between God and man could not occur if God did not rule the cosmos through His providence. Our faithfulness to God would not be genuine if we did not admit that everything that occurs in our life—both good and evil—occurs by God's will or permission.

In the Old Testament church, before its transformation through the God-Man Jesus Christ into the Church of the New Testament, it was pleasing to God to order Moses and Aaron to cover all the sacred objects and vessels of the altar with red covers whenever the Ark would be moved during the wanderings of the Jews across the desert of Sinai. The Levites were assigned to carry these vessels. This commandment is given in detail in the fourth chapter of

Numbers: "Aaron and his sons shall enter [the tabernacle] and take down the overshadowing veil and cover the ark of the testimony with it. Then they shall put on it a blue leather covering; and on top of this they shall spread an entire-ly blue cloth, and then insert the carrying-poles" (Numbers 4:5–6). After this, there are instructions concerning the packing of the table of presentation and the golden altar with its vessels. All of these commandments were necessary to prevent the rest of the people from seeking to see the holy objects merely out of idle curiosity. For the penalty for anyone who would see, much less touch, a sacred vessel was death.

Thus, those who carried the sacred vessels never saw a single one of them, but only felt their weight upon their shoulders. In a similar way, everyone who completely submits to the will of God avoids searching into the inscrutable reasons for God's providence and wisdom. He will not ask why God allowed one thing, commanded another, yet forbade a third, and so on. Every one of us must bear this limitation on our curiosity with eager-ness. It is enough for us to be sure that the burden we bear, wrapped in blue or scarlet covering—that is, hidden in the unseen depths of God's will—is for our salvation.

VI

Finally, in order for a human will to be acceptable to God, it must be fruitful. A fruitful will, like fertile ground, produces from its heart (the inner man) many exalted thoughts and desires, and it dedicates all of them eagerly, as the first fruits, to God's glory. Some of these fruits include wisdom, a mind that gravi-tates toward heaven, prayers filled with love, groans from the heart ascending to heaven in words such as these: "O all-beloved God, how I want not only to suffer, but to die for You, even if it were the most painful and dishonorable death."

This heavenly agitation of the heart unites God and man so intimately in every good deed that the union is palpable, even if invisible. This union is so complete that God reveals His mercy in a way that allows His beloved to truly refer to God as Father: "Even so, Father, for so it seemed good in Your sight" (Matthew 11:26). Such a true Christian will say to himself, "I received and continue to receive everything good from God's hand. Can I not bear a little deprivation for His sake?" Thus, a true Christian accepts everything eagerly, as given to him by God. Even the ancient philosophers knew this to be true. Epictetus said the following:

Never dare to say that you have lost this or that object. Instead, say that you have given this or that object to God. Did you lose a child? No, you gave him to God. Did someone steal your estate? No, it was given to God. But you will say, "A wicked man stole it from me!" Why do you ask who took it? He who gave it took it back. As soon as it is taken, you should care for it as much as you care for another's estate. You should care for it as much as a traveler cares for the inn where he spent the night.

Every person who desires truly to commit himself totally to God must think in such a manner. If he loses anything, he should say, "God gave it to me, and God took it back again." In other words, a Christian does not pay any attention to the person who stole, but only to God Who allowed it to happen, to God Who returned to Himself that which He gave before. Therefore, a true follower of God will repeat the words of Christ in any situation: "Even so, Father, for so it seemed good in Your sight" (Luke 10:21). In addition, dear reader, search deeply into the meaning and significance of this wise and mystical divine utterance. The Heavenly Father told His Son in ancient times through the prophet, "I will... give You as the covenant of a race, as the light of the Gentiles" (Isaiah 42:6). It is as if God were saying, "It is not enough for Me that You brought to Me the remainder of the Israelites who are still faithful to Me; I want You to illumine and convert the pagans who do not know Me."

This prophecy preceded Christ's birth by eight hundred years, and the Son, Who has in His divine essence one desire with the Father, accepted it. The humble human nature of Christ accepted it with eager readiness, as the Evangelist Matthew writes, "At that time Jesus answered and said, 'I thank You Father, Lord of heaven and earth'..." (see Matthew 11:25–30). Note here that in Matthew's account no one asked Jesus a question. Christ answered the Father in heaven in the spirit of His constant oneness with Him after He had truly fulfilled the will of His Father by preaching to the people, especially His disciples, the mystery of the redemption of the entire human race. With what joy and exultation does He glorify the holy will of His Heavenly Father:

I thank You, Father, Lord of heaven and earth, that You have hidden these things from the wise and prudent [at least in their own estimation] and have revealed them to babes [i.e., His disciples, who were like children in their spiritual simplicity and the purity of their hearts]. Even so, Father, for so it seemed good in Your sight. All things have been delivered to Me by My Father. (Matthew 11:25–27)

It is as if Christ is saying to His Father, "Father, I will do everything that You command Me to do." In the same way as the Father spoke to His son across the abyss of ages through the Prophet Isaiah, so God speaks with every one of us from before the ages, for He foresaw every one of us in space and time. He foreknew, with perfect clarity, everything about our birth, life, and death, and he prepared the perfect help for the personal salvation and blessedness of every one of us, making it fit exactly to our character, our moral and spiritual qualities. For God foresees our life in its entirety—past, present, and future—in all of its actions and particular circumstances, as if every person's life were laid out on the palm of His hand. He cooperates in the salvation of every person invisibly, but wisely. In other words, He uses many different means or events, both sweet and bitter, both pleasant and abhorrent, to save us.

Therefore, we must firmly believe in God's direction of the cosmos and especially in God's providence for mankind. We must be attentive to ourselves. Do we thank God for everything He sends us during our entire life, be it pleasant or unpleasant (but always conducive to our salvation)? We must wisely conform our desires with the will of God as expressed in important events in our lives. Those who commit themselves to God hear God's voice resonating in their hearts, especially during these important events. Every time we receive God's blessing on our intended action, or every time we do not, we must humbly thank God with a submissive spirit, repeating the words of our Saviour and Redeemer. "I thank You, Father, Lord of heaven and earth" for everything You have sent me, for supporting my life, for correcting my mistakes, and for saving my soul. "Even so, Father, for so it seemed good in Your sight."

 CHAPTER 8

How Human Will Can Conform to Divine Will in Various Everyday Circumstances

I have already noted what preparation is useful and helpful to unite the human will with the divine. Now I must show through various examples how this can be accomplished in life.

I

"And though I bestow all my goods to feed the poor, and though I give my body to be burned, but have not love, it profits me nothing" (1 Corinthians 13:3). In such a case, any good deed that I do will simply not be a good deed.

St Pimen[24] always gave this counsel: never act according to your own will if it contradicts God's will; may your will be always in agreement with God's. And if your desire truly does not contradict the will of God, then God will reveal this to you through the Gospels or by inspiring in your heart the thought of holding off on doing your intended deed, and instead to commit it to God's will, saying, "If my desire is pleasing to God, it will happen; if it is not, it will not happen. As God wants, so do I."

Worthily glorified is Ruth the Moabitess in Scripture. When her Jewish mother-in-law Naomi, the wife of Elimelech, became a widow—having lost in Moab her husband and both sons—she returned to her home city of Bethlehem. She blessed her daughters-in-law Orpah and Ruth and counseled both of them to remain in their own country in the homes of their parents. Orpah agreed, but Ruth refused to leave Naomi, a poor and helpless widow. Ruth said to Naomi,

Do not ask me to leave you, or turn back from following you; for wherever you go, I will go; and wherever you lodge, I will lodge; your people shall be my people, and your God, my God. And wherever you die, I will die, and there I will be buried. May the Lord cause this to happen to me, and more also, if anything but death parts you and me. (Ruth 1:16–18)

Any person who loves God ardently, with his entire heart and soul, will say the same thing to God as Ruth did to Naomi. Such a person can speak no other way. Before it pleased God to carry Prophet Elijah away from this world in a chariot of fire, the prophet spoke to Elisha, "'Stay here, please, for the Lord sent me to Bethel'. But Elisha said, 'As the Lord lives, and as your soul lives, I will not leave you'" (4 Kingdoms 2:2). He repeated this answer three times to his master, desiring always to remain by his side.

Here is another example of a united human and divine will. Jehoram, the King of Israel, desiring to punish the King of Moab for not sending him tribute, invited Jehoshaphat, King of Israel, to help him attack Moab. Jehoshaphat answered, "I will go. I am as you are, my people as your people, my horses as your horses" (4 Kingdoms 3:7). In the same way, we must unite with God in all the powers of our soul, in every deed we do, as Ruth united to Naomi, as Elisha united to Elijah, as Jehoshaphat to Jehoram. Let each of us say to Him with undoubting faith, unfailing love, and firm hope, "Your will, O my God, is my will. Your heart is my heart. I submit myself completely, O God, to Your merciful and righteous goodwill. I confess Your mercy and justice over myself."

Let us preserve such oneness of will with the divine in all actions and deeds, in our work, in caring for our subordinates, in all our labors and studies, in our losses, in sicknesses, and in the very hour of our death, having unshakeable hope in the redemptive sacrifice of Christ for our sins. Brother-Christians, we will then see God's great mercy to us and the eternal blessedness prepared by Him for our sake. Let us commit ourselves completely to His will, having nothing on our lips except these words: "Let Your will be done in me, O merciful and righteous God, my Redeemer!"

All of Christ's virtues and benefactions were revealed most vividly and majestically in His sufferings, and also in the quality of His last humble, ardent prayer in Gethsemane. After completing His final Old Testament Passover meal in the high room in Jerusalem, and after instituting the greatest of Mysteries by giving His disciples His own All-pure Body and Blood in the form of bread and wine (for the sake of His union with them and to give them eternal blessedness and to help them remember Him in this life), Jesus went with His disciple to the Mount of Olives (as was their custom). When they arrived,

> He said to them, "Pray that you may not enter into temptation." And He was withdrawn from them about a stone's throw, and He knelt down and prayed, saying, "Father, if it is Your will, take this cup away from Me; nevertheless not My will, but Yours, be done." Then an angel appeared to Him from heaven, strengthening Him. And being in agony, He prayed more earnestly. Then His sweat became like great drops of blood falling down to the ground. (Luke 22:40–44)

There is no better, no shorter, no more perfect, no more God-pleasing prayer than this: "Not my will, but Yours, be done" (Luke 22:42). Not as I wish, O Lord, but as You wish. Your will be done, O Lord, even if the entire cosmos will come tumbling down. Some of the three hundred and fifty Holy Fathers of the Seventh Ecumenical Council had the custom to repeat this prayer three times: "O All-good Jesus, may Your will be done!"

St John Cassian[25] offers the following question:

> What does this petition in the Lord's prayer—Thy will be done on earth as it is in heaven—mean? This petition means nothing other than this: human beings must be like the angels. And since the will of God is fulfilled by the angels without question, those who live on earth must do likewise, not seeking their own personal will, but the will of God.

No one can utter this petition from the Lord's prayer sincerely, except one who believes with his heart and confesses with his lips, that God alone arranged all things on earth for the good, both things that help us prosper and many misfortunes that strike us down. He provides for the salvation and benefit of every one of us more assiduously, diligently than any of us do for ourselves. For He knows better what each person needs for the benefit and salvation of his soul. Therefore, he who completely rejects his own will when it contradicts the will of God—thereby reconciling his personal will with the will of God in his actions—is "at the very gates of heaven" (St John Cassian) or, better yet, has the kingdom of heaven inside him (see Luke 17:21). Truly, in heaven there are countless myriads of blessed saints who have the same will as the will of God.

Abba Mark asked Abba Arsenios, "Abba, why do you not come to visit us?"

St Arsenios answered him wisely, "I have better and more pleasant company—the inhabitants of heaven. They all desire one and the same thing; they all have one and the same will. On the contrary, here on earth, you will find as many different desires as there are people in a community."

Whoever submits to the will of God both in happiness and in misfortune understands the meaning of King David's words, "Behold, what is so good, or what is so fine, but for brethren to dwell in unity?" (Psalm 132:1). Who are these brethren? They are Christ and the righteous man, for the very King of Heaven is not ashamed to count Himself among such brethren.

II

When Solomon tried to find a vivid image to express the wonder of a truly wise man, he said, "The wise man's eyes are in his head" (Ecclesiastes 2:14). St Gregory the Great explains these words as follows:

> Whoever strives with his mind to examine the organization and direction of the visible world and its unshakeable laws, will see the invisible hand of God, His wise providence, His ever-present power and holy will. Such a person is truly a lover of wisdom (see Romans 1:20). For such a person, no matter how many eyes he may have (that is, thoughts of the mind), they will all be in his head (that is, in his spirit acting through the mind).

The philosopher Epictetus lived a life that seemed to him better than any happiness. He had a single servant and a single clay lamp to illuminate his house while he studied and wrote. However, someone bought this clay lamp after his death for one thousand denarii, in memory and in honor of such a famous man. Lucian of Samosata,[26] one of the later Greek philosophers (second century A.D.), ridiculed many other philosophers, but he had only praise for Epictetus. Epictetus wrote, among his many other works, a wonderful work called the *Enchiridion* (*The Handbook*). This book has so much in it that is wise and beneficial that a pious Christian, not a pagan, could have written it. It will be a reproach to many Christian writers who left writings filled with lies—Christian writers who spent this life unrepentant, unfaithful, and unfeeling.

Epictetus famously said, "All philosophy lies in two words: sustain and abstain." He insists that it is very beneficial and safe to follow the dictates of the will of God and to submit to it eagerly and without question. He considers this to be the surest path to achieve both temporary and eternal good things. It would be good to offer his thoughts on following God's will:

> I give up every personal desire in obedience to God. Does the Almighty desire for me to fall ill? Then I desire to be sick. Is it pleasing to Him to give me some kind of gift? I accept it with reverence and gratitude. Is something unpleasing to God? It does not please me either. Does God want me to die? I am ready to die, for who can forbid me anything that is contrary to my will or convince me otherwise, if it is (as I am sure) pleasing to God?

O Christian, is not your callous heart moved by a pagan's faithfulness to God? Are you not horrified at your own stubbornness and foolishness? Epictetus has many other wise sayings concerning many other subjects. He has an unshakable conviction that the person who commits himself with his whole heart to the will of God shall walk his life's path in peace. What does it mean to "commit oneself entirely to God?" It means complete submission to God. Whatever is pleasing to God should also please me. What God does not desire, that I also do not desire. How can this be done in actual fact?

Such complete submission only occurs by God's blessing and by His all-wise providence and just rule over the world, never infringing on the freedom given to all reasoning creatures. Whatever God has given me is mine and within my authority. But what God has kept for Himself is subject to His authority alone.

He gave me a free will, and He does not want to limit my freedom in any way. He inscrutably made my body from the earth in such a way that it would serve only me and no one else without my will. He subjected all of visible, irrational nature to my authority, for the support of my earthly life, but He left to Himself the ultimate authority over the world and the cosmos. He subjected to my authority and direction my entire family, my wife and children, and the property that I have acquired through my labors until He should demand an account from me. For God gave me all this without expecting a return by His goodness alone. So why would I oppose God?

If we do not begin to freely and eagerly submit to God's plan, then God will lead us to it anyway against our will. Seneca,[27] a philosopher who lived during the reign of Augustus, in his work concerning freedom, wrote,

> You ask what is total freedom? It means to have no fear of any people or even God (for He is not terrifying to the good, being beloved of them). It means not to want anything shameful or excessive. It means

having complete authority over oneself, or—which is the same thing—
to belong to oneself entirely. In all this consists complete freedom, our
most precious treasure.

However, no one can belong to himself if he does not first belong to God
in such a way that his desires align in all ways with God's. Every person who
desires to belong to himself or to become independent must reject all external
things and turn within. He must (as much as possible) keep himself out of others' business and constantly watch his own behavior and actions. He must not
react to any insults, for everything that is unpleasant he endures with meekness, since it was allowed by God. If he does this, only then can he begin to
belong to himself and have complete, reasonable freedom. Blessed Augustine
says something similar concerning total freedom:

> A virtuous person, even if he is surrounded by misfortunes or is
> burdened by labors, yet he remains free. On the contrary, an evil person,
> even if he were to rule an entire kingdom, remains a slave, for he has
> many masters: the iniquitous desires and passions that lurk within.

III

The brave warrior Judas Maccabeus, when inspiring his soldiers to bravery
before battle, said to them: "Be ready at dawn to fight with these Gentiles who
have gathered against us to destroy us and our sanctuary. For it is better for us
to die in war than to look upon the evils the Gentiles would bring to us and the
sanctuary. But as God's will is in heaven, so He will do" (1 Maccabees 3:58–60).

Joab encouraged his brother Abishai, "Be of good courage and let us be
strong for our people and for the cities of our God; for the Lord will do what is
good in His sight" (2 Kingdoms 10:12). It is a very laudable and honorable thing
to have a courageous heart in all things, a heart that greets every event with
trust in the goodness and providence of God. For it often happens, even with
wise men, experienced military commanders, and holy men—all of whom usually act wisely and courageously—that their intentions do not reach a good end.
But such men ascribe any lack of success to the lack of God's blessing on their
intention, and so they greet their lack of success with joy, because they did not
act in opposition to God's will.

All of this is confirmed by the Preacher, who said, "I returned and saw
under the sun that: The race is not to the swift, nor the battle to the strong,

nor bread to the wise, nor wealth to men of understanding, nor favor to men of knowledge; for time and chance will happen to them all" (Ecclesiastes 9:11).

What the Preacher calls "chance" is not accidental to God, merely to our human perspective. It is not strange that even a wise man can make mistakes in his intentions; however, we often consider this to be a misfortune and ascribe our failure to some evil fate or spirit. Truly there are events and phenomena in the world that do not depend on human reason, whether they are good or bad. God's power, foreknowledge, and providence knows of them pre-eternally and foresees all the circumstances of their appearance. God makes these events coincide with certain places, times, and people to bring them into accordance with His wise direction of the cosmos. However, these ways and paths are invisible to us, and often the means chosen by God to achieve His goals are incomprehensible to us until they are accomplished. Only afterward can we come to understand God's care and providence for us and for the human race.

God occasionally repeats these unexpected events—either merciful or threatening to us depending on the manner of our life—in order to remind us not to ascribe anything to our own efforts, reason, or work ethic. Instead, He wants us to pay attention every moment to our inner spiritual life and become convinced that everything in the cosmos occurs only by the goodwill or per-mission of God, in accordance to our good or evil deeds, which will determine either our blessedness or our perdition.

The ancient pagan nations honored chance (fortune) greatly. They even burned incense to it. Now, in the light of the Holy Gospel, what is chance? It is nothing but a pernicious delusion of the mind, the very spawn of hell! The light of the grace of the Gospels has shown us the true reason for our prosperity and our misfortune (i.e., our sinfulness, consisting of breaking the command-ments of God and the laws of the state). By its nature, sin is a lie, a nothingness, the work of the father of lies and those unfortunate people who are deluded by him (see John 8:44). Everything else in the world—prosperity or misfortune—occurs by the foresight and providence of God for our eternal salvation.

The all-holy will of God moves all the works of mankind like a wheel that spins unevenly. Sometimes it moves fast, sometimes slowly; in this manner, all unexpected events that seem to us to occur by blind chance in reality direct us wisely to the best of intentions. "I am the Lord God, and there is no other. I am He who prepared light and made darkness, who makes peace and creates troublesome things" (Isaiah 45:6–7).

Fortuna was often depicted with two faces and in two colors. A statue of Fortuna had a white and cheerful face on the front, and a black, surly face on the back. She revealed herself in one of two opposite faces: the first face was a symbol of prosperity; the second a symbol of misfortune, calamity, all the evil that Fortuna sometimes sent to her followers. These are childish fables and games. Happiness or misfortune, poverty or prosperity, God sends them all.

Here it will not be excessive to quote Seneca, who interprets the apparently undeserved misfortunes of some and the prosperity of others in the following manner:

> Some people become fairly upset and even silent at the memory of the evil end of some virtuous men. Socrates was forced to kill himself in prison. Rutilius was forced to live in exile. Pompey and Cicero bowed their heads to the swords of their pupils. What should every person then expect for himself, seeing good repaid by the greatest evil? Examine this, and understand for what reason every man suffers evil. If he bravely suffered for the truth, then try to emulate him. If he perished because of laziness or because he did not purse virtue, then there is nothing useful to be learned from him. Thus, some people were worthy of a better end and will receive a reward from God and respect and emulation from other people. Others have deserved the contempt of mankind and separation from God.

In this sense, Job, David, and Jeremiah often express lament or sorrow when remembering the misfortunes or unjust deaths of the righteous and the undeserved prosperity of lawless, lazy, and slothful men in this life. But this is not blind chance or fortune at work. These things have no significance or power. All of this occurs by God's foresight and providence for our correction, to show us by the example of men of history that we can expect to be rewarded according to our deeds. Thus, we vividly see the mad chaos resulting from laziness, carelessness, and sloth. We also see examples of the consequences of general moral corruption in the family, society, government, and in the world at large. By this, the Lord wakes people up to turn to Him and to have a care for the improvement of their moral health.

IV

In one of the most brutal episodes of the Old Testament, men of the tribe of Benjamin raped a concubine of a Levite repeatedly until she died. When Israel demanded that these men be put to death, the tribe of Benjamin refused. Israel united as one man and decided to attack the city of Gibeah, where the crime occurred. In order to be assured of their success in this righteous work, they inquired of the true God: whom should they choose to lead the attack? The Lord said, "Judah, as leader, will go up first" (Judges 20:18). Israel was pleased with this answer, and so it was easy to muster a great army. They were sure of victory over Benjamin.

However, they were defeated handily, losing twenty-two thousand men in the process. But the Israelites did not despair. They prayed and fasted and asked God a second time whether or not to attack Benjamin. They received the same answer: "Go up against them" (Judges 20:23). This time, they again hoped for God's help and fought bravely, but again they lost the battle, this time losing eighteen thousand men.

How can this be explained? God ordered them to attack and punish the evildoers twice, and both times the armies of the Israelites were defeated, and they lost nearly forty thousand men. Who can understand and explain these commands of God?

A third time all of Israel gathered at Bethel before the Ark to pray for God's mercy with bitter tears, an extraordinary fast, and many burnt offerings. Humbly they confessed their sins before God and begged Him to deliver the nation of Israel from a heretofore-unseen temptation, lewdness, and outrage. They begged Him to give them an exact order. Should they fight the enemy a third time or not? If yes, they asked Him to give them unmistakable signs of their victory.

God gave His third command through Phinehas, the grandson of Aaron, who ministered before the Ark of the Covenant. "Go up, for tomorrow I will deliver them into your hands" (Judges 20:28). If we are to judge like weak humans, it would be understandable if the Israelites lost faith at this moment and doubted, for twice God commanded them to enter the fray, and twice those who fought by God's command were slaughtered. Who would have the courage to go again to a sure death? Who would prefer such military uncertainty to a safe and peaceful life at home? But the firm hope of the Israelites overcame all these doubts. They attacked Benjamin a third time and defeated their enemies completely. In this battle, Benjamin lost twenty-five thousand warriors, and in all the other cities of Benjamin, civilians were put to the sword, property was looted, and the cities themselves were destroyed and burnt to the ground by Israel (Judges 19, 20, 21).

In this horrific episode, two moments are worthy of special attention. The first is that the judgments of God are not comprehensible in their vastness. The second is that for those who patiently hope in God dishonor never remains. Of this we will speak in more detail later.

In all these and similar situations, the safest thing to do is to fall down with heart-felt prayer before God. And even if our good deed sometimes begins badly, we must never lose hope or despair. Instead, we must have a firm hope in God's help, no matter what we do. Ignoring all doubts, we must look at God with the open eyes of our faith and we must commit ourselves to His holy will.

Sometimes in the life of those around us we also encounter unexpected events. For example, those who are moderate in food and drink become seriously ill; healthy and strong-bodied people fall to tuberculosis; the innocent are punished; hermits are attacked by impure thoughts or apparitions. Deliverance against the enemy comes by the same means both in societal and individual life—only by following the will of God.

In everyday life, sometimes the proverb is true: "The more, the better." But when we examine the manner of God's direction of the world, sometimes the opposite is true, "the less, the better." In other words, as St Paul says, "work out *your own* salvation with fear and trembling; for it is God who works in you both to will and to do for His good pleasure" (Philippians 2:12–13).

V

A certain man who wanted to become a monk asked St Pitirim, "Tell me, honored father, how must I act in this life in order to become a true emulator of the saints?"

Abba Pitirim answered,

> If you want to find a calm life with no problems here on earth and in the next life, then begin every action with the following question: "who am I, that I choose to prefer my own will and desires to the will of God and His command?" In addition, strictly follow the commandment of Christ to never judge anyone (Matthew 7:1). If you follow these two rules, you will emulate the saints no matter what your earthly calling, for God has saints in all social classes, callings, and professions.

What a wise, beneficial, and salvific counsel! Truly, God is subject to no law, and He gives account of His actions and commands to no man. May all human wisdom fall silent before Him, and may it revere His divine will, falling down before His wondrous works and salvific signs. The Lord alone lives eternally (i.e., without beginning or end), and He alone is all-holy. He created everything that exists with His mighty Word, and everything is founded, lives, and moves by the Breath of His mouth (see Psalm 32:6). To no one did He give the responsibility of interpreting His actions. How can we examine and measure the power of His might and His great works? How can we even speak of the greatness of His mercy? (see Sirach 18:1–4).

It used to be the custom in large cities for people to synchronize their watches with the main clock in the town square. In the same way, each one of us should synchronize our constantly changing desires and wills to the will of God, expressed in the books of divine revelation. Let us further become convinced by the experiences of history that, despite all attempts of the unfaithful and ungodly, revealed truths justify themselves in deed. There are many examples of this in world history.

True followers of Christ, never doubting the truth of the Gospels, utter a constant call to Christ the Lord in the inner heart:

> O beloved Christ, my Saviour, who has redeemed Me by Your precious Blood, nothing gives me such joy as the constant sense in my heart of the active grace of Your Holy Spirit. Your Spirit leads me to submit my desires completely without complaint to Your pre-eternal goodwill and dispensation concerning me. For Your holy will and my love for the greatness of Your glory and honor is greater than all other things.

Here is an example, an image of the willing submission of the human will to the divine.

Borgia, the King of Crete, lived for twenty-two years in blissful marriage with his beloved wife Eleonora. When his wife fell ill and no medicines could heal her, the pious king, who did not want to be parted from his beloved wife, prayed to God both at home and by adding petitions for her in the liturgy. He also fasted and gave alms. One day, when he humbly prayed with tears alone in a locked room, he suddenly heard an inner voice (as he himself later recounted). It said, "Do you wish and desire for your wife to become healthy and live for a long time with you? Very well, it will be as you ask, but this will not be for your benefit."

He was shaken by this voice, doubtlessly believing that it was the voice of God mystically telling him that he did not understand the nature of his own prayer. The King prayed again with tears, saying,

> O Lord, my God! Why do You assign to my will that which belongs only to Your holy power? I am obliged to fulfill Your holy will always without complaint. I humbly submit to it, for who knows what is good

for me better than You, O my God? Let Your will be done not only concerning my wife, but also concerning my children and myself. Whatever pleases You, make it so. Let Your will be done, not mine.

Until this moment, the physicians could not accurately predict whether or not she would recover. Now, after this prayer of her husband, the doctors were sure that she would die.

VI

The previous example illustrated how we must act in all doubtful or confusing situations. Here are several more examples for our instruction. King David was so committed to the will of God that God Himself was a witness to it: "I have found David, the son of Jesse, a man after My own heart, who will do all My will" (see 1 Kingdoms 13:13). It is as if God were saying that He searched long for a man pleasing to Himself, capable of fulfilling His will, His providence. He waited long and finally He found him. This praise of the future king of the Jews, given by God Himself, is greater than any other honor available to earthly kings.

Christ the Lord, obedient in all things to His Father, offered Himself to us as an example and model of submitting to the will of God, saying, "For I have come down from heaven, not to do My own will, but the will of Him who sent Me" (John 6:38). When the disciples offered Him food in Samaria, He answered them, "My food is to do the will of Him who sent Me, and to finish His work" (John 4:34). Notice what the Father orders His only-begotten Son to do. That which even the lowest servant would not do, the Son fulfills to the letter. And on which of us, cruel-hearted ones, did He lay such a heavy, unbearable, and shameful burden as He laid on His own Son? Whom did He deliver to such shame, beatings, and tortures, as His Son, Who humbled Himself, being obedient to the Father even as He approached the Praetorium of Pilate, the shameful whipping post, the heavy and shameful cross (that through Him became a majestic sign of the greatest of victories), the tomb (which was not even His own), and even the very gates of Hell?

"For I have come down from heaven, not to do My own will, but the will of Him who sent Me." We, who are the slaves of God, should endure the heaviest and filthiest labors, the most extreme deprivations, since the only-begotten Son of God endured far more, and all in order to do the will of His Father! Therefore, Christ the Lord, having summarized all the commands of God, said, "Not everyone who says to Me, 'Lord, Lord', shall enter the kingdom of heaven, but he who does the will of My Father in heaven" (Matthew 7:21).

In conclusion, every person who has committed himself completely into the disposition of the will of God is so great that he will reach the heights of the highest mountain with no problems. All dangers such as storms, hail, thunder, and lightning are beneath his feet; he stands higher than them. He looks at any changes in his earthly life without fear. He has but one fear in his soul, and that is to always align his will and his desires to the will of God and to completely submit himself to it. Therefore, he constantly turns to God with the words, "Thy will be done on earth as it is heaven (concerning me and within me)."

 CHAPTER 9

On the Meaning and Significance of the Prayer "Thy Will Be Done on Earth as It Is in Heaven," and with What Spiritual Disposition One Must Utter These Words

The disciples of Christ asked Him, "'Lord, teach us to pray, as John also taught his disciples'. So He said to them, 'When you pray, say: Our Father in heaven, Hallowed be Your name. Your kingdom come. Your will be done on earth as it is in heaven'" (Luke 11:1–2). But, O God, how inscrutable is this prayer for us! We are very different from the blessed spirits of heaven. They live in heaven; we have been exiled from paradise and live on earth, in the valley of tears, filled with all the misfortunes of earthly life. Everything the heavenly hosts desire, they receive, and they have nothing that is not pleasing to them. We, on the other hand, are far from the heavenly life, and we hardly hope even for occasional goods and pleasures.

We encounter opposition, sorrow, and filth everywhere. Even if we encounter something good, it rarely happens by goodwill (i.e., without compulsion), but more often for other reasons, less noble. On this earth, every day brings us sorrows and insults from countless debauchers, traitors, thieves, rascals, and other evil men. There, in heaven, everything follows a good order, everything is triumphant and joyful, and it is very easy and pleasant to do the will of God, to submit to the command of God, since nothing contrary to His will can possibly confuse a soul in heaven. Here on earth, thousands of calamities persecute us and overwhelm our spirit, burdening us with sorrows and cares. No sooner do we find a moment of rest than a new trouble, a new war assails us. Everything that is evil has gathered against us, calamity after calamity follows in steady succession, and we can hardly find one free moment in which to remember God and to pray calmly to Him.

We, weak mortals, are neither zealous nor diligent in prayer, and so we cannot hope to equal the inhabitants of heaven. We cannot say together with them, "Your will be done on earth as it is in heaven," for we are so different from them! O Lord! Transport us to heaven, and then we will rival even the angels in our eagerness to do Your will.

Is it actually like this in real life, beloved Christian? No! We do not properly understand the words: "Your will be done on earth as it is in heaven." It is not for the aforementioned reasons that we do not do God's will on earth. The true reason we do not do the will of God on earth as the angels do in heaven is not found in the external obstacles surrounding us. No, it is found hiding within us. We are weak in spirit; we do not labor to fulfill the will of God to the letter. How easily we fall, defeated by our own sinfulness, even in the simplest of tasks. The smallest sorrow, like the sigh of a tiny wind, overwhelms us and confuses us. Immediately, we are filled with terror, as though we are about to die. Calm down, you frightened ones of little faith!

God never commands anything that a person cannot fulfill. God never gives a task too difficult to complete. Brothers, let us focus all our energy on doing the will of God on earth in the same way as the angels do it in heaven. If we do not have enough strength to do the will of God in actual deed, then God will accept our sincere desire to try in lieu of the actual deed. St Cyprian said, "Christ taught us to pray in this way: Your will be done on earth as it is in heaven. This does not mean that God should do everything that He wants on earth. No, it means we ourselves must try to do what God wants and what He expects from us." Thus, whoever desires to follow Christ should not limit the full meaning of these words, but in their full significance, he should say, "Your will be done on earth as it is in heaven." He should ask God to give him the knowledge and wisdom to do His divine will.

I

This is how we should pray the Lord's prayer.

1. We must pray with pure intention. *Your will be done*, for I desire with my whole heart to follow it, not expecting anything in return, not for a reward or to receive anything from You, not because You, Lord, have enriched me already with Your mercies, not because You have protected

me from my enemies, as Satan slandered Job before God (Job 1:9–11). I desire it not because I fear the eternal torments of Gehenna, but in the simplicity of my heart I follow Your will. I desire that which You desire only because You wish it, only because this is Your will, O my God!

2. We must pray with love. *Your will be done.* I only seek one thing; I only have one thought—to do Your will in all things, Lord! May the majesty of Your name, O my God, be spread and glorified through me, Your worthless servant. This alone I consider to be the greatest honor and reward: to be worthy of pleasing You, my Creator, Who gave me a mind and a free will as a pledge of intimate communion with You, my Creator and Saviour. St John Chrysostom said, "You do not understand what it means to *please God*—that is, to pray to Him, to glorify His power, righteousness, and mercy, and to do His will—if in pleasing Him you seek another reward. The greatest reward is our living communion with God."

3. Our desire to do the will of God must be quick and freely given. *Your will be done, Heavenly Father!* I am ready to fulfill it without delay and by my own desire. Whoever ruminates at first whether or not to fulfill the commandments of God does not want to do them. Whoever cheerfully consecrates himself to the service of God is always ready and never delays to fulfill His holy will. A free will that does a good deed loses the grace of God in measure depending on the degree of sluggishness with which it does that good deed. Therefore, every true Christian must always repeat, together with David, "My heart is ready, O God, my heart is ready" to fulfill Your will, whether easy or difficult for me (Psalm 107:1).

4. We must do the will of God with pleasure in our hearts. Some tasks are completed quickly and easily, but unwillingly, "heartlessly," so to speak. And so, St Paul instructed the Corinthians, "He who sows sparingly will also reap sparingly, and he who sows bountifully will also reap bountifully. So let each one give as he purposes in his heart, not grudgingly or of necessity; for God loves a cheerful giver" (2 Corinthians 9:6–7). Whoever plans to dedicate everything he does to the will of God will not consider any sorrows he meets along the way to be difficult, but instead he will accept them as good fortune and easily endure them, saying together with Christ the Lord, "My food is to do the will of Him who sent Me, and to finish His work" (John 4:34). *Your will be done on earth as it is in heaven.*

5. Our fulfillment of the will of God must be total and complete. A person who truly desires to fulfill the will of God and to be pleasing to God does not search for self-justifying excuses or apparent reasons for delaying the fulfillment of God's will. He does not say, "I will do Your will, O Lord,

but not now," or "I will listen to You, Lord, I will obey You, just don't command me to do it *now*," or "I am ready to wash and kiss everyone's feet, only don't force me to do it to my enemy," or "I will not agree to endure humiliation, except in cases when no one can see it," or "I am ready to do everything except that *one* thing." Such people are not faithful or submissive to the will of God. The faithful reject nothing; they do not run away from afflictions, but humbly and completely commit themselves to the will of God, saying, "O God, if it pleases You that I suffer such great and heavy sorrows and trials, here I am! I am ready for everything; I will accept everything eagerly. I will not refuse anything. Command even heavier punishment for me; only may Your holy and righteous will be done in me!"

6. Every person who fulfills the will of God must be longsuffering. May Your will, O Lord, be done by me and with me, over the course of tens, hundreds, thousands of years. Your will be done in all the endless ages. "I have inclined my heart to perform Thy statutes always" (Psalm 118:112). Do You wish, O Lord, that I wait for my salvation for a hundred, a thousand years? I will wait. If You wish this, I wish it as well. For those who have truly loved the Lord, it is desirable and pleasant to utter the words of His prayer constantly. This prayer is like the wings of the seraphim that raise us to the heights and exalt our mind and heart above the heavens, to the very throne of the Most High.

II

The chosen ones of God, the saints, rejoice more in completely fulfilling the will of God than in their own personal dignity and honor. Therefore, all of them are content with God's reward and the deserved honor they receive from Him, and not a single one of them considers himself greater than another. Entrusting themselves always to God and burning with a common love for Him, not only do they align and liken their will to His, but they allow their will, as it were, to be taken over and completely transformed into God's. They, and only they, act together with God. They rejoice and desire that God alone will act through them and in them, never ascribing anything to themselves. They rejoice that God wills all of us to have eternal blessedness with Him, that God wills to abide in all of us, not for us to find blessedness in the world outside of God, or to find pleasure in earthly good things and to forget about God or to not know Him, our Creator, at all.

In this manner, the transfigured human will attracts to itself God's all-encompassing love and the intimacy of His communion. We can truly say that God's will swallows up man's will; however, at the same time, God in no way limits any person's free will, for the person submits his will freely to God. This union of the human and divine will in the bond of love gives the greatest joy and happiness to the chosen righteous ones of God, who believe unstintingly in the eternal life with God, who love Him with their whole hearts, who love their both neighbors and all of creation ardently. Having within themselves a firm hope in the steadfastness of the Incarnate Word's promises—which are established in the historical destinies of churches, nations, and kingdoms that live and act in the spirit of Christ—they consider themselves fortunate and successful. On the contrary, they consider those who are weak in constant fulfillment of the commandments of Christ—or those who reject His teaching outright—to be truly unfortunate and, ultimately, already perishing.

The chosen ones of God desire that all nations and tribes will honor the name of God, and His wisdom, power, mercy, and truth as holy. They want all people (as the creations of the One God) to live together in peace and harmony. They hope that those who know God will instruct those who do not know Him, that the elders will teach the young all good things, that the strong will protect and care for the weak, that every person will treat others the same way that he wishes to be treated, not only in words, but in actions. The crown of their triumph and joy will be the universal glorification of the endless perfections of God, the greatness of His power, and the immeasurability of His might and dominion.

As good, well-behaved children do not envy their parents' happy life, their riches and contentment, but instead desire them to have ever more good things (even more than they wish for themselves), so the chosen ones of God rejoice in that ineffable blessedness in which God abides. They rejoice in it as much as they rejoice in their own blessedness; contemplating God's blessedness, they sing ecstatic songs before the throne of God, songs that St John heard while writing the Revelation on the island of Patmos: "Alleluia! For the Lord God Omnipotent reigns! Let us be glad and rejoice and give Him glory, for the marriage of the Lamb has come, and His wife has made herself ready" (Revelation 19:6–7).

Such a transfiguration, or more accurately such an intimate union of the chosen of God with the divine will, is accessible even to us. We must affix our reason carefully to the contemplation of God's perfections (as much as they are revealed to us): His power, eternity, wisdom, beauty, and endlessly inconceivable blessedness. Let our heart rejoice in how God, One in essence and glorified in Trinity: the Father, the Son, and the Holy Spirit, is eternal, infinite, and endless goodness, the source of all benefits (both spiritual and material), dependent on no one, self-sufficient completely, generous to all His creation, abiding in all invisibly. The summary and crown of all His perfections is His Love, the very essence of the Divine, the life of God, "for God is Love" (1 John 4:8). No greater or more perfect love can be found than the love with which God loves Himself in Himself and His creation. "For God so loved the world [i.e., all people as the creation of God] that He gave His only begotten Son, that whoever believes in Him should not perish but have everlasting life" (John 3:16).

Among people one will not find a more perfect love than a love that is very similar to that of God. Philosophers define love in the following way: to love is nothing but to desire to actively do good for another person. If this seems a self-evident truth, then the conclusion should be obvious as well: the more we desire to actively do good to a person, the more we love him. If we apply this principle to love for God, we can make the following conclusion: we cannot desire good for God, since His perfections are greater than we can ever expect to have ourselves (for His are limitless). Consequently, we can only show our love to God by acknowledging with our heart that His limitless perfections belong only to Him and dedicating ourselves completely in our actions to His perfect, holy will. If we do this, the will of God will be done on earth as it is in heaven.

III

A will that completely obeys the will of God brings people close to God, so close in fact that they become like lightning. In other words, they become ready to do the will of God instantly, like a flash of lightning, concerning which Job expressed himself thus: "Can you send out lightnings, and they shall go? They shall say to you, 'What do you want?'" (Job 38:35). It would be accurate to call such people—that is, those who reject and despise their own will for the sake of fulfilling God's will—Christ's lightning. If we follow our own sinful will, we rise up to the heights of pride, disdain for the lesser brethren in Christ, and even to self-deification. But since God desires the opposite from us, then we must strive to be pleasing to God, to do what God requires of us, and cheerfully submit to Him. When we live like this, doing His commandments is easy. We do not tire or lose strength if something difficult or sorrowful meets us on the way. Instead, presenting ourselves before the Lord, we say, "What do You command, Lord? Here we are, ready to die by Your will. Command us, tell us what You desire for us to do."

As lightning does not come from the water or the earth, but from many dense clouds combined into a single mass, so also our God-pleasing will is born and strengthened in our soul when our external senses are enclosed on all sides by prayers and thoughts of God. On such wings, our wills ascend to complete submission to God's will. Let us sensibly and dispassionately consider these things: a million angels please the unapproachable Light with completely obedient service. Even the Son of God lovingly submitted to His Heavenly Father and did His will without complaining in the manger in swaddling clothes, during constant travels, labors, and sufferings on the Cross. By calling this to mind, we cannot for a moment hold ourselves back from doing the will of God. With the quickness of lightning we will hurry to do His will, crying out with a pure heart, "Our Father in heaven, Hallowed be Your name. Your kingdom come. Your will be done on earth as it is in heaven."

A certain chief hunter of the Tsars once told one of his subordinates, "It is required of you to come with me tomorrow to the hunt." His subordinate answered, "It *need not be required of* me, for I will follow you with great pleasure." Everyone who is truly committed to God should likewise do nothing by necessity or out of a sense of duty, but should cheerfully fulfill all his Lord's commands. He should find pleasure in the doing, and with this small labor—the readiness to do the master's will cheerfully—he wins true freedom. Epictetus said, "I consider that which God wants to be better than anything that I want. I emulate Him as a student and follower; I desire with Him; I seek with Him. Whatever He wants, that I wish as well." What is more worthy and honest than these words of a pagan?

IV

The famous Agathon, desiring to unite his will with God's in the most intimate possible union, was ready to zealously endure, for the sake of Christ, all labors, diseases, sorrows, and afflictions, anything that can be expressed in words or even imagined. He was even ready to accept the sufferings of hell only for the sake of submitting His will to the will of God. He wanted to love God so ardently that even if God, in His holy will, refused to give him this gift, then he would never stop praying to God for permission to love Him. He had the habit of asking his conscience regularly, "Why do you not cry for your sins as often as you used to?"

His conscience answered him, "I do this because you have completely given yourself to God's will and you submit to Him in all things. You never refuse to do God's will. Whatever happens to you—whether it is pleasant or abhorrent—you thank God for everything, and you eagerly submit to His holy will."

It is appropriate to include here Blessed Augustine's reflection on God's commandment to Adam concerning abstaining from the Tree of the Knowledge of Good and Evil. This reflection takes the form of a conversation between Adam (the questioner) and God (the instructor).

Adam asks God, "If this tree is good, then why must I not touch it? If it is evil, then why was it planted in Eden?"

God answered, "It was planted in Eden because it is good (that is, pleasant to look at and beneficial). But you must not touch it or eat its fruits, because I want you to be My unquestioning, obedient, and virtuous servant. For I am the Lord, your Creator, your Life-giver, your Benefactor. You are my servant."

Let this conversation be for us a resolution to the thousands of doubts that we have concerning the reasons for this or that phenomenon in God's ruling of the cosmos. Whatever our limited mind cannot understand should be resolved with the following answer:

> God is our Lord and the Master of everything that exists in the cosmos. He reveals His will to us through the Holy Scriptures and through the activity of His providence for His creation. He commanded us to act according to His will without any doubt in its holiness, wisdom, and justice. For He is the Lord, and we are His servants, and so we must serve our Lord with a pure conscience, fulfilling His holy will in that calling or profession into which He has had the goodwill to place us.

Our cunning adversary asked the woman in Eden, "Why did God forbid this?" It would have been more natural to ask why Adam and Eve must not eat the fruit of that tree, for the answer to the question would be simple: "God has forbidden it." But the cunning serpent foresaw this answer, and so turned it into a question: "Why did God forbid this?"

As we have already seen from several historical examples, to ask why God does something when His will is already clearly revealed is foolish. The first and most important reason is that God did it because it pleases Him. Abraham was commanded to sacrifice his son Isaac. Could Abraham not have found plenty of reasons to resist God's will in this? But he did not resist God and silently submitted to His command. It was enough for Abraham that God desired it.

V

Consider this example: many parents, desiring to test the intelligence of their children, ask them, "Would you like to go on a walk today, for example, to the gardens, to drive around the city, or to visit our friends in the village? Or would you prefer to play some game and take a rest from your studies?"

The children answer, "As you wish. You are better suited to counsel us whether it is more useful for us to go on a walk or to continue studying."

Such an answer is proof of the children being raised well in complete and well-established intelligence. If the children ask to take a walk, without their parents' suggestion, when they should be studying, or if they try to avoid their responsibilities by any means possible, or if they yawn in a bored manner during classes and immediately rush to some spectacle after school, or if they spend all their time in useless and improper conversation, or do mischief with more eagerness and attention than they ever dedicate to their studies, then they give their parents no reason to hope for a good future. In that case, the father, mother, or instructor must seriously say to the child, "Listen, my son (or daughter), cease your pointless amusements, mischief or bad habits, go to school and study diligently, be well-behaved in all things. Otherwise, it will go very badly for you!"

Whenever a child is thus disciplined, the boy or girl usually makes a face, begins to cry and complain quietly. If the child is taught at home, then he begins to flip through the pages of books instead of reading them carefully, and he answers his parents' criticism with cries and complaints. This is the behavior of foolish and badly behaved children who don't listen to their parents and who do not do what they instruct or command.

Even though we are adults, often we act as these children do. Like foolish children, we often spend our time in pointless amusements and pleasures. We often oppose the will of God when God, the best and kindest of all Fathers, prevents our worldly amusements or lays before us some kind of unpleasant work or difficulty in our lives. If we want to deserve the mercy of God and eternal salvation, let us become like the wise children. Let us never say anything to God in our prayers except this: "O Lord God, our Father, as it pleases You, so let it be. We are ready to follow Your will and command, to go where You will and to avoid going to those places that You forbid; to do what You will and to not do what You forbid; to labor and to suffer, as long as it pleases You, our Father and Lord."

Epictetus impressed on us the necessity of such complete submission to God's will, saying, "Slothful man! What do you ask of God? Do you ask only what is good for you? And what is best for you, except what your conscience reveals to you as pleasing to God?" Another wise man also said,

> Suppose God gave someone a free choice in his manner of life. Suppose God even asked him, "Do you want Me to free you from all spiritual and physical afflictions and to place you immediately into Heaven?" Such a question can only be answered thus: "Lord, do with me as You will. You can remove all afflictions from me or not. It will be most pleasant to me if You do everything according to Your holy will."

Truly we will receive greater grace and mercy from God if we answer thus, than if we act by own our choice. For God, while He desires us to do good, chastens us, His children, like a wise parent. Therefore, if you see that virtuous people, beloved by God, are burdened by sorrows, wearied by misfortunes, laboring under all manner of unpleasantness, then be assured that they possess humility, tears, meekness, purity, and other virtues. If, on the contrary, you see sinful and angry people living in all manner of luxury, excess, and contentment in earthly goods, know that they are brazen in their obstinacy and often squandering their entire inheritance. They perish from their sins and unbridled passions.

God does not spoil His beloved children; He does not keep them in luxurious excess, but He tests them, humbles them with trials, sorrows, and insults, in order to make of them worthy servants for the common good: pillars of the Church, bedrocks of society, illuminators of nations, and so on. Therefore, let us offer ourselves to God as pure, unfilled vessels in all afflictions, so that God can fill us with His grace, thanks to our obedience. Blessed Jerome, while rebuking Julian the Apostate, wrote to him:

> You consider yourself to have reached the heights of virtue if you donate some small part of your riches to God-pleasing deeds? You are mistaken. God desires you to bring yourself, your moral-reasoning activity, as a sacrifice to Him for the duration of your life.

CHAPTER 10

Which Signs Indicate That Our Will Agrees with God's Will?

The Romans considered any soldier who did not have firm muscles, a large chest, wide shoulders, and the ability to lift and carry heavy weights to be a bad soldier. A bad soldier took no care of his weapons, never cleaned or polished his sword. Finally, a bad solider did not fully trust the military capability of his commander. Likewise, no one can consider himself a true Christian or call himself a follower of Christ and His divine will if he does not find within himself obvious signs that all his own desires are in active agreement with the will of God. Whoever wants to make sure of this and test himself, whoever wants to finally become adept at aligning all his desires and actions with the will of God, should examine himself carefully to see if he finds the signs or spiritual qualities I will be discussing in this chapter. At the same time, he must also labor to preserve them in himself and not to suppress them by his passionate attachments.

I

The first sign or unique quality of a true Christian is diligence to do everything eagerly, being careful that none of his actions be contrary to the commandments and will of God. Therefore, he never begins a deed without first calling on God for help. Every true follower of Christ will not dare to begin any work without appealing to God with at least a short, but heart-felt prayer. If he is faced with a useful and important work that is difficult to complete, let him ask for God's help not once, but many times, until God gives him wisdom and instructs him how to accomplish this work. People in positions of power or government should keep this counsel always in their minds: "Do nothing without God's assent, given to you mystically in zealous prayer."

The mind of a mortal man is limited; it cannot encompass everything and often assesses things incorrectly. Many misfortunes and problems all over the world arise from this problem. How many famous houses are ruled badly! How many kingdoms and regions lack proper justice and right behavior! How many unjust, destructive wars are started because of this! All this occurs because rulers disdain the commandment of Christ to "take heed [of yourself and your responsibilities], watch and pray; for you do not know when the time is" (Mark 13:33). The beginning of all the many evils in the world is a disregard of this commandment. For rulers, commanders, and kings are often people that act not by God's law or even civil law and common sense. Often their own interests, passions, and ignorant arbitrariness guide them. They do not ask the Lord God's blessing for the illumination of their mind. They put their trust in their own mind and powers, and think that they are like the ancient titans who tried to overturn a mountain. Therefore, their social actions, as well as their private affairs, suffer absolute ruin, with the damage often extending to the lives of many around them. Many examples from history prove this.

The elders and ruler of Israel sinned greatly when they included the pagan Gibeonites among the chosen people without receiving God's preliminary permission (see Joshua 9). Our own delusions are often similar to theirs. We often seek things of great importance, but we do not ask God about them. We desire to enter the priesthood, to get married, to buy a large track of land with workers already attached to it, but are these plans pleasing to God?

This is not how the praiseworthy, glorious Maccabees acted. They did not begin a single battle without first ascertaining God's will for it. In their humble hearts, before every battle, they prayed ardently to God, and not only did they pray, but they inspired all their fellow soldiers to pray with them as well. They never began a war without first having a service in the congregation of the people. Thus Judas Maccabeus, seeing and understanding the strength of his enemy, raised his hands to heaven and called to the Lord Who works miracles and sees all that occurs on earth, both just and unjust. He prayed to God for help, knowing full well that this victory would not depend on the number of soldiers or their weapons, but on God who gives it by His own good will to those who seek His mercy and protection. And it was not only Judas Maccabeus who prayed for God's command to begin or not to begin the war. By his example and his speech, he inspired his entire army to a prayerful disposition of soul and to true courage, bringing examples of God's previous help and mercy to the chosen nation, whenever they would all turn to Him with a repentant heart.

Having thus asked God for help, Judas and those with him entered the fray against the host of proud Nicanor, who attacked them on a Sabbath. They killed over thirty-five thousand warriors of the enemy, and were overjoyed by such obvious signs of God's mercy and help (2 Maccabees 15). What a fine example of how beneficial it is to run with a humble heart and pray to God for help and protection during any sorrow or affliction!

St John Cassian advises us to have these inspiring words in mind before beginning any work: "O God, do not deny me Your help. Help me, Lord, by Your good will." He also recommends this short prayer:

> We beg You, O Lord, to anticipate our every task, even before we begin it, with Your Holy Spirit. Help us, direct us to accomplish this task, so that our every prayer and action will always receive its cause from You, will be perfected by You, and will successfully reach its accomplishment through You.

Abba Pambo[28] had a custom. When anyone asked his advice about anything, he would answer, "Wait a little and leave your task to God," and Abba Pambo would never give anyone concrete advice until he had first asked the Lord for guidance. This custom brought Abba Pambo such benefit, that when he was already lying on his deathbed, he said, "I cannot remember a single useless word that I regret and of which I should repent."

Truly, to anyone who asks the Lord with faith, God answers in the depths of his soul in the words of the Psalmist: "Thou hast heard the desire of the poor, O Lord; Thine ear hearkeneth unto the disposition of their hearts" (Psalm 9:38). Whoever does not initially lay the blessing of God and His holy will at the foundation of his intentions and tasks will not have any success. The very consciousness of our relationship with the Lord obliges us to ask His blessing on all our tasks and to diligently weigh them in the light of their worthiness before God.

II

The second sign of true piety and eagerness to act in agreement with God's will is a lack of fear when faced with afflictions or difficulties. Not merely a lack of fear, but cheerfulness, even eagerness, to suffer them. This eagerness is justified in the following way: the Lord God's grace is closer to those who are in sorrows and afflictions than to those who wallow in luxury and know no deprivation. The Lord loves not only the poor and indigent, but He blesses those who act as their benefactors. David, magnifying such benefactors, says,

> Blessed is he that considereth the poor and needy; the Lord shall deliver him on the evil day. The Lord preserve him, and keep him alive, and bless him upon the earth, and deliver him not into the hands of his enemies. The Lord comfort him on his sick-bed; Thou hast turned all his bed in his sickness. (Psalm 40:2–4)

According to the interpretation of St John Chrysostom and St Ambrose of Milan (ca. 340–397 A.D.), God visits those who are in sorrows or grief and sweetens their afflictions with various joys and His mercy, as though God Himself changed their bedding like a gentle nurse to make it more comfortable for them, lessening their pain and calming them with His co-suffering and love. The Most Pure Virgin Mary and Christ the Lord both give great consolation and relief to the sick and grieving, if they are worthy of such a visitation and acceptance of this grace-filled heavenly gift and intercession.

Seneca, even before the full illumination of the world by the grace-filled teaching of Christ, uttered many thoughts worthy of divine wisdom:

> I ask and beg you most fervently not to fear those means (even if they are something stern and sharp) by which the immortal God arouses the soul to greater labors. Grief gives birth to virtue (self-improvement). It is truly right to call those people pathetic who, living in excessive luxury and not knowing deprivation, fall in spirit, defeated and incapacitated by sloth, in the same way as a long calm on the sea makes sailors lazy. Whoever God loves and tests, those He often punishes with afflictions and visits with sicknesses. In a word, He trains them. While those whom He, apparently, keeps in a state of calm, forgiving them much, those slothful and lazy ones He prepares to be a sacrifice to coming evils. You have left the true path if you think that there are some people who are taken out of the general fate of sinful people to bear sorrows and afflictions in this life. Every person will have his turn, every person will be visited unexpectedly by his own personal calamity, his unique turn of the dice, or his fate. If someone seems to be free from any troubles, know that he is merely given a respite until a later time, when he will not be able to avoid them.

Ask yourselves: why does the All-good God visit virtuous people with diseases or other calamities? It will be effective to answer this question by asking a different question whose answer is more easily accessible. Why is it that during a war the most capable and brave soldiers are sent to do the most risky and dangerous missions? The answer is not difficult. The commander chooses the most capable and brave soldiers for night raids on the enemy, to scout the best possible flanking movement around the enemy, to find the best path across a ford or a mountain pass for his division, and not a single one of the chosen soldiers complains to his commander for this assignment. He does not say, "My commander gave me this assignment because he wants to kill me." On the contrary, each of these soldiers eagerly tries to accomplish his mission with the greatest success, despite all difficulties and dangers.

Those among us Christians who are weak in faith or lacking in patience should act like these brave soldiers, especially when God allows us to suffer and bear something grievous, heavy, or sorrowful. We should encourage ourselves and strengthen ourselves with the thought that God has acknowledged us worthy to bear such a burden, and that He would never lay on us a burden too heavy for our weak human strength.

The wisdom of God says, "For God tested them and found them worthy of Himself" (Wisdom of Solomon 3:5). St Paul confirms this by saying, "No temptation has overtaken you except such as is common to man; but God is faithful, who will not allow you to be tempted beyond what you are able, but with the temptation will also make the way of escape, that you may be able to bear it" (1 Corinthians 10:13). Therefore, I beg you, brothers, avoid all sensuality and flee from delusive happiness and excess, all of which weaken and paralyze the soul and body. God acts like a teacher with his best students, demanding more exacting work from them and forcing them to work out very difficult solutions to problems.

Ancient history shows us a wonderful image of certain aspects of the proper upbringing of children in the example of Sparta, a city distinguished among the Greeks for bravery, patriotism, and disdain for riches and luxury. One cannot say that they were monsters lacking natural parental love for their children, but their parental love was motivated by their desire to make their children the best possible citizens and human beings. Their love was expressed in appropriate forms of training meant to maximize their physical and moral strength, helping them to endure courageously the worst possible afflictions in this life. Parents exhorted their children with tenderness and encouragement to ever-greater endurance in hunger, labors, inspiring them to disdain effeminacy and luxury completely.

Therefore, it is not so unusual that God, knowing in advance what means can give us the best chance of rising to the highest level of moral perfection, tests us, His children, with various difficulties and teaches us to rise up from the low levels of our virtue to ever higher ones. All training in virtue seems cruel and laborious for the frail body. Has God allowed misfortune to attack us? Let us bravely endure it. This is not God's wrath, but a kind chance given to us for ascetic labor that always carries a reward with it. The more labors we endure, the braver we will become. A person can achieve complete victory over evil only through patience. As gold is purified by the fire, so a person is strengthened by hardship.

And what is so unusual about this? A tree growing in the deep woods is never firm, strong, and resilient unless it is first subjected—in its early years—to strong winds. Only through the heavy pressure of wind do the atoms of the wood get compressed against each other firmly and strongly, while the roots dig ever deeper into the earth. Trees that grow in calm, sunny, and moist plains live only for a short time before rotting.

From everything said here, it should be obvious that the most clear sign of the accord between the human and divine will is courage in the face of troubles and sorrows, when we, willingly having rejected ourselves (i.e., our self-will), bear the Cross of Christ on our backs. In other words, we do not refuse to follow the dictates of the divine will along the difficult, narrow, and sorrowful path of a Christian life, courageously enduring all offences, grief, diseases, and other misfortunes that God allows.

Thus, whoever loves God with his whole heart and keeps the will of God with all his soul can boldly turn to God with prayer during times of troubles and sorrows:

I regret, O my God, that You did not reveal Your holy will to me earlier, for I would have hurried to do it even before You called me to do it. Do You wish to take back the lands, honor, and glory that You gave me? I have long been ready to return them to You. Do you wish to take my children? I commit them to Your will. Do you want any part of my body? Take it. It is not much to take, for soon I will leave it all behind. Do You want my soul? Why would I deny You even this? Everything that You gave me, take from me, for You love a cheerful giver. I do every task You send me freely, without compulsion; I suffer nothing that I did not agree to in advance. I do not work for You, O my God, like a slave. Rather, I bring my own will into agreement with Your holy will.

This is a true image of a human will in accord with the divine.

III

The third sign of the accord between the human and divine will is Christian humility, that is, the effacement in the self of any self-opinion, anything that goes beyond human, mortal, organic life. This virtue is particular to Christianity; it would hardly have even been known to the ancient idol-worshippers. Whoever is not infected by exalted self-opinion ascribes all the good he does not to himself or his mind, but to God's goodness and power. The only thing he considers to be his own, in the narrowest possible sense, are his delusions and falsehoods, keeping in mind always the words of Blessed Augustine: "Everything good attempted and accomplished by you, ascribe to God and admit that without God nothing is possible, but with God, everything is possible."

The person who puts no trust in his own wisdom and strength is truly a good and faithful servant. With undoubting trust in God's help, he never refuses to do those labors that are required of him in his calling. He does his work the better and the more successfully the less he trusts in himself, being sure that by himself he is nothing, but with God he can do everything. He labors to the best of his ability, but he expects the good fruits of his labors only by God's good will, enduring with a generous heart all that is in and of itself not evil, but often seem to be so to those who are suffering from it (such as slander of detractors, excessive workload, too many taxes, personal insults)

On the contrary, those who are proud and self-confident can expect a very different result from their labors. These people forget about God and their responsibilities to him; they lay all their hope on themselves, their own wisdom, adroitness, ability, and strength. These people are so arrogant! They raise themselves up in the estimation of the society of their peers by praising themselves to the skies, while the quality of their labor in the most important and socially useful work ends up being deficient, since they are often lazy and careless in the details because of their excessive self-confidence.

Those who have committed themselves fully to God's will, those humble laborers in the vineyard of Christ, act differently. They are like the balance beam on a set of scales with two measuring cups attached to them. The heavier the weight they place in one cup, the lower it goes, while the higher goes the opposite cup. This is a symbolic image of the dignity of the people of God as opposed to the people of this world. The more a person humbles himself before God and man, the higher the grace and mercy of God raise him up. And vice versa: the higher he places himself before God and despises his brother through his arrogance, the lower he places his human dignity.

A serious military commander who is assigned the defense of a city against attack makes sure to examine in advance all the weak points of the walls in order to fortify them. He makes all necessary arrangements for food stores in case of a siege; he builds stores for weapons and artillery. Simply put, he takes care to meet the enemy bravely and is ready to give him a strong fight, for he knows that you can never trust an enemy. Similarly, every Christian must prepare in advance for the unexpected meeting with his enemy by saying, "I will not be spared sickness or death. Therefore, is it not better to protect myself with confession and communion more often, to arm myself with prayer and fasting?"

On the contrary, a self-confident and ignorant person who relies on his own strength usually thinks that he is basically ready to repel all enemy attacks. Or he always waits for a more appropriate time to take the necessary measures to prepare for battle. Or finally he is so sure of victory that he has no doubt he will have time to prepare when the time comes. Solomon wisely discusses both of these types in his proverbs: "A simple [i.e., a foolish] man believes in every word, but an astute man comes to repentance. A wise man fears and turns away from evil, but a man without discernment persuades himself to mingle with a lawless man" (Proverbs 14:15–16). This kind of evil self-confidence needs more explanation in the next section.

IV

The fourth sign of agreement between our will and God's is our complete trust in the Lord God in all things. Such trust makes it possible for us to remain internally calm even when someone publicly insults us. It humbles the naturally occurring thought to avenge one's enemy. A trusting person thinks within himself, "God sees and hears this lie, this insult. There will come a time that God will reveal the lies of the enemy and will turn it back on my enemy's head." In this way, the fully natural desire to avenge oneself is put down.

Only through a firm trust in God can we become victors over all enemies and take the moral high ground over them, for a person who firmly trusts in God is sure that even if his enemies try to raise all of hell against him, they would not harm him any more than God would allow them to. You may perhaps remonstrate, "My enemies are unstoppable, constantly trying to do me evil in every possible way. If they cannot personally injure me, they will try to attack me with material deprivations, such as losses in my business or the destruction of my property." Truly, this is so.

This is the way a person who firmly trusts in God acts in such a case: In order to calm himself fully, he commits every action, task, and object prayerfully to God for His help in accomplishing it or preserving it, firmly trusting in His providence. He leaves every possible circumstance to God's disposal, as though completely giving up personal control. Everything good that happens—in his business affairs, for example—he considers a blessing of God. Any misfortune or unsuccessful venture he ascribes to a special providence of God that has something better planned for him. It is useless for an enemy to attack a person with such faith in God with any material deprivations, since all that such a person has belongs to God. "There is no wisdom, there is no courage, there is no counsel for the ungodly" (Proverbs 21:29).

No matter how unfairly Laban tried to treat his son-in-law Jacob, changing his wages ten times in the hopes of lessening it, it was all for naught, since Jacob trusted only in the Lord. As Jacob himself said, "God did not allow him [Laban] to harm me" (Genesis 31:7). Sennacherib, King of Assyria, was angered against Jerusalem and threatened to raze it to the ground. However, neither he nor his armies could avoid the heavy hand of God's punishment, for God heard the prayers of King Hezekiah and the Prophet Isaiah. He sent His angel, who singlehandedly defeated the Assyrian army. Sennacherib returned to his own land, where his own children killed him (2 Chronicles 32:21–22). Thus God saved Hezekiah and the inhabitants of Jerusalem from the hands of Sennacherib and his armies.

Therefore, I advise every Christian to have such a firm hope in God and to leave all vengeance to Him alone. "Vengeance is mine; I will repay, says the Lord" (Romans 12:19). Even the pagans teach us this.

Tissaphernes (445–395 B.C.), the commander of the Persian armies in Asia Minor, made peace with Agesilaus II, King of Sparta, but only in order to gain time before finding a more fitting time to attack his enemy, for he soon afterward ordered that all Greeks leave Asia, breaking his truce. Agesilaus answered Tissaphernes' emissaries, "Tell your general this. I am very grateful that he has broken our peace, for by doing this he has deserved the ire of gods and men both, and has made enemies in high places. Because of this, my own armies have grown considerably, for his cunning and treachery have made him many enemies." This is a truly Christian answer, as we see in the Gospels: "God has raised up a horn of salvation for us … from our enemies and from the hand of all who hate us" (Luke 1:68–71).

He who trusts in God with his whole heart turns all his enemies into tributaries and even slaves, for He has God as his helper, since he prays to God concerning all his desires. He keeps to such a rule constantly:

Whatever I ask of God can either benefit or harm for me, but this is known completely only to God. If what I ask is beneficial to me, then God will send it to me immediately, or sometimes he will delay it in order to test me and train me in patient endurance. But if God does not answer my petition, though I repeat my request many times, then it becomes obvious to me that I asked God to give me something that is either useless or harmful.

Only he who has completely committed himself to the direction of God's will can act by this very wise rule. Those who do not acknowledge the mysteries of God's rule over the cosmos and His providence for every single one of His creatures either never even bother to call on the Almighty for help, or if they do pray, they do it half-heartedly, only because custom dictates it. Instead, they prefer to ask help of other people with fervent and pathetic requests, and if they do not succeed with their first attempts, they will try other people, always seeking for someone's patronage with presents and bribes, making the fulfillment of their desires contingent on a dishonorable and sinful "business deal."

St John the Theologian saw Christ the Lord in a heavenly revelation. Christ held seven stars in His right hand. What do these stars signify? St John himself explicates this mystery: "The seven stars are the angels of the seven churches" (Revelation 1:20). The crowns of all churches are in the hands of Christ. If the crown (i.e., the episcopal see) is vacant anywhere, then many seekers appear, eagerly desiring to bow their heads under this crown. However, they often do not follow the straight path to Christ, but more often than not, they first go to the hands of princes, rulers, and governors, and only at the end do they turn to Christ for help. The same happens when anyone seeks any other ecclesiastical or civil honor or dignity. Everyone seeks the love, mercy, and help of men; few seek from God the aid they need to first become worthy bearers of the crown by their moral perfection or their labors of righteousness, mercy, and compassion for the state. Here we often see clear delusion and ignorance concerning the right path to receiving ordination or earthly glory and honor. Those who desire to deserve true respect from men and mercy from God should act otherwise.

First of all, they ought to seek the mercy of God concerning the forgiveness of their sins with their whole heart. They must seek His good help in order to align their free will and actions with the will of God, for scepters and crowns are in the right hand of God; principalities, ruling power, honors, and dignities are determined by God and distributed by His all-wise will. Consequently, we must always ask Him first. "As a flow of water, so is the heart of the king in the hand of God. Wherever He wills to incline it, there he turns it" (Proverbs 21:1).

A gardener always keeps a source of water (such as a fountain) at his disposal. He directs the water not always to the closest and best trees, but often to the farthest and the weakest, or wherever else he wishes, depending on the needs of the garden. God acts like this gardener. He has the king's heart in His hand, and He directs it where He wills—without ever violating the free will of the man—like the gardener's water, helping him properly govern the ship of state with its various ecclesiastical and civil laws and the many people under its authority. God gives dignity and authority to those whom He has chosen from before the ages in His foreknowledge, calling them in their proper time to serve His righteous work of directing the world. "For whom He foreknew, He also predestined to be conformed to the image of His Son, that He might be the firstborn among many brethren. Moreover, whom He predestined, these He also called; whom He called, these He also justified; and whom He justified, these He also glorified" (Romans 8:29–30).

Therefore, it is extremely unwise to turn with fervent requests, gifts, and prayers to other people, forgetting the immanent God, having no hope in Him, barely—only in passing, so to speak—praying to Him at all. What a frightening, incredible blindness these people have! Water taken from the source is always pure, healthy, and beneficial.

V

The fifth sign indicating the accord of our will with God's is endurance in humble-minded silence of universal dishonor, slander, and other accusations against our good name and deeds. There is no more sensitive wound for a righteous Christian soul than brazen insult and slander of his good intentions and actions, all done for the glory of God and the salvation, instruction, and benefit of mankind. However, a true follower of Christ will silently endure all such cruel blows, always gazing with his mind's eye with reverence at the much-suffering Jesus, who remained silent during countless accusations and tortures, during the unjust judgment of the Jews and the Romans. All the elders and rulers of the Jews gathered, accusing Him vehemently. Jesus remained silent. Many false witnesses ascribed many crimes to Him. Jesus remained silent. The people insisted, screaming, that He be crucified. Jesus remained silent. Already crucified and nailed to the Cross, He was not spared countless mockery and vitriol. Jesus remained silent (cf. Matthew 26:63, 27:12).

Like the Lord Jesus, the most blessed Virgin Mary, the Mother of God, though she felt the greatest pain and grief, remained courageous in her endurance, meek and silent. She acted no differently than her Son, that is, Mary also remained silent and committed everything to the will of God and His divine providence. She heard Her beloved Son, a completely innocent man, being slandered and abused. Mary remained silent. She saw Him weighed down by His Cross, faltering and unable to go one, nailed to the Cross, in horrifying tortures, exclaiming to His Father, "My God, My God, why have You forsaken Me?" Then, she saw Him die from His countless wounds and heavy tortures. Mary remained silent (cf. John 19:25).

Many pious people emulated the Son and His Mother. When they were falsely accused of the vilest sins, they remained silent. This was true in the time of the meek King David, who became famous for his humble silence in the face of personal insults. In such cases, he said to himself in his heart, "I will take heed to my ways, that I sin not with my tongue. I kept my mouth as it were with a bridle, when the sinner stood up against me. I was mute and held my peace; I kept silent, even from good words ... I became dumb, and opened not my mouth, for it was Thy doing" (Psalm 38:1–2, 10). The reason for his silence is simple: it is the Lord who allowed David to be insulted, and David remained silent because without God's will, without His permission, no one would be able to insult David. It is the Lord's will that sealed David's lips.

Severinus Boethius, an exceptional Roman writer, virtuous man, and philosopher, said,

Who but the One God can be a protector of virtue and the banisher of all that is evil? He, as the One who rules and orders our hearts, gazing at all from the heights of His divine foreknowledge and providence, knows and appoints what is good and salvific for every person. If it seems to us that something in the world occurs not by the righteous order and direction of God, then that is merely the disorder of our limited, human minds. In essence, this order is the true and all-righteous divine direction of the cosmos. And every person who submits to the will of God becomes sure of this, noticing how the true and just are God's dispensations concerning every person individually and all tribes, nations, and governments in general. He then comes to believe in God's wise providence for everyone and everything, and he accedes to it in silence.

Sometimes, even in large houses, you see something similar between masters and servants. For example, a master with a cheerful, good-hearted character enters the home of his steward and finds no one there. In order to teach his steward a lesson about not leaving his home unlocked, he turns the place upside down, leaves a huge mess, and quickly leaves before the servant can find out who left the home in such disarray. The steward, seeing all his things thrown about and turned over, becomes very angry and incensed at the person who ruined the good order of his house; but then he finds out that his master did it. So he calms down and remains silent.

Like this servant, David "became dumb and opened not [his] mouth, for it was Thy [God's] doing." Likewise, every person committed to the will of God feels inner heaviness from his misfortunes and offences, but he patiently bears them, comforting himself with the providence of God and knowing well that sorrow and useless complaining will help him not at all. He then directs his gaze to heaven and says, "I lifted up mine eyes unto the hills, from whence will my help come. My help cometh even from the Lord Who hath made heaven and earth" (Psalm 120:1–2).

When Ataxerxes and Haman feasted with Esther, all the Jews cried bitterly, but soon Haman's feasting—he was gleefully preparing to slay innocent Jewish blood on the next day—turned into his own downfall. God marvelously revealed to the king that Haman hated Mordecai and all the Jews, and the king ordered the Haman be subjected to the same punishment that he had prepared for all the Jews (Esther 7).

Let every person repeat this unquestionable truth: "When the Lord will make you sorrowful by allowing some deprivation or insult, do not forget that He will ultimately turn it all to your benefit." If the moon were always full, never changing, never waxing or waning, then astronomers would never have discovered that it reflects the light of the sun. In the same way we come to know—through various deprivations and afflictions—that every good is a gift from God.

Did someone fall ill? Then he will come to know by experience how precious health is and how strictly he must safeguard and protect it. This he would have never known if he was always healthy, for we have an inherent carelessness that never values or guards anything good, beneficial, or pleasant until we lose it. Only then do we understand what we lost and regret its loss.

Do others dishonor someone? Then only by experience will he understand how much sin dirties the good name and glory of his neighbor. Did someone become poor? Only then will he truly understand how badly he treated the poor (before his destitution) and how one must, by God's command, love everyone and care for them, especially the poor and helpless. Therefore, remain silent and contemplate all that I have written above, humbly committing your-self in all things to God's will.

However, I do not think that every person who bears a heavy burden must remain silent until he despairs. May God protect you all from despair! There-fore, beloved brother in Christ, speak up! But speak with your heart; speak to God. May your tongue remain silent, but pray with your mind. Go deep inside yourself and reverently contemplate the silence of Christ before Pilate, the si-lence of the most pure Virgin Mary before her wicked compatriots, the silence of David before his opponents. Does a most honored and dignified person slan-der you? Be silent! Is a low or unworthy person dishonorably rebuking you? Be silent. Is your equal defaming you? Be silent.

Yes, it is difficult and painful to act this way, but it is extremely praisewor-thy, salvific, and beneficial. Ignore your abuser; turn to God, your Comforter, and pray for your enemies, as David did, in David's own words: "Instead of the love that I had unto them, they would defame me, but I gave myself unto prayer. And they rewarded me evil for good, and hatred for my love" (Psalm 108:4–5). By being silent, you will tame your enemies, and your prayer will mol-lify God. Therefore, remain silent and give yourself over completely to the will of God, having David's words in your heart at all times: "It was Your doing, O Lord (not my enemy's)."

VI

The sixth sign of a human will in concert with God's will is readiness to accept all hardship and deprivation, to subject oneself to the worst dangers, to endure all sorrows and difficulties at the limit of human endurance, all for the sake of the glory of God and the fulfillment of His commandments, firmly trusting in God's providence and help. How great-hearted was the Apostle Paul, as we see in his own words, "I have learned in whatever state I am to be content. I know how to be abased, and I know how to abound. Everywhere and in all things I have learned both to be full and to be hungry, both to abound and to suffer need" (Philippians 4:11–12).

David, always prepared for greater and greater labors, joyfully sang to the Lord, "For You, O Lord, are my lamp; The Lord shall enlighten my darkness. For by You I can run against a band of troops; by my God I can leap over a wall ... The Mighty One who strengthens me with power, Who has prepared my way blameless" (2 Kingdoms 22:29–30, 33). David considered it nothing to walk by the path indicated by God until he sweated from the exertion. He girt his waist with truth; he put on the breastplate of righteousness; he put on the shoes of the preparation of the gospel of peace to speak to the world (see Ephesians 6:14–16); more than everything else, he protected himself with faith in the coming Messiah and the helmet of His salvation. He wielded the spiritual sword of the word of God and prayer. Armed thus, he willingly went by the appointed path.

Each of us must come to know and contemplate God's desires, in order to prepare ourselves to be patient in suffering and blameless of sins in this life, to eagerly forgive our enemies, to think and speak well of everyone until they reveal themselves to be otherwise. Why should we not act as God desires? Yes, until this moment our self-will was a hurdle, even a stonewall, preventing us from following God's directions to a God-pleasing life. But since the light of His holy grace has illumined our souls, such a wall should not frighten us. "By my God I can leap over a wall." We can do everything by the power of Christ Who strengthens us (Philippians 4:13).

Everyone who reverently reads or listens to the lives of the saints will often repeat the words of David, "Wonderful is God in his saints, the God of Israel; He will give power and might unto His people" (Psalm 67:36). He is eternal: He has always been, always is, and will have no end. He is our blessed God and Creator. He gives power and strength to His people, to all who live by His commandments. We see this in the lives of the Apostles and their successors and the followers of their teaching. The Apostles, chosen by God to preach the name of the Lord Christ and His salvific teachings and deeds, had great boldness (fearlessness, courage, and faith) and performed wondrous works. What walls of falsehood, superstition, and ignorance did they not scale by the power of truth and living faith? For them there was nothing uncomfortable or insurmountable in the work of preaching the Gospel. In a relatively short amount of time, they flew all over the known world as if on seraphic wings of divine love. Through them the prophecy of Isaiah came true: "But those who wait on God shall renew their strength; they shall mount up with wings like eagles; they shall run and not be weary; they shall walk and not hunger" (Isaiah 40:31).

They had unshakeable trust in God, and by fulfilling His will, which girded them like a belt, they walked over the whole world and sailed the seas with no fear, preaching to all the nations under heaven concerning the kingdom of God, teaching all to believe with conviction in our Lord Jesus Christ, despising all the threats of their enemies. Like a man dying of thirst feels a fire burning within him, so the Apostles saw the world covered in flames, and they thirsted to save all mankind, their hearts alight with the fires of love that "much water will not be able to quench ... nor will rivers drown it" (Song of Songs 8:7). In other words, no persecutions could ever stop the spread of the Gospel of Love.

With such fiery love in their hearts, the Apostles hurried to spread the good news of the Gospel of the kingdom to the whole world, from end to end. There was no nation, country, city, or village where they did not preach Christ. The Apostle Paul, that chosen vessel of grace, filled with fire that burned away all tares, preached the Gospel from Jerusalem to Illyricum and covered all the lands between those two points, converting to Christ mostly Gentiles, as he said in his Epistle to the Romans:

> For I will not dare to speak of any of those things which Christ has not accomplished through me, in word and deed, to make the Gentiles obedient—in mighty signs and wonders, by the power of the Spirit of God, so that from Jerusalem and round about to Illyricum I have fully preached the gospel of Christ. And so I have made it my aim to preach the Gospel, not where Christ was named, lest I should build on another man's foundation, but as it is written: "To whom He was not announced, they shall see; and those who have not heart shall understand." (Romans 15:18–21)

He spread the good news of Christ's teachings to all peoples living in the lands he traversed, including Romans, Persians, Parthians, Medes, Indians, Scythians, Arabians, and many others (see St John Chrysostom's Homilies on Paul's Missionary Journeys).

St Andrew the First-called also spread the Gospel. Having in himself the fire of the Holy Spirit, he preached first in Bithynia and all countries adjacent to Pontus, reaching even Chersonese on the Crimean Peninsula. By a special providence of God, he even reached Russia. A local tradition tells that He placed a cross on the hills where Kiev would eventually be built, as if prophesying that the Russian people would eventually be enlightened by the holy faith of Christ. Having preached the Gospels in Great Scythia, he returned to Thrace and visited Greece and the Peloponnesus.

Equally on fire with the love of God was the Holy Apostle Thomas, called the twin. He was called to Caesaria of Philippi, the cities of Galilee. He who touched the wounds of Christ after His resurrection preached Christ to the Parthians, Medes, Persians, Bactrians, Brahmans (members of the Indian Brahman caste), and in India, where he was pierced with spears by heathens and died for Christ.

Other Apostles, alight with the fire of divine love, zealously preached faith in Christ. They realized David's prophecy: "Their sound [preaching] is gone out into all the earth, and their words [concerning eternal life] unto the ends of the world" (Psalm 18:5). In all the ends of the world they sought to quench their hearts' thirst for the salvation of all nations by bringing them to faith in Christ, so that the converted would be found worthy to enter together with them into the mansions of the Heavenly Father prepared by Christ, where no one will hunger or thirst, neither will they be burnt by the sun or any heat. No misfortunes or sorrows, no persecution or slander, no wounds, beatings, hunger, nakedness, not even death for Christ could prevent the Apostles from accomplishing such glorious labors. Even the assembled hosts of demons could not frighten them, since they trampled those hosts underfoot. No other discomfort or obstacle that they met on land, sea, or any other place could stop them. Everywhere they preached the glory and honor of God with courage, strengthened by His power, never fearing any labors or afflictions.

Thus, they easily overcame all obstacles in their way, and they prepared the entire world for Christ by their preaching, as Isaiah prophesied: "All the ends of the earth shall see the salvation of God" (Isaiah 52:10). By fulfilling the will of God with their whole heart, they were unassailable in all misfortunes and persecutions. For every person who loves the Lord wholeheartedly and with his whole soul, whoever gives himself to God's will completely, can hope to overcome everything and to find the words of the Lord coming true for him: "Assuredly I say to you, if you have faith as a mustard seed, you will say to this mountain, 'Move from here to there', and it will move; and nothing will be impossible for you" (Matthew 17:20).

PART III

CONCERNING THE BENEFIT TO THE HUMAN WILL FOUND IN FOLLOWING GOD'S WILL ALWAYS

 Chapter 11

The Peace of Soul That Comes from Following God's Will

In the two previous parts we indicated the path by which man can come to know God's will and align his own will with it. In this book, we will endeavor to explain what benefit one can receive from this harmony between the human will and the will of God.

I

The Lord is so merciful and generous in His outpouring of gifts and riches, that He not only predestined us for eternal blessedness in the next life, but even in this life He sends us sweet bread, a small foretaste of the future blessedness, providing a glimpse, as it were, of our future eternal joy. He does this because He wants to encourage us and strengthen us by the promise of receiving eternal good things, to bring us to a place of cheerful expectancy founded on hope and trust. In this way, even in this many-cared, many-labored, and unpleasant world, God does not forget us. Even here we are given a taste of the heavenly feast, and though we still walk in the valley of the shadow of death, we find in it some consolations and heavenly pleasures. To receive these gifts, God does not require great labors from us. It is enough for us not to contradict God's desires. Here is an example.

On Mount Tabor, the Apostle Peter sensed within himself a tiny part, a reflection, of heavenly blessedness. Even so, he could not contain his ecstasy and exclaimed, "'It is good for us to be here; and let us make three tabernacles: one for You, one for Moses, and one for Elijah', because he did not known what to say" (Mark 9:15 and Luke 9:33).

O Holy Peter! It is not yet time to taste the full consolation. It will be given in a different, better world, but not in this hour.

St John says in Revelation, "When He [the Lamb Who said, I am the Alpha and Omega] opened the seventh seal, there was silence in heaven for about half an hour" (8:1). According to the interpretation of St Gregory the Great, this silence is the inner peace or the spiritual consolation of those who do the will of God on earth, as well as the angels in heaven. Therefore, the people who do God's will live on earth as though they were already in heaven. King David, belabored by the cares and inconstancy of earthly life, exclaimed with a sigh, "Who will give me wings like a dove's? And I will fly away, and be at rest" (Psalm 54:7). Where can one find a restful place except in God and in our submission to His holy will? Truly, only this holy submission to God's will, done with a free will and reason, can sweeten and console this earthly life. For there is nothing more pleasing to the one who loves God than to do His holy will. "Your will be done on earth as it is in heaven." This is the first and most trustworthy means to achieve consolation for our soul—to give ourselves completely, with our whole soul and heart, to the will of God to serve Him constantly, and to do His commandments. O Lord, let Your will be my will; Your desire, my desire; and Your disinclination, my disinclination.

II

A certain writer mentions, in his letters, an encounter with a God-inspired monk, whose clothes used to heal the sick merely by touching them. For this reason, the monk was greatly honored and respected by the sick, and even his fellow-monks were amazed and astounded by the fact that he was not remarkable for any extreme feats of asceticism. He was a monk like all the others, in no way distinguishing himself from the lives of the other (i.e., he was not a strict faster, he did not limit his sleep overmuch, he did not labor physically to excess). He had only one rule, which he did without fail. He never allowed himself any passionate attachment to anything or anyone except to God. In other words, he eagerly accepted everything that happened to him and thanked God for it. Once, when he was healing the sick with absolutely no medicines, the abbot asked him what means he used to heal the sick.

The monk answered,

I myself am amazed that I can return health to them. I am even ashamed that my clothing has this power, for I did not come to deserve such a gift from God through any ascetic labors. I am hardly equal to my brother monks, and in no way do I transcend them.

"Yes, this is truly so," said the abbot. "We see that you are an unremarkable man and are in no way better than the others." He then continued to ask him questions, desiring to find out his other qualities and reveal the secrets of his very heart.

The virtuous monk answered,

I know that God gave me His grace to always agree with His will concerning me, so that I never have even a thought contrary to God's will. I never fear any mishap that can disturb my mind or weaken my heart to such a degree that I begin to complain to someone about my sorrow, or even reveal it to anyone. I greet all successes in the same way, never allowing them to give me such sweet pleasure that I find more joy in them than in any other day of my life. I accept everything that God sends me—both positive and negative—and I never ask God to arrange anything by my will. Instead, I desire that everything occurs by God's will, that is, I wish everything to be as it is. Therefore, nothing pleases me too much, nothing grieves me too much, and nothing makes me so happy as doing God's will. I only ask one thing in my prayers to God. Let His divine will be done in me and in His creation always.

The abbot was astounded by all this, and asked the monk, "Beloved brother! Tell me, what were your thoughts yesterday, during the fire we suffered? Did you not also grieve with the rest of us when that evil man burnt down our monastic building, when all the grain we gathered and all the cattle we owned was lost?"

The monk answered,

I want you to know, holy father, that none of these losses brought me any sorrow whatsoever, since I have the habit of thanking God for both sorrowful and joyful occurrences. I am sure that everything that occurs with us is part of God's providence and is for our benefit. Therefore, I do not worry about the amount of grain we have for our sustenance. I am firmly convinced that God can make each one of us satisfied with a crumb as well as a loaf. So, joyfully and cheerfully, I live this life with no worries.

The abbot continued to press him, asking him many question in order to force the brother to explain his thoughts and frame of mind more fully. Among the many answers, I would like to highlight one:

By offering myself as a sacrifice every day to the altar of God's will, I have become so adept at submitting to it that even if I were to find out in advance that God has decreed to send me to hell, I would not oppose Him even in this, for I would know that this is pleasing to God and that God desires this. I will only add one thing. If it were possible for me to change this decree of God's solely by my utterance of the Lord's Prayer, I would not dare or desire to do this. I tell you truth! I would only pray to God the more fervently that He would do with me according to His all-holy and all-righteous will, and that He give me His grace to strengthen me for the ages of ages never to even think of anything contrary to His will.

The abbot was terrified at this answer and seemed to be transformed into stone. After a long mutual silence, he said to the monk:

Go, beloved father, go and continue to zealously do everything you have told me. Keep your promise to God. You have found heaven outside of heaven. Understand that God gives such grace only to a few; there are not many people whom nothing or no one is capable of upsetting. Such a person (who accepts every event, whether good or bad, as sent by God) is surrounded in his life by strong and unassailable walls.

III

Having peacefully parted with the monk, the abbot, filled with surpassing wonder, began to think to himself:

Now I know how this person, whom we considered to be useless, whom we despised and mocked, is given the grace to heal the sick. O how highly does the grace of the Holy Spirit raise a man when he accords his own will in all things with God's. Is it even possible that

God would condemn such a person to eternal torments? No, this does not agree with God's endless goodness! I am forced to admit that the road by which this person leads his life is not a long or uncomfortable path. Rather, it is the shortest and easiest path to reach the heights of indubitable and reliable spiritual consolation. He does not require great ascetic labors such as heavy fasting or prolonged exhaustion by keeping vigils entire nights without sleep. All this is rewarded only by a true desire in all things to submit to the will of God.

We should all renew this desire and support and strengthen every day in actual deed, so that we will never prefer our own will to the all-wise and all-powerful will of God. St John Chrysostom said, "A desire awakens the strength to overcome all things, just as apathy makes everything impossible for us. The only reason for all our weakness is apathy. Great is the power of desire that makes us mighty in all things that we want, and weak in all things we do not care about."

Let us imagine that a person raises his spirit to God in prayer every morning, crying out with the following words from the heart:

O Lord, my God! I am—all of myself—at Your complete disposal; I am ready to accept everything that You send me. Now I have reasonably and completely understood that without correcting my life by the light of Your commandments I can do nothing good by myself. Therefore, I promise You to try with all my strength never to do anything contrary to Your holy will!

Now, let us imagine that despite the good intention of his spirit, this person enters, that very same day, some shameful place such as a tavern or a gambling hall, and there he partakes of various dishonorable games and other lawless amusements, becoming guilty before God and man. How are we to categorize the actions of such a person?

He has mocked God and man. With one hand he gives bread, so to speak, but with the other a scorpion. Therefore, to humbly submit oneself to the will of God and yet to simultaneously steal another's money, to slander another's name or impugn another's honor, to eagerly encourage others' envy, to become angry, to rage at others—these are actions that mock God. This is an eager and willing exposure of one's heart to all possible passionate desires and sinful actions. What signs of love will we find in such people? The lips say, "I love you," but the hands slap you in the face. The lips say, "I cannot be parted from you," but, at the first opportunity, the hands hurl you off the top of the highest mountain into a deep abyss.

And yet we all act thus! And we have the gumption to excuse our carelessness (or worse!) with such hypocritical words as these: "I cannot act in any other way." St John Chrysostom answers us:

> No one can justify himself by saying that he allegedly wanted to do something good, but could not. Doubtless he did not because he desired not. Let the one who desires to do good but who claims he cannot do it be punished the same way as one who desired evil. Let the one who truly wishes good and does it in actual fact receive his reward in the kingdom of heaven (which is within us, as Christ Himself said).

IV

The aforementioned conversation between two monks is easily understandable for anyone and instructive for all. Truly, it should be obvious to us that the path to acquiring the highest blessedness of spiritual calm and consolation—found in firm and unassailable trust in God and in complete commitment of oneself and one's life to the will of God—is accessible to everyone. The door to this Eden is not locked for anyone who constantly desires only to emulate God's desires. Such a person has already entered heaven, and no matter what a person's social status, sex, or age, he will not be cast out of this heaven. There are, in short, two instructive rules that can be summarized from the conversation between these two monks. Anyone who truly keeps these truths in his heart will receive all benefits from God.

1. We must be firmly convinced, and always remember, that everything occurring in the world at large, and in our life in particular, occurs by God's providence, which, by correcting our sins, brings everything finally to our perfection and blessedness by those means and ways that it pleases Him to employ, according to His inscrutable (for us) judgments. His own providence corrects all transgressions against His eternal laws, and order is restored. Seneca describes this eloquently: "One cause gives rise to another, provoking a long series of phenomena, both in the natural order and in the life of each person individually." Therefore, we must be courageous and patient, for all events in human history occur not as we think and imagine we understand them, but as they occur in actual fact (i.e., in God's plan). It has long been customary to say, "That which grieves you will bring you joy," for even though the life of each

differs from all others in many ways, yet each person will suffer and die. Being all of us perishable, we should endure everything from all others, since all their actions are also perishable (i.e., all petty human offences are nothing, for every person will die). Why do we become angry? Why do we complain so much? Let us instead be ready to bear all humiliations and calamities in our life. Let our physical nature have its way with our body, leading it ever to death. We will still remain joyful and courageous in our immortal soul, firmly believing that nothing dies in our spiritual being, that our self can never be destroyed.

2. We are required to do everything that is contained in our immortal and reasonable soul. In other words, we must follow our common sense, our conscience, and our heart, leaving all our external being to the disposal of God's will. In short, we must be content with our lot (i.e., everything God has given us). We should not seek to acquire material benefits that others—richer and more honored than we—enjoy. We should envy no one. Such a disposition of our spirit will give us calm and spiritual consolation that nothing can disturb or destroy. This peace is the armor, so to speak, of all virtue.

Those who love the moribund and ephemeral goods of this earth never find such peace. They do not realize how material goods fool their owners into thinking that they are eternal and always present; and so the lovers of earthly goods always strive to be respected solely because of these goods they possess. As a result, they tend to trust more and more in their own successes, instead of trusting in God's providence, in which they have little faith. Such people fall into despair and sorrow at the slightest offence, especially when they like foolish and frivolous children, who have lost some trinket, lose these inconstant earthly goods.

On the contrary, a person who has not become proud of his advantages, who does not despair at their lessening or complete loss, will never despair in his spirit, for he trusts in God's providence completely. His heart is armed with the shield of all virtues. With imperturbable calm, he bravely opposes all temptations and desires only that which it pleases God to do with him and his life.

CHAPTER 12

Is It Possible to Avoid Sorrow Entirely?

Solomon, that profound depth of human wisdom and wonder, said, "No grave trouble will overtake the righteous" (Proverbs 12:21 NKJV). The wise king is here speaking of those troubles that attack a virtuous man contrary to his will, by accident. It is as if he is saying the following:

> Any evil done by the will, any fall into sin, upsets every decent person and fills his heart with regret and compunction. But external troubles, such as misfortunes, insults, deprivation, unfair loss of honors or dignities, sickness, the death of those nearest to us—none of these things can severely confuse and grieve a righteous man, for he often considers such trials to be blessings and ascribes them to God's mercy, God's intention to train him in endurance. And so he thanks God for it, for to a wise man every trouble gives a reason for attentiveness to one's heart, and so it becomes a cause for virtue.

A certain wise philosopher said, "Chance is inherent in the life of man, but it only brings harm to an ignorant man. Similarly, sorrow is also inherent, but it causes compunction in the soul of a righteous man."

The Apostle Paul witnesses that a righteous man always overcomes sorrow with repentance and courage: "I am filled with comfort. I am exceedingly joyful in all our tribulation" (2 Corinthians 7:4). It is as if he is saying, "I rejoice not only in hunger and thirst; not only in bonds, prisons, and wounds; not only in troubles and persecutions; but in all our sorrows. I do not merely find a certain consolation, but I am truly filled with joy when they beat me with rods, when they stone me, when I suffer shipwrecks and float for entire days in the abyss of the sea."

St Martin of Tours (316 or 336–397 A.D.), though subject to insults by Sulpicius Severus for many years, never became angry with him, never expressed his sorrow at these attacks, remaining calm in his soul. Truly, nothing can upset a righteous man, no sorrow or trouble. St John Chrysostom confirms this by saying, "There is nothing more serious or sorrowful than angering God." It means that if a man is righteous, nothing else can grieve him, not sorrow, not slander, not anything else. But in the same way that a small spark thrown into the sea immediately goes out, so every sorrow, even the heaviest, if it falls into a pure conscience, quickly dissipates and disappears. Again St John, desiring to offer this same thought to our contemplation, likens our mind to the visible sky by saying,

The sky is higher than rain-bearing clouds, but when it is covered with them, it seems to be dark. In actual fact, it continues to shine brightly as it did before. In the same way, when we seem to suffer, that is, when we are enveloped by sorrow as the sky is by clouds, let us not despair. If we become ill or grieve in our human weakness, then for how long will it burden us?

Blessed Augustine said,

Even if there is something burning or sharp in our suffering, a brave mind will overcome any pain. I do not pretend that the ocean is not deep, because its shores have shallow water. I do not pretend that the sky is always dark only because it is sometimes covered in clouds. I do not pretend that the earth will bear no fruit only because a harvest occasionally fails.

The same analogy can be brought to the fruitfulness of a good conscience. It can sometimes fall to the evil influence of painful sorrow, but a God-pleasing life lessens this evil influence and completely destroys it, just as weeds growing between stalks of wheat are not visible in a good harvest.

Thus, something sorrowful that occurs in the life of a righteous man will not kill him with excessive grief. He will come to know sorrow, but he will not succumb to it. His sky will be covered with dark clouds, but it will not transform into darkness. His land will have weeds peeking out of it, but the wheat will cover it. Not to sorrow in troubles is not human, but to be defeated by them is unworthy of a soul of high quality.

I

This high quality of a soul is known not only in Christianity, but it was well treasured even by the ancient pagans. Horace[29] describes the type of such a valiant hero-philosopher. The valiant man always keeps his promises and never changes his given word, and this is made obvious when threats and deprivations have no ability to change his righteous oath or principled position. He will not change it even when afraid of his fellow countrymen, who demand that he do an evil deed. He will not fear the threats of torturers or even the tortures themselves, which would so easily sway a weak-willed man. In vain will the torturers strive to convince him to change his mind or to betray his oath. He will remain stalwart as an immoveable pillar. Even if the whole worlds were to burn to ashes, even if the sky were to come crumbling down, a heart that trusts in God will not fear, for this heart is strengthened, not by vain promises, but by the invisible presence of God Himself: "He suffered no man to do them wrong, and reproved even kings for their sakes, saying, Touch not mine anointed, and do My prophets no harm" (Psalm 104:14–15).

Truly, "The souls of the righteous are in the hand of God, and no torture will ever touch them" (Wisdom of Solomon 3:1). The Prophet Zechariah adds, "For the one who assails you is as one who assails the apple of His [God's] eye" (Zechariah 2:12). The beloved disciple of Christ expresses himself thus, "We know that whoever is born of God does not sin; but he who has been born of God keeps himself, and the wicked one does not touch him" (1 John 5:18). In other words, no evil can defeat him.

> Sennacherib, king of Assyria, destroyed all the cities of Judah during the reign of Hezekiah, but he could not take Jerusalem. He could not even besiege the city; he could not even gaze upon it. This is described in detail in the Book of Isaiah: "Therefore thus says the Lord concerning the king of Assyria: 'He shall not come into this city, nor shoot an arrow there, nor come before it with shield, nor build a siege mound against it. By the way came, by the same shall he return says the Lord.'" (Isaiah 37:33–34)

The same happens to people who fear God. A righteous man who orients his actions by God's law and will remains unassailable from all sides. No misfortune defeats him; no excessive grief destroys him. Even if every member of his body is stricken with disease, even if every possible misfortune attacks him, he raises his mind and heart bravely to God and runs to Him with firm hope in His aid. Even in a time of extreme need, he still conforms his own desires to the will of God. And why would he not act in this way? He has a loving heart, and its striving toward the Eternal Good can never be tied down by passionate attachment to anything earthly, if only he has that desire to always strive toward the eternal embrace of God's will.

In some ecclesiastical chronicles, we find mention of a certain wise, great, and virtuous man who was stricken by terrible afflictions. He welcomed it, however, with the following words, "I greet you with joy, you terrible sorrows that are so filled with God's mercy and blessing!" Something similar happened to Socrates,[30] who accepted the poisoned cup with great joy. The Apostle Andrew also greeted the cross on which he was to be crucified while still far away, and when he reached it, he embraced it and kissed it.

II

You may say beloved reader that it is easy to write about this in books, but in reality things are different when we actually encounter hunger, dishonor, the loss of property, and the terrible pain of illness. No one finds joy in these things, for all this fiercely beats down a person who would be otherwise stronger than iron, if he were not beaten down by fate. Excuse me, dear reader, but you seem to me like one of Job's friends who were his alleged comforters. To them he said, "You are all bad comforters. What order is there in words of wind?" (Job 16:2–3). My eyes weep to God; yes, I weep, I admit it, but this is no comfort to me. That I weep for my God, however, is the truest, most constant joy, "for the Lord will not cast off the innocent. Nor will He accept any gift of an ungodly man" (Job 8:20–21). He will not extend His hand to the one who is ready to do all evil, but He will decorate unhypocritical lips with a smile and inspire the tongue to praise Him. What do you want from me? "The hand of the Lord has touched me" (Job 19:21); but it is better to be beaten by His hand than to be caressed by any other. The right hand of the Lord heals with a mere touch; its strike gives not disease but health; not death but life.

I answer you, dear reader, in the same way. And I also offer you a question: If, while sparring, someone strikes you with a metal gauntlet and makes you bleed, is that the fault of the gauntlet? No, this is the hand's doing, but will you then take the hand to court? No, for it was a man who hit you. Thus God sometimes covers His striking hand with leather, sometimes with wood, sometimes with iron. Today He punishes with hunger, tomorrow with dishonor.

Today He allows you to be insulted by this person, but tomorrow it will be another. Sometimes He punishes you through your relatives, brothers, or your own immediate family. It is one and the same hand of God that chastises, not always in the same manner, but differently every time. Sometimes He visits you through other people. So why do you rail against these others? This cunning person has harmed me, that thief left me with nothing, and that liar stole my honor along with my property. What are you saying you fool? Why are you taking a gauntlet to court? Pay attention to the hand of God that gives you mercies as well as punishments. God sent all this to you.

Remember King David, who never complained about his afflictions and remained silent, firmly keeping in mind that it was God who allowed him to be afflicted. Solomon, when speaking of the difference between good days and days of misfortune, said, "In the day of what is good, live in that goodness. But in the day of trouble, consider also that God made one harmonious with the other, that a man may not find out anything that will come after him" (Ecclesiastes 7:14). Why are we so ungrateful to God, when we shower our physician with praises after he completed a successful operation? We said to the doctor, "What a wonderful job you did! Even though the incisions were painful to me, I am grateful to you, because you have healed me." We praise this doctor, who is able to skillfully extract the poison from an adder and use it for our benefit. This amazes us. So why do we then not accept with joy the afflictions and insults God sends us with the purpose of correcting us and turning us back to the path of salvation?

Let it be known to everyone that God knows all our deeds, and He knows for what reason we need this or that affliction, even if we do not understand it. And we dare to secretly murmur at God, saying, "O Lord! How heavy is Your punishment! Your hand is unbearably heavy?" On the contrary, beloved Christian! When you utter such brazen complaints to God, you are very mistaken. It is not He who is cruel. It is not His hand that is heavy in punishment. He, seeing with His gaze your entire past, present, and future, chooses to send you, by His mercy, everything that is most beneficial to you, even if it were to be your very death. Your soul is eternal, and you do not know what your future holds, you impatient fool of little faith, more fickle even than the weather! God has desired to heal you, to make you strong in spirit, and you think that He prepared a poisoned cup for you? Listen to the words of the wise man: "The fear of the Lord is the stronghold of a holy man, but destruction is for those who work evil" (Proverbs 10:30). The righteous man is firm down to his very core (in his heart), and nothing can shatter his foundations, nothing can frighten him. He remains calm in spirit amid all afflictions.

III

Seneca wrote to his friend Lucillus: "I wish for you to be always joyful; let there always be joy in your home. It will never depart from your home if it always abides within you yourself." Any external joy will never fill the heart totally; instead, it often results in boredom or even leads to sorrow, for it is not constant. Do not imagine that every person who laughs is joyful. The only true happiness and joy is the joy of a heart that is courageous, rising above all that is earthly. Truly this is so. If every one of us strives to have a heart that ascends always to God, the greatest, eternal Good; if we live in accord with God's commandments and will to such a degree that no glory will puff us up and no sorrow will destroy us; then our true joy will be our own inner knowledge that we stand above the pleasures of this world, despising them so much that we tread them underfoot.

If, with God's help, we reach such a state of spiritual ascent, then the merciful God will send us, in the bitter moments of our temptation, His own unassailable strength. He will cause our hearts to be filled with true and constant joy, before which the pleasures of the world and sin will be revealed to us in all their worthlessness, powerlessness, and filth, as unworthy of the attention of a reasonable human being and a true Christian. All the pleasures and amusements of the world divert, not our human soul, but our animal nature, which when undirected by the soul lowers a man to a likeness with irrational animals.

A wise man looks differently on impure amusements and pleasures. Even pagan Seneca said, "The joy that comes from the spirit of a man is true and strong. It constantly grows, and remains with a man until the very end." Understand his words correctly. The end he speaks of is the full development of perfection in a person, as St Paul also said, "till we all come ... to the measure of the stature of the fullness of Christ" (Ephesians 4:13). This should be obvious, for only virtue gives constant, eternal, secure joy. Even if a virtuous man is struck with sorrow, it comes over him only like a cloud briefly obscuring the sun, but the light and warmth of the sun is not fully blocked. This is a true image of the pure heart, contrite and humbly committed to the will of God. For as the firmament of heaven, extending out beyond the moon, has a brightness that is never darkened by a cloud or shaken by earthquakes or subject to storms, so the mind of man, joyfully having given itself to the guidance of God's will, remains always meek, bright, convivial, and peaceable in the calmness of its depths. Nothing can ever shatter this calm.

A righteous man will remain neither in perpetual joy nor in sorrow. He will have joyful days and sorrowful ones, depending on the providence of God. His days will not always be full of clement weather. There is something mysteriously pleasant in this union between joy and sorrow or even heavy suffering, for it gives inner peace and consolation through the accord of the mind with providence. It is moral superiority combined with meekness (the emblem of Christ's teachings).

Ignorant and angry people do not have any of this. Instead, inside them is a battle of various passions that they themselves give birth to. These passions incite and multiply entire legions of sorrowful and unpleasant thoughts in the mind and heart. The virtuous man, on the contrary, committed in all things to the will of God, never complains even in the most terrible of troubles. He despises all afflictions. Everything evil that comes into his sphere of influence he corrects and covers with his good counsel. Thus, he transforms evil into good. Finally, he never complains to God about other people who cause him sorrow.

This is the peace and moral height of a mind that is submerged in a life of virtue; this is the greatest and strongest joy of a righteous soul that cannot be defeated or grieved by any external affliction. For those who meekly and humbly do the will of God accomplish what is written in Scripture: "But whoever listens to me will dwell safely, and will be secure, without fear of evil" (Proverbs 1:33 NKJV). St Ambrose of Milan confirms this: "A wise man is not brought low by physical illness, nor is he sorrowful in afflictions. Instead, he remains good-humored and patient in sorrows, for blessedness and happiness are not found in the pleasures and delights of the body, but only in a conscience purified of all stain."

IV

Of course, one cannot say that righteous men do not feel the pain of afflictions, for no virtue or power can fully diminish human suffering. However, they do not fear it; they do not fall into despondency. They have a strong spirit that allows them to rise above any pain and makes them indomitable. Seneca noticed this quality of the virtuous man: "Nothing evil can happen to a good man." In other words, no occurrence, no matter how uncomfortable, can bring evil to such a man. He continues,

> In the same way that many rivers flowing into the ocean do not change the salty taste of seawater, so the many misfortunes and attacks against a virtuous man do not pervert his mind and heart. He always remains unchangeable in his views and actions, while everything contrary to his wishes (which he considers to be either sent or allowed from above)

he turns ultimately to his own benefit. Every external difficulty makes him stronger than that difficulty. I am not saying that he no longer senses that particular difficulty, but he overcomes it sufficiently so that he no longer considers it, remaining always calm and content in his soul. In a word, he becomes greater than any misfortune. He considers any negative event to be a practical means to becoming wiser and more moral.

Such virtuous men included in their ranks the much-suffering Job, King David, the Apostle Paul, and many others.

King David said, "Yea, though I walk through the valley of the shadow of death, I will fear no evil, for Thou art with me; Thy rod and Thy staff, they have comforted me" (Psalm 22:4). The Apostle Paul encouraged the faithful with the following words: "If God is for us, who can be against us?" (Romans 8:31). St Paulinus the merciful, bishop of Nola (fifth century), said, "If God is our helper in battle with the enemy, then even a spider's web will protect us better than stone walls. On the contrary, if God has left me, and He is no longer with me, then the thinnest thread of a spider's web becomes a more effective obstacle to my goal than stone walls.".

In order to illustrate this vivid image, St Paulinus offers the following example. A certain Nolan priest named Felix used to rebuke the pagans for their foul worship of idols; for this reason, the pagans persecuted him and wanted to kill him. Escaping from these persecutions, he hid in the narrow space between two old stone houses. He found a cleft through which he crawled, and so his persecutors could not find him. Even though they carefully examined this cleft through which the priest crawled, they saw that a complete spider's web covered the opening, and so concluded that the priest could not have crawled that way and ceased searching for him. Unbeknownst to them, the spider had spun a new web the moment that the priest had passed through.

Truly it is said, "Many are the troubles of the righteous, but the Lord delivereth them out of all" (Psalm 33:20). "I sought the Lord and He heard me, yea, He delivered me out of all my troubles" (Psalm 33:5). For this reason, we, together with the Apostle Paul—whom God saved from certain death in Asia—exclaim to God, "Blessed be the God and Father of our Lord Jesus Christ, the Father of mercies and God of all comfort, who comforts us in all our tribulation, that we may be able to comfort those who are in any trouble, with the comfort with which we ourselves are comforted by God" (2 Corinthians 1:3–4).

No sorrowful calamity can overcome a righteous man, for just as no one can touch the apple of Christ's eye without Christ's permission, so without God's will not a single hair can be plucked out of the head of a righteous man (Luke 21:18). Knowing also that any calamity comes about only by the will of God, the righteous man greets it with prayerful words, "Your will be done on earth as it is in heaven," for he is convinced that everything that happens to him will serve for his benefit. For this reason, Isaiah, when listing the many calamities threatening Jerusalem and the entire Jewish nation for their immorality and sinfulness (i.e., for the proliferation of social and personal sins against God's law), declared to all who have a clean conscience that they have God's protection and goodwill, saying, "Say to the righteous that it shall be well with them, for they shall eat the fruit of their doings" (Isaiah 3:10 NKJV).

O, you most holy and marvelous prophet! This good man lost his wife to disease, but you say, "Tell him that it is for his benefit." That other man's house burned down, and you still say, "It is for your benefit!" That man is subjected to a horrible personal insult and dishonor—"It is good for him!" That man buried his children and yet, "It is for his benefit." That good man lost all his money, but tell him that it is doubly good for him, for I believe he would have perished if he were not deprived in good time of his gold and precious things.

When Jacob traveled to the home of Laban (his future father-in-law), night caught him while he still traveled, and he lay down to sleep. The earth served him as a bed, and a stone was his pillow. As you see, his bed was not luxurious, but he fell asleep and saw a miraculous vision, a ladder founded on earth whose top reached the heavens. Angels of God ascended and descended this ladder, and he could see the Lord Himself above it (Genesis 28:11–13). Let this vision be for us an image and explanation of any apparently unfavorable circumstance that we may meet on the road of life. Many of us only see the rock that is under our head, but let it be known to all sufferers that around them the angels and God Himself invisibly encourage them, seeing every moment their troubles. This is why no bitter misfortune can defeat people with pure consciences and hearts, with a humble spirit: "He who trusts in the Lord shall be careful" (Proverbs 28:27).

When Alphonso V (1396–1458), King of Naples (1442–1458) and Aragon (1416–1458), called the Magnanimous, was already old, he read Livy and Julius Caesar every day, he translated the letters of Seneca, and—lest anyone think that he only bothered with secular writers—he read the entire Bible fourteen times through. He also read all the major interpretations of the Bible, and not quickly, willy-nilly, but with great attentiveness and reflection. This virtuous and wise king left, among many other words of wisdom, the following aphorism, which was his last. When asked whom he—in his great wisdom—would call a truly happy and fortunate man, he answered, I consider such a man to be extremely fortunate and blessed—a man who commits himself completely, with great reverence and a pure heart, to God. Such a man, no matter what happens to him in life, considers it to be God's arrangement for his life, and so he accepts it, praising and thanking God for it."

Even an angel of God could not have spoken more beautifully.

V

Heraclius, an outstanding dignitary of Alexandria (fifth century A.D.), left us the record of his conversation with Abba Dorothoeos, who had already lived for sixty years in a cave. Heraclius tells how he visited Dorotheos, and the Abba asked him to gather some water from a well. He went, and seeing a water snake in the well, he returned with his bucket still empty. Abba Dorotheos chuckled, looked at Heraclius for a long time, and said, nodding his head, "If God allowed the devil to throw adders in all the wells of the world, would you then not take water from any of them?"

Abba Dorotheos then left the cave and went himself to the well, filled the bucket with water, signed it with the cross and began to drink, saying to Heraclius, "No evil thing will overcome a righteous man, even if it is bitter to his senses."

We have already mentioned that calamities may upset even a righteous man, yet they will never defeat him. In other words, his inner man (his "I") remains constantly at peace and gathers yet more strength. Here are some examples that prove this to be true. St John Chrysostom offers us two obvious proofs.

1. When our body is afflicted with various diseases or pains, it often occurs that one pain drowns out the others, making them, as it were, disappear. For example, a person who has an injured finger, a headache, and a stomachache does not complain about his finger, because he does not feel that pain in comparison with the other more severe pains. Instead, he complains bitterly about the pain in his head and stomach. St John says that whoever has lost his riches, whoever has been dishonored or lost his good name, whoever has been deprived of civil or ecclesiastical rank, should awaken in himself the awareness of his terrible sins. He should sigh from the depths of his heart, remembering how much Christ his Redeemer suffered for his sins. He should vividly imagine how He was scourged, how He was led—weak from physical and emotional sufferings—along the streets of Jerusalem toward Golgotha, how He was nailed to the Cross, how even on the Cross He endured all manner of insults, mockery, rebukes, and the most painful of deaths. Then he should remember

his own future suffering in accordance with his sinfulness (i.e., his transgression of God's laws). This true sorrow in his sins, if he feels it deeply, will soften and drown out any external sorrow. In this sense, Christ the Saviour told His followers not to fear those "who kill the body [that is, all physical sufferings, including death] but cannot kill the soul. But rather fear Him who is able to destroy both soul and body in hell" (Matthew 10:28).

2. For his second proof, St John Chrysostom takes an example from medical sciences. He says that bandages are not placed on a healthy part of the body, but it is placed on an afflicted part. A lotion or a poultice for healing the eyes is useful for the eyes but not for the shoulders. Certain liquid medicines are useful for the stomach. A healing cream is placed on an open wound, not to the part of the body adjacent to the wound. In the same way, unhappiness resulting from poverty, dishonor, chronic illness, or any other affliction cannot be removed by excessive grieving (which is itself harmful to our health), or by our tears, or by our useless moaning. There is nothing joyful in such grieving, and it will not return riches, honor, or health. In fact, such grief will only increase one's suffering. This is because neither sorrow nor tears are actual medicines for our losses or sufferings. They are only useful to heal our sins.

Chrysostom offers us many more examples. Is anyone punished by a confiscation of property? He sorrows, but this sorrow will not cancel the punishment. Has someone lost a son? He cries over him, but this will not resurrect his son. Has someone been dishonored? He weeps, but his tears do not restore his honor. Has someone fallen gravely ill? He suffers, but his pain does not restore him to health; it only makes it worse. Notice that none of these aforementioned people benefited from their sorrow, but it only increased their pain.

On the contrary, if someone has sinned, he repents and grieves over his fall into sin. He confesses his sin before God, and through this he destroys the sin. This person has experienced sorrow for the sake of God, and by this he has in no way harmed himself, for sorrow for the sake of God leads him to genuine repentance for salvation. Earthly sorrow, on the other hand, only brings death. Consequently, sorrow can be either medicine or poison; therefore, it should be used wisely. In conclusion, I will repeat myself a thousand times: No affliction ever defeats a righteous man.

 CHAPTER 13

Fashioning One's Will to God's Is a Pleasing Sacrifice to God

We believe and confess that the bloodless sacrifice (at the liturgy) of the Lamb of God, Christ the Lord, in the form of bread and wine, is a pleasing sacrifice brought by us to God. In other words, when we participate in this mystical service to God, we offer ourselves to the Lord completely as a sacrifice. Consequently, we must submit our will to God in all things completely. Blessed Jerome, in his letter to Lucanus, expressed this beautifully:

> To bring sacrifices of gold is the work of beginners, those not yet grown up. Socrates, Antisthenes, and other lovers of wisdom did this. But it is proper for a Christian to bring himself to God, to his Redeemer, the Lord Christ. That is, he must dedicate his entire life to the uncomplaining fulfillment of God's will in all deeds and actions. A person has given everything to God when he has brought his own self as a sacrifice to Him, rejecting his own will, pride, and other sins. This is all that God demands of us, saying, "My son, give me your heart, and let your eyes observe my ways." (Proverbs 23:25)

You may be sure that you will give everything to God when you give Him your heart (that is, your own self).

I

This sacrifice of personal will to God will only be pleasing to Him if the one bringing the sacrifice abides in the grace of God, that is, lives a life as sinless as possible, correcting his transgressions by constant repentance. St Basil (330–379 A.D.), while interpreting the words of Psalm 28:1, says,

> Before you bring your sacrifice to God, test yourself assiduously—do you belong to the grace-filled sons of God? If you are truly a son of grace, then bring your gift to the altar. Only in this case will your offering be pleasing to God. Sorrow in the depths of your heart if your conscience accuses you in sins, and apply all your effort and firmly resolve to avoid falling into sin, because sin removes God's mercy from you. "A contrite and humble heart God shall not despise" (Psalm 50:19). Say to yourself, "I desire nothing more than to have opportunity to give myself completely to my Creditor, and thus to become a cheerful slave of the Lord."

Blessed Augustine also says, "Believe in God without doubt, and give yourself to Him as much as your circumstances allow. Do not desire ever to belong to yourself or to have full jurisdiction over yourself, but consider yourself to be a slave of the all-merciful and compassionate God."

Such a relationship with the Lord will make you pleasing to the Lord, and He will not stop bringing you into ever-closer intimacy with Himself. He will not allow any evil to befall you, nothing bitter, except that which is absolutely necessary for your correction, even if you do not understand how such events may serve for your benefit. Blessed Augustine confirmed this teaching in another place, when he said, "We can bring nothing to the Lord, except the heartfelt repetition of Isaiah's words, 'Be our master, O God!'"

Some bring offerings to the Church—wax for candles or oil for lamps—but these are monetary offerings, and so they are not enough nor are they especially virtuous. Some give God an oath never to drink wine—not to say never to get drunk!—while others generously give to the poor and destitute. These are truly worthy gifts, but they are no greater than other oaths, for in what way can the poor help you save your soul? God has redeemed your soul (He has turned it away from sin, redeemed it from its evil effect, and turned it to the path of virtue). Thus, bring Him as a gift that which He has already redeemed. Bring Him your soul as an offering.

You ask me, "How can I offer my soul if it is already in His power?"

Listen: Bring your soul, that is, your own self, in your good manner of life, in your pure thoughts, in your good deeds. This is the nature of Hannah's offering her son Samuel,[31] Joachim and Anna's offering the Mother of God,[32]

St Gregory the Theologian's[33] parents' offering the great future saint to God. Such offerings yielded the greatest and most famous of saints. If it is so useful to bring one's children as offerings to God, how much more useful is it to bring one's self as an offering to Him! King David accomplished this fully, committing himself to God's service with these prayerful words: "Willingly shall I sacrifice unto Thee; I will praise Thy Name, O Lord, for it is good" (Psalm 53:8).

It is pleasant for us if someone willingly offers his services to us. Many admirers of Socrates gave him precious gifts from their excess wealth. Aeschines, a disciple of his who was very poor, said,

> I have nothing to give you as a gift worthy of you, and by this I truly know myself to be truly destitute. All I have is myself, and I offer myself in service to you. Disregard the poverty of my gift; see that others give you gifts from their excess, leaving themselves much more than they give. But I give you everything I have. May my gift be pleasing to you.

"Truly, you bring me the greatest and most precious of gifts," answered Socrates, "except that you consider yourself to be of little value. However, I will try to do everything in my power to return you to yourself in much better state than you are now."

Aeschines thus surpassed, by his heartfelt offering, even the great Alcibiades.[34] Truly his gift was more precious than all the riches offered by prosperous youths. It would be useful for us to pay attention to how a wise mind can find the greatest wealth even in the worst poverty. The truth is that an object is not valued by its price at market but by the eagerness with which it is given as a gift to another. It is the greatest sacrifice to God, or better yet, it is a complete sacrifice to offer one's own will to His every single day. Such a sacrifice should be offered not once a day, not twice, but many times (as often as necessary), especially when one finds oneself burdened by various earthly attractions or misfortunes, when one is surrounded by problems or when everything is going exactly as he wishes. Whatever the situation, he should turn to God in prayer, saying, "O Lord, my God, I bring myself completely as a sacrifice to You, let Your goodwill rule over me. Let Your will be done in me."

Such an offering will arrange our lives perfectly. In afflictions, we will receive endurance. In our happiness and success, we will remain chaste and moderate. Such an offering lessens our sorrow during troubles and restrains our mouth from improper complaints against God. It distances us from lack of patience. It also increases our reward for good deeds and, more than anything, it attracts the mercy of God. In a word, this sacrifice is an indomitable shield against all troubles, trials, and temptations.

II

While offering the aforementioned way of relating to God—that is, sacrificing oneself completely to His will—a certain teacher of the church had the following observation:

> I have no more than these two copper coins, that is, my body and my soul. To be completely honest, I only have one coin—my will. Should I not give it into the disposition of the One Who made me, a worthless creature, so rich with His benefits? For He redeemed me by the price of His own earthly life and sufferings! If I do not want to submit myself completely to His holy will and its dictates after His redemption, with what eyes, heart, conscience will I stand before the merciful face of our God?

St John Chrysostom, speaking of the Apostle Paul's daily offering of himself to God (through those labors and sufferings that he endured for the sake of the preaching of the Gospel), said,

> Abel brought an offering that was more pleasing to God than Cain's, but if we compare Paul's offering with Abel's, then Paul's offering will be more exalted and glorious than Abel's, as the heavens are in comparison with the earth. For Paul brought to God not animals, but himself, every day, many times, and he considered this to be not enough, and so he eagerly tried to dedicate the entire world to God.

During the time of Diocletian, the priest Epictetus and the monk Astion[35] (commemorated on June 7/20) lived piously in the East, and during the persecutions were seized and imprisoned by Latronianus, the military commander of Halmyris. Epictetus said to Astion,

> Beloved Astion! When they bring us tomorrow to the tribunal, and the judge asks us our names and parentage, let us only answer thus: "We are Christians. This is our only name and parentage." If it pleases God that we should suffer for His sake, let us say nothing to the persecutors

during our tortures, except the prayer, "Lord Jesus, Thy will be done in us."

On the next morning, a public tribunal was set up, and the two accused Christians were brought before the judge. In the presence of the entire city, the judge asked them, "Where are you from, what is your name and your ancestry?"

Epictetus answered, "We are Christians and are born of Christian parents."

"That is not what I asked you," countered Latronianus. "Tell me your names. I already know what faith you profess."

The martyrs answered a second time, "We are Christians. We worship the Lord Jesus Christ alone, and we despise your idols."

Hearing this, the judge became very angry and ordered them to be stripped naked and beaten without mercy for a very long time. The martyrs, red with blood, raised their eyes to heaven and loudly prayed, "Lord Jesus Christ, our God, Thy will be done in us." Latronianus began to laugh and rebuke the martyrs, saying, "Where is this mediator from whom you ask help? Let him come to help you and deliver you out of my hands."

The martyrs only answered, "We are Christians. Let the will of God be done in us."

This only angered the judge the more. He ordered them to be hanged and their bodies to be torn with metal hooks. However, the martyrs still only said, "We are Christians, and let the will of our God be done in us."

The judge considered it to be a great dishonor to be defeated by these martyrs, and he ordered to have them burned by torches, but still he heard no other words leave their mouths. Finally, having suffered such tortures, the saints were imprisoned.

A certain pagan named Vigilantius watched this spectacle. He sat near the judgment seat and heard the repeated words of the saints. After reflection, he came to the conclusion that there was some mystical, unexplainable magic in the words that had the power to lessen or completely remove the sensation of the pain of the tortures. He began to repeat these words to himself and keep them always in his mind, as a powerful protection against all evil and need. Wherever he would go—at home or while walking or before going to sleep or after getting up from his bed—he would have nothing else in his memory, except the words, "We are Christians, and let the will of our God be done in us."

For three days Vigilantius exercised his mind thus with God's help. On the fourth day, inspired by the invisible power of God, he began to exclaim before the assembled court, "I am a Christian. Let the will of my God be done in me." Then he went to the prison where the holy Christian martyrs were being held and accepted baptism along with his entire household. As a result, when the holy martyrs were beheaded for confessing Christ, he buried the sufferers' bodies with gratitude.

However, let us return to the story of Epictetus and Astion. On the next day after their first interrogation, they were brought back for further questioning. The judge, as cunning as a fox, asked the martyrs with false gentleness, "Well! Will you worship our gods or do you persist in your foolishness?"

Epictetus answered, "In vain do you, Latronianus, labor to convince us. We do not honor your hellish horrors. You will sooner deprive us of health and life than of our confession of Christ, our God. One thousand times we have repeated and we will continue to repeat to all the people that we are Christians, and let the will of our God be done in us."

The torturer once again boiled over with rage and began to roar like a lion. "Bring the strongest salt and vinegar you can find this instant! Remind these reprobates about their wounds. Do not spare yourselves, and apply as much vinegar and salt to their wounds as you can." Again the martyrs uttered no words except their previous phrase, and they were miraculously protected from further harm, and the judge returned them to the prison.

After thirty days, they appeared again before the tribunal in perfect health. Now their mouths and teeth were struck with stones, and their bodies were beaten with rods. Yet they continued to repeat, "O Lord, our God, Thy will be done in us." Finally, the judge condemned them to death by beheading. As they were led out of the city to the place of their execution, the holy martyrs strengthened each other and generously praised the Lord, crying aloud, "Praise the name of the Lord, for His will is done in us." When they arrived, they began to sing the hymn of the three youths: "Blessed are You and praiseworthy, O Lord, the God of our fathers, and praised and glorified is Your name unto the ages. For You are righteous in all You did for us, and all Your works are true" (Daniel 3:26–27). "We thank You that Your will, not the will of man, was accomplished in us." In that very moment, when they were supposed to be beheaded, they began a praiseworthy argument about who would receive the glory of being executed first. Epictetus was already an old man, but he was willing to give the honor of the first death to Astion.

Astion replied, "Beloved father, holy priest of God, let your will, and the will of God, be done." With these words, he lowered his head under the sword. Holy Epictetus then embraced and kissed the body of his beloved student, and eagerly submitted to the sword himself. Thus, both of these saints died in a God-pleasing manner.

III

These martyrs are mirrors, in which the pious accord between the human and divine will is clearly reflected. They are examples worthy of emulation for every Christian who finds himself in the midst of a temptation to resist the will of God. In such cases, let every person strengthen himself with a short, but constant prayer:

I am a Christian. Let the will of God (not my will) be done in me. Even if this temptation is unpleasant and difficult for me, still let the will of God be done in me. Though I did not foresee or expect such sorrows, still let the will of God be done in me. Though that man maliciously did me evil, let the will of God be done in me.

Jehu, the great commander of Israel's armies, wrote letters to the rulers of Samaria and the elders of their city with specific instructions. Without hesitation, they chose honored men and sent them to Jehu with the following answer: "We are your servants; we will do everything you tell us" (4 Kingdoms 10:5). How often and in how many different ways did God declare His will to us in the Holy Scriptures, so that we would act in accordance with it! This is true: we are obliged to cheerfully follow the will of God, repeating the words of the Samaritans, "We are your servants; we will do all you tell us." For this reason, St Anthony the Great often repeated, "If we always commit ourselves and all our actions to the hands of God, then not a single demon will be capable of entering single combat with us."

Elijah the Tishbite once argued with the priests of Baal concerning the worship of the One True God. In order to resolve this disagreement, Elijah and the priests of Baal agreed to call on their respective deities to call down fire from heaven to consume their offerings. Baal's priests prepared their sacrifice for burning and began to call on Baal from the morning until the noontime, exclaiming, "Baal, hear us!" But there was no answer, though they hopped around their altar in their customary way. At midday, Elijah began to laugh at them, saying, "Cry out with a loud voice, for he is a god; for either he is always meditating, or he is too busy, or preoccupied with other business. Perhaps he is sleeping and has need to be awakened from his nap" (3 Kingdoms 18:27). And so they screamed more loudly and began to cut themselves with knives and spears until they bled, but it was all in vain. Midday passed, and they continued to thrash about until the evening with no success.

Then Elijah told them to move aside so that he could perform his sacrifice to the Lord before all the assembled people. He made an altar out of twelve stones (the number of the tribes of Israel), laid wood on it, and placed a prepared sacrificial ox on top of the wood. Then he commanded all of his preparation to be doused with a great deal of water, all the while exclaiming aloud to God,

O Lord God of Abraham, Isaac, and Israel, answer me, O Lord, answer me this day with fire, and let this people know You are the God of Israel, and I am Your servant; and for Your sake I do all these works. Hear me, O Lord, hear me with fire, and let these people know You are the Lord God, so as turn the heart of this people back. (3 Kingdoms 18:36–37)

And immediately God sent fire from heaven and the sacrifice, though wet all through, was consumed.

It often happens that Christians labor and suffer during services in church. They mortify their bodies with fasting, they come to church often, and they perform other feats of asceticism. All this is good, but we rarely receive fire from heaven, rarely do we burn with true eagerness to fulfill the will of God and to completely avoid contradictions between our will and desires and those of God. How rarely do we speak these words—even when we do, our heart does not participate—Thy will be done, Lord! It often happens that we sacrifice this or that thing for the glory of God, and invite others to do the same, and yet we receive little benefit from it. This is because we do not bring—for all our external gifts—the true sacrifice of our will and desires to God's holy will. We do not even care about doing this.

Two people once asked St Macarius[36] to teach them how to pray. In answer, he said to them, "Do not use many words in your personal prayers. Instead, raise your hands to heaven and repeat often: 'Lord God, let it be as You will and as it pleases You.' He knows what we need better than we do."

This is an excellent instruction on how to pray. St Pachomius the Great[37] prayed in the same way. He only asked the Lord for one thing: that he do the will of God in all his actions.

Such uncompromising commitment to God's will is the best and most pleasing offering we can give to God, for all other sacrifices—abstinence from food or drink, charitable donation, patient endurance of insults—are partial. However, by completely committing himself to the will of God, a person can give himself as a gift to God. Then God becomes his true Master, overseeing him personally, managing all the things and events in his life.

I offer two further remarks worthy of frequent repetition.

1. When you, the chosen one of God, commit yourself to Him and His divine will completely and unconditionally, when you bring your will as a sacrifice to His, I beg you never to regret it afterward. Whether your life is easy or difficult, do not be sorry about the promise you gave to God. You know how children are sometimes. Whenever they are insulted by one of their friends, they immediately say, "I will no longer be your friend. I prefer to be by myself!" even though five minutes before they would have sworn undying friendship. I beg you, Christian soul, do not be like these children. Do not abandon God, even if God allows you to be punished, even if He seems to abandon you to fiery tortures, crushing you with many sorrows and afflictions. Instead, constantly call to Him in the brokenness of your heart, "O Lord, have mercy upon me. I am Yours, O my God. I am Yours! Your will be done in me."

2. If you ever fall prey to a serious sin such as drunkenness, judging others, or lust, you should ask yourself: "To whom does this body of yours that committed the sin belong? Does it not belong to God? Was it not brought to God in sacrifice a hundred times, a thousand times? And now you make it the instrument of terrible sins? Do you not realize that you afflict God as well as your neighbor with your sins? And how much more do you harm yourself with this madness by stifling your own conscience! Wake up! What are you doing? You have lost both your faith and your conscience. Your tongue, your eyes, your hands, and your whole body were committed by you countless times to the service of God, but now you commit them by your actions to the demons? What are you doing? You are subjecting yourself to terrible dangers, to eternal perdition. Know that our God is not mocked: "Whatever a man sows, that he will also reap" (Galatians 6:7). If you do not want God to forsake you eternally, piously submit yourself again to His divine will before you fall into eternal punishment. Do all that the Law and divine revelation demand of you.

The entire blessedness of the Israelites consisted of following God's direction on the way to the Promised Land. The cloud and the pillar of fire indicated this way.[38] In the same way, our eternal salvation is contingent on our walking the earthly path unwaveringly, according to the directions of the fiery Law of Love. If we do this, we will be illumined by the grace-filled cloud of God's providence for His Church and for every one of us in particular until the end of our journey, when we will enter the land flowing with milk and honey (i.e., the eternal kingdom of God). Consequently, the true and righteous path to heaven is the path that follows God's will. He will unerringly lead us into the kingdom of God's love for mankind.

CHAPTER 14

Human Perfection Is Contingent on the Coordination between One's Desires and Actions and God's Will as Revealed in the Law or in One's Own Life

Every human action is judged by its desired end. This ultimate purpose determines the quality of our actions, that is, whether our actions lead to our eternal blessedness or perdition. If we assume that there is a choice among many ultimate goals in life, it would behoove us to determine what is the best possible goal in life. The truest, most blessed, eternally joyful, self-sufficient, most noble and beneficial goal in life is the constant striving to do God's will. This striving gradually brings us closer to God Himself and to eternal blessedness in His kingdom. There are no better or more beautiful actions than those that bring us closer to God and attract His mercy to us sinners.

True and *righteous* are the words of St Basil the Great:

> To give yourself eagerly in all actions and deeds to the will and guidance of God, that is, to reject your own self-will and to accept with gratitude everything God sends us—both pleasant and unpleasant—this is the perfection and highest degree of Christian holiness. By virtue of this evangelical self-rejection and bearing of Christ's Cross, God raises up and glorifies all the saints. This cheerful rejection of your own will, according to the teaching of the Holy Fathers and teachers of a God-pleasing life, is considered the only sure principle of spiritual peace and calm for a person who believes firmly in God's providence, since it never leaves anyone without first directing him to his best

possible end. This principle establishes in us a firm hope in our eternal well-being, so that a person no longer even wants to trust in his own powers; he ceases to belong only to himself, but becomes God's, living no longer for himself, but for God. Whatever God sends him, he is content and gives thanks to God for it, though he be in prosperity or in chains.

Such submission to God is the most pleasing sacrifice to Him, for such a sacrifice God honored David with the highest praise given to anyone in the Scriptures, calling him a "man after My own heart, who will do all My will" (Acts 13:22). For David truly came so close to God with his heart that he was always ready to cheerfully and eagerly accomplish any command of God. Every person should be guided by the example of King David.

I

The sunflower is a flower that constantly turns to the sun—morning, noon, and evening—not only during sunny days but also even during cloudy ones. The will of man should emulate the nature of this flower and turn to God and His divine will every hour, not only in the bright days of life but also during the dark, difficult days. The holiness of a person's life, according to a certain wise theologian, is the constant striving toward perfection for the duration of life, the gathering of all possible virtues together with God's will. Whatever is pleasing to God, let it be pleasing to you, O Christian. Whatever God does not wish, that you must avoid. While following His holy commandments in every moment of doubt, you must say to God in your heart, "Lord, You have commanded this. I will do it immediately."

When God forbids something, say, "Yes, Lord, I eagerly abandon this, and I will do nothing abhorrent to You." By willingly submitting our will to God's, we express complete humility before God, to Whom we are required to worthily and righteously submit in all things, according to the words of the prophet, "Doth not my soul wait still upon God? For of Him cometh my salvation" (Psalm 61:1). Yes, my soul will submit to Him, for He is the consolation of my soul, He is my salvation. He is my foundation, my haven, and I will never waver in my obedience to Him. For to God, as to the Creator, every creature is obedient except for man, but God desires that man, gifted with reason, submit to Him willingly.

II

In the Old Testament, Moses brought the groans of the Israelites to Pharaoh, asking him to release them from the land of Egypt. "The God of the Hebrews has called us to Him. Let us go three days' journey into the desert and sacrifice to the Lord our God, lest at any time death or slaughter happen to us" (Exodus 5:3).

Many call the road to heaven "three miles long" (a mile being used metaphorically). The first mile is the mile of correction, the second is the mile of illumination, and the third is the mile of union. Truly to walk toward God along this path is very easy, if only a person aligns his will with God's. Christ the Lord said that no one is good except for God (Luke 18:19). The Holy Fathers interpret this saying as the foundation of that postulate that "the reason of God is the rule of all truth, an unchangeable rule that is the foundation of knowing all that exists." The will of God should be such a rule, an unchangeable signpost, for all our actions leading to the acquisition of true good.

St John Chrysostom said, "That which is according to God's will, even if it seems to us wrong and undesirable, is always God-pleasing and beneficial. On the contrary, everything that is done without God's direction or contrary to His desires, even if it seems to be pleasing to God (such as some virtuous deed), is actually foul and lawless in the eyes of God."

We see an example of such a situation in the third book of Kingdoms. By the command of God, a prophet was sent for the instruction of King Ahab, who had forgiven the defeated king of Syria and allied with him contrary to God's desires. This prophet, in order not to accuse the king openly, but in order to force Ahab to accuse himself, did the following. As he came to the king, he told another Israelite to beat him "by God's command," but that person did not want to strike the prophet. The prophet immediately foretold a terrible future for the man: "Because you did not obey the voice of the Lord, surely, as soon as you depart from me, a lion shall kill you." And as soon as he left him, a lion found him and killed him (3 Kingdoms 21:36).

The Scriptural account continues,

> Then he found another man and said, "Strike me down." So the man struck him and inflicted a wound. The prophet departed, and waited for the king of Israel by the road, and disguised himself with a bandage over his eyes. Now as the king passed by, he cried out to the king and said, "Your servant went out against the army in the war, and behold, a man brought a man to me and said to me, 'Guard this man. But if by

some means he escapes, your life shall be for his life, or else you shall pay a talent of silver.'" So it came to pass that your servant was looking here and there, but he was not to be found. But the king of Israel said to him, "Behold, you destroyed the ambush meant for me." Then the prophet hurried to take the bandage off his eyes; and the king of Israel recognized him as one of the prophets. He said to him, "Thus says the Lord," Because you freed a man meant for destruction at your hand; therefore, your life shall be in place of his life, and your people in place of his people. (3 Kingdoms 21:37–43)

St John Chrysostom says that it would seem that there is something very wrong in this account. The one who beat and bloodied a prophet of God remains unharmed, while the one who did not beat him (fearing to beat a man of God) received a terrible punishment. This is how dangerous it is to refuse to follow the commandment of God's will. It is not useful to ask too many questions about the reasons why certain things are allowed, while others are forbidden. The Omnipresent, Omniscient, and All-Good God is the first principle of all that exists, and His holy will is the highest, most unchanging law for the will of man, for the free activity of his reasoning creature. To follow God's will in all things or to conform one's free desires with God's will (which is the same thing) are the highest and final step of Christian perfection.

 CHAPTER 15

Conforming the Human Will with the Will of God Is the Greatest Good in Life

The brother of the prodigal son (see Luke 15:11–32) was extremely upset that his brother, who had wasted his entire inheritance by living dissolutely in a foreign land, was mercifully received back in the house by their father. The merciful father even ordered the slaves to prepare a great feast to celebrate the salvation of the son he thought to be lost. The elder brother was so upset that he refused to enter the house. His loving father went out to him and began to entreat him not to cause trouble on such a joyful day. But the son, opposing his father to his face, said,

> I have served you for so many years and have never acted contrary to your wishes, and yet you consider me to be your slave. You never even gave me a goat so that I could have a feast with my friends, as though my obedience and submission were not pleasing to you. But when this vagabond returned, you offered him all the best of your house, as though you are grateful for his sins. Who can look at this impassively?

The good father, desiring to calm the anger of his son, said, "My son! You are always with me, and everything that is mine is yours. Do you not know that you are as much a master of this house as I am? We have one common inheritance for our life, and all the profit of the land belongs as much to you as to me." With these words, the father calmed the anger of the older brother and reconciled the two brothers.[39]

In the same way, the merciful God preserves and pacifies every person who gives his heart to His holy will. God encourages and strengthens His beloved's heart to remain faithful to His will, telling him in secret,

You are always with Me, you abide constantly in My mind and memory if you submit to My will without complaining. I always look on you with love and preserve you, so that you will not lack My grace. All that is Mine is yours: My heaven, My angels, and especially My Only-begotten Son. I Myself am yours, and will be yours, as I promised faithful Abraham: "I am your shield, and will be your exceedingly great reward." (Genesis 15:1)

The Beloved Heavenly Father does not limit Himself even to such gifts. He, through His beloved Son, our Lord Jesus Christ, declared that the person who has committed himself fully to God's will may, in certain situations, receive a special grace to accomplish deeds that are only possible with the direct aid of divine power. "Most assuredly, I say to you, he who believes in Me, the works that I do he will do also; and greater works than these he will do" (John 14:12). Truly, God gives such grace-filled authority to those who have decided, with the help of God's grace, once and for all to direct themselves according to the will of God and to battle all personal desires contrary to that will. This is God's dominion, God's kingdom. This is the beloved promise, the constant communion of the heart with God, Who is love. God wants to share His kingdom with man without dividing it, for everything that is God's also belongs to faithful mankind. Even God Himself belongs to man, being his eternal, indomitable power and shield.

St Paul speaks of this at length:

If anyone defiles the temple of God, God will destroy him. For the temple of God is holy, which temple you are. Let no one deceive himself. If anyone among you seems to be wise in this age, let him become a fool that he may become wise. For the wisdom of this world is foolishness with God. For it is written, "He catches the wise in their own craftiness"; and again, "The Lord knows the thoughts of the wise, that they are futile." Therefore, let no one boast in men. For all things are yours: whether Paul or Apollos or Cephas, or the world or life or death, or things present or things to come—all are yours. And you are Christ's, and Christ is God's. (1 Corinthians 3:17–23)

All are yours not because they belong to us, but because everything serves for our spiritual and physical benefit, helping us achieve our highest, final goal—eternal blessedness with God and in God. *The world* is ours together with all its created things, for these are necessary for our bodies and souls. Our life is ours, in order for us to consecrate it to the service of God and our neighbors, which will be counted for our advantage. Our death is ours as well, since through it, as through a door, we will enter eternal life. Our present life—prosperous or torturous—is ours, for through it we can become virtuous. The future is ours, because it is the harvest of the seed planted in life. We reap what we sow: "And we know that all things work together for good to those who love God, to those who are the called according to His purpose" (Romans 8:28). "Thou hast given him his heart's desire, and hast not denied him the requests of his lips" (Psalm 20:3).

I

The son of Themistocles[40] once boasted that all the citizens of Athens were under his direction and disposal, because they all wanted the same things he did. When all were amazed at the words of the brazen youth and refused to believe him, he added, "Whatever I desire, my mother desires as well [for she loved her son beyond reason]. Whatever my mother desires, that also my father Themistocles desires. And as everyone knows, whatever pleases Themistocles pleases all of Athens. Therefore, I conclude that all the citizens of Athens submit and are obedient to my authority."

Of course, this is an anecdote. But, like this young man, a righteous man who has completely rejected his own will and entrusted himself with faith into God's hands can say with pure conscience, "That which I desire, all the hosts of heaven also desire (for I never want anything other than what God wants), but that which God wants, that also all the holy angels and saints desire as well." To such a person the Heavenly Father speaks a kind word: "You are My son, and all that is Mine is yours." Only reprobates remain opposed to God.

But there will come a time when even they will be given to the disposal of the righteous: "The righteous shall have dominion over them in the morning" (Psalm 48:15). Truly, during the night of this life, much that is unlawful occurs, but all such evils are covered by a mystical darkness. Though some stubbornly oppose God, God only remains silent for a time, but when morning comes, when the last day of the earth comes, when all shall resurrect, then the righteous will judge the sinners and even the darkness of hell will not cover their sins. They will be deprived of their honor and might, all their power and authority will turn to dust like a beggar's rags. God will reject them. Then truly these words will come to pass: *All are Yours, O Lord!*

Brocard[41] told of miraculous things during his travels across Palestine (he only wrote about what he saw with his own eyes). He wrote that a stone's throw from the gates of Jerusalem is a place where Christ once taught the people. A stone lies there where the woman stood as she declared in inspiration, "Blessed is the womb that bore You, and the breasts which nursed You" (Luke 11:27). No sand ever covers this hill, though it is a desert place, and the surrounding area is covered in sand like snow. Both in summer and winter, this place is decorated with naturally occurring greenery that never withers.

It is appropriate to compare this eternally green hill to a person who always keeps the will of God in his heart. Such a person says, "My Lord! Are You not mine? Truly mine? I beg You and beseech You. Preach in my heart. I hear You and will do what You tell me with my whole heart." The mind of such a person never darkens with the clouds of troubles or sorrows. Whatever evil befalls him, he always says,

Lord, You are always merciful to me, and You forgive my sins even more than I deserve. I have deserved much greater punishment. I see and feel that all this is too gentle a punishment for me. Still, I direct my attention not to the sufferings I endure, but to Your holy will. It is pleasing to You to send these troubles, this sorrow, and I dare not say anything to contradict You, for all this is beneficial to me, for it pleases You. I am completely content with whatever Your goodwill commands of me, and at Your slightest command I will show myself ready to submit to Your direction. Command me, be my Master, direct my fortunes, change them as You see fit. I would be very foolish and godless if I would think to correct Your arrangement of my fate, or if I dare to suggest an improvement in the way You run the world.

Such a person will never be defeated by evil occurrences or deprivations, nor will he ever be forced to complain about God or to depart from His side. Whether in good times or bad, he always flourishes and is constantly green like the miraculous hill in Palestine.

II

Jehu, the commander of Israel's armies, asked Jehonadab as he rode in a chariot (after Jehonadab was anointed to the throne of Israel by Elisha's order), "'Is your heart right with my heart, as my heart is right with your heart?' And

Jehonadab answered, 'It is.' Jehu said, 'If it is, give me your hand.' So he gave him his hand, and he brought him into the chariot. Then he said, 'Come with me, and see my zeal for the Lord of Hosts'" (4 Kingdoms 10:15–16).

As Jehu did to Jehonadab, so Christ, the King of the world, does the same to all of us sinners. He came to Samaria—which literally means "a field, either sowed or covered with weeds"—to uproot the unrighteous seed of Ahab and the servants of Baal, that is, pride, a dissolute life, service to idols, and every kind of sin. Christ, like Jehu, found His own Jehonadab–that is, a person with good will–and He asked him, "Is your heart right, as my heart is toward your heart? And if it is, give me your hand, sit in my chariot, and continue your life's journey with Me, that is, follow Me in self-rejection, in the submission of your self-will to the will of God."

To such a good person Christ God always reaches out His right hand, the hand of His grace. He raises him to His own chariot, to the height of His self-rejection. Christ says to him, "Come with Me on My way. I will lead you by the Way of the Cross. This is the true, straight path leading to eternal life. Do not be afraid. I am next to you, and I will not let you fall, but will lead you by this road to the kingdom of heaven. Come with Me, so that you will always abide with Me and never be far from Me."

Reliable and true is God's direction of the world. Righteous Job did not fear it, but prayed God to send him the patience necessary to endure the arguments of his friends, who constantly tried to convince him that he was not without fault in his troubles, but rather that he suffered for his sins. It was as if he were saying to God, "Keep me near You, and then let everyone rise up against me, for I will remain undefeated, even if a thousand blows rain down on me. Covered by Your right hand, I will remain unharmed."

When a person enters Christ's chariot, he becomes a friend of Christ, or even becomes a member of Christ's family, as He Himself said, "For whoever does the will of My Father in heaven is My brother and sister and mother" (Matthew 12:50). St Euthymius (377–473 A.D.) said, "Great is the power given to those who do the will of God. This power gives its practitioners a quality that is above the human. By the command of God, it makes them relatives of Christ! Truly, this is the greatest good in life, this unity of one's own will with the desires of God's will."

St Euthymius had the habit of saying that whatever you desire, that becomes your self, your very essence, your personality. For the will, when joined sincerely in heartfelt union with God's will, is so strong that it transforms the entire person—that is, his feelings, desires, and actions—into a pure, innocent, and virtuous being. In a word, that which we strongly and conscientiously desire becomes our soul's very essence. No one desires to be seriously and completely humble, obedient, or generous if he does not display this in his actions. A true desire is made manifest in action. Whatever you want, that you become.

St Euthymius continues,

> If your powers are insufficient to accomplish great deeds or sacrifices for the sake of the poor, then at the very least cultivate the greatest of intentions and unlimited desires to act. Are you a poor man yourself? You can still have a rich heart so that, if you had any money, you would immediately and eagerly give it all away to those who do not have anything. You have insufficient power and money, but you can so incline and consecrate yourself to self-sacrifice for the sake of God and your neighbor, as though you have inside yourself a thousand different souls, a thousand heads on your body, and all this you would not refuse to lay aside for Christ and for your faith in Him.

Are others attacking you? Then entrust yourself completely to the will of God, repeating the words of the Lord's prayer—Thy will be done in me—and you will attain the greatest success. Truly, whoever cannot rule over himself is greatly unfortunate and destitute. Such a person is the target of attacks of various earthly evils, all of who fight over him: "To whom does he belong?" He is like the Greek cities that argued about Homer: in which city was he born? Such an inconstant, unbelieving man subjects himself constantly to the attacks of various foul passions and sins. Sometimes, he is attacked by arrogance, love of money, constant irritability at one particular person, or envy. Sometimes he is attacked by drunkenness or lusts of the flesh, and he has hardly ever belonged to himself, much less to God, for he has never thought about his immortal soul or God, for he has no control over himself.

A certain poet once wrote an ode to the Emperor Heraclius,[42] in which he said, "Though all his enemies he trampled underfoot, he remained a slave to lust and anger." About such a person it would be fair to say that though he may have everything, yet he has nothing, for he has lost himself. He does not rule over his self, but is a slave of money, impure desires, and many other evil deeds. "A patient man is better than a strong man, and he who controls his temper is better than he who captures a city" (Proverbs 16:30). If you want to subjugate all things to yourself, first of all you must subjugate yourself to the will of God. You will only be able to do good when you yourself are led by the will of God.

III

The all-merciful God has His special chosen ones and close friends in every age of history. These He has foreknown to complete His great works, and so He reveals to them His many exalted and profound mysteries and invisibly participates in all their good deeds, instructing and teaching them internally in their heart and enlightening their minds. Among these chosen ones of God, some are in the first tier, so to speak, some in the second, and some in the third. In other words, not all the chosen ones of God are equally intimate with God nor do all receive the same grace and calling to perfection in the works of the Lord. And yet all are called saints.

According to the wise Seneca, between such good men and God there is a friendship that binds them through virtue. Have I said friendship? That is too weak an expression. It would be more correct to say that spiritual unity with God is like the marital union between a man and a woman, for it is the union of Christ with a member of His Church (see Ephesians 5:20–33). Through his virtuous life, the saint differs from God Himself only in time, space, and power; he is God's disciple and His zealous emulator. All of us Christians are either already truly God's children or only so in potential.

Epictetus, among his universally appropriate aphorisms, said, "If Caesar accepted you into his family and exalted you, then who would not fear your countenance? Now that you have become a son of God, do you not respect yourself and your exalted dignity? Why then do you stoop to bestial desires and enticements of sin?"

Truly, we are a holy race, the offspring of God (Acts 17:29), the sons of the Most High, but only because God has decreed this by His mercy and grace, and if we do not desire to lose this gift, we must preserve it by the holiness of our lives. The first stage of a God-pleasing life and holiness is the complete commitment of oneself and all of one's will to the will of God and His direction. The highest step of a holy life is reached only by those who have deeply penetrated the height and power of God's will and God's inscrutable plans and omnipotence for the direction of the cosmos.

Therefore, the Apostle Paul, desiring that his followers gradually reach such a level of the knowledge of God, wrote to them, "[We] do not cease to pray for you, and to ask that you may be filled with the knowledge of His will in all wisdom and spiritual understanding" (Colossians 1:9). He is not content that his disciples should only know the will of God, but he desires that they reach the highest levels of this knowledge, the fullness of knowledge. He eagerly wants them to penetrate the meaning of the actions and dispositions of God.

St Paul knew well that if he would beg God concerning this benefit for his disciples, then they would easily and effectively move forward in the pursuit of all virtue. How good and fair would it be, if man would always find pleasure in that which has always been pleasing to God in all times!

Note: The ancient Romans often included this flattering address when writing petitions to the emperor: "I am a servant dedicated to your divinity and majesty." The pagans did this only out of a desire to flatter and win the favor of the emperor, but when we Christians pray to the almighty God for the forgiveness of our sins and help in all our needs, we must show genuine signs of our humility, not out of a desire to flatter God, but from a profound acknowledgment of our sinfulness and for the sake of the genuine greatness of the Creator and Lord of the cosmos. And so we should say,

O Lord my God! I, Your unworthy slave, the creation of Your hands, with all humility subject myself entirely to Your almighty dominion. I subject the free will You have given me with love to Your all-wise and all-holy will. For I acknowledge that only my humble submission to Your will constitutes the perfection of human life. This is truly heaven on earth!

 CHAPTER 16

The Agreement of the Human Will with the Divine Is Truly Heaven on Earth, the Only Genuine Blessedness in Life

"Blessed shalt thou be, and it shall be well with thee" (Psalm 127:2). Whoever has acquired such blessedness—that is, the complete agreement of one's actions with the will of God—will cheerfully accept everything as coming directly from the Lord's hand. Such a person is a true image of blessedness even on this earth, in this temporary life. O, blessed are you, and it will be well with you! You taste such sweetness now and you will taste such joy, such happiness that hardly anyone in this world has ever tasted, especially not those who have never rejected their own self-love and self-will. This blessedness is prepared for the chosen ones who unite with God through sincere self-rejection and true active love for God and neighbor.

Everyone knows these words of St Paul: "The kingdom of God is not eating and drinking, but righteousness and peace and joy in the Holy Spirit. For he who serves Christ in these things is acceptable to God and approved by men" (Romans 14:17–18). In the future life, there will be no troubles (no fickle happiness or sorrow), since there will be no yesterday or today that differs from one another as they do in this life. In that life, there will be a constant, single stream of eternal heavenly sweetness, which is unchanging, constant, all encompassing, and complete. This we read in Psalm 89:5: "For a thousand years before Thine eyes, O Lord, are but as yesterday when it is past, and as a watch in the night."

In a similar way, those who have been found worthy of God's mercy—that is, those who have completely subjected their will to the will of God—are never fickle in their spirit. If something sorrowful that disturbs their soul occurs, they calm themselves with wise reflections. Their only source of joy and consolation is God's goodwill for them. This removes them from all confusion and sorrow perpetrated by others, even if such sorrow repeats itself, sometimes increasing day by day. However, their loyalty to God's will creates such a sweet consolation and calm in their souls that they, being firmly convinced that all that happens to them is either willed or allowed by God, consider even the worst deprivations and sorrows to be for their correction or for their greater reward. And so they rejoice in all misfortunes, for even in the midst of deprivations and afflictions they see God's will and continue to hope for their salvation, even more than when everything goes well in their life. But even when they enjoy peace and spiritual calm, they are still sure that truly nothing can harm them, for "they that trust in the Lord are as mount Zion; he that liveth in Jerusalem shall never be shaken" (Psalm 124:1).

I

This is the reason for the total inner peace of soul and conscience that was characteristic of the early Christians. They, like we, were subjected to many different misfortunes—diseases often afflicted their bodies or sorrows often confused their hearts—for whoever was most pleasing to God was usually subjected to the most frequent troubles. Where did they find their unchanging constancy of mind? How could they be so cheerful and so filled with joy? How could they maintain such triumph in their lives, as though every day were a feast? All this truly occurred from their complete unity with God's will. Vainly did so many different calamities attack them, for all such attacks were harmless, as is written in Scripture, "No grave trouble will overtake the righteous, but the wicked shall be filled with evil" (Proverbs 12:21 NKJV).

Therefore, all those virtuous people were at both prosperous and joyful, for in all their actions, they saw the will of God and revered it, finding in it their sole comfort, joy, and riches. But even the Greek philosophers knew the virtue of such a manner of life, and they often contemplated it. They considered human happiness to consist in aligning one's life to the influence of the guardian angel (whom they called a genius) that was assigned to them at the beginning of life. They believed this to occur by the command and will of the most high Ruler of the world.

Epictetus gave the following wise utterance concerning this:

> Show me any sick man who, in spite of his sickness, is still happy. Show me any man afflicted by troubles who is still happy. Show me a dying

man who considers himself fortunate. Show me a dishonored man who is still joyful. The source of joy for each of these is his own mind and heart. These are those fortunate ones who, thinking of God or being with God, never accuse Him or other men. Even when physically imprisoned, such men never considered themselves to be lacking anything. They were never irritated, never overcome by anger, never envious, never antagonistic to anyone. In short, they, remembering that without God's will nothing occurs, ascribed everything to the will or permission of God, and so they accepted everything without complaint, as though it were from the hand of God.

What can one say against these words? What can we imagine to be more exalted or more honorable than these words?

Once two friends had a discussion. One of them said that if everything occurs by God's will and is accomplished by it—so that not a single bird would fall into a snare without Christ's word and God's foreknowledge and desire— then we should always be joyful. If only we would understand this truth with our mind and believe it with our heart, then nothing adverse would ever affect us, and we would live this life as though we were already in heaven.

His friend answered, "Yes, in this case, we would be completely safe and fortunate, but very few people come to know this truth with their minds, not because it is difficult to understand, but because their hearts do not cleave to it completely, instead wasting time in empty amusements."

However, there is another reason why more people do not live thus. This truth is not clearly and instructively explained in sermons. Many amusing books and tales are written, but they hardly help the soul to perfect itself for its eternal salvation. This wisdom must be constantly imparted and taught, together with useful examples from experience, and then all will come to know that every person who has given his entire soul and heart to God already lives in this present life as though he were in heaven, since God lives in him, and wherever God is, there heaven is as well.

The righteous Job was dedicated to God after his deprivations and during his time of prosperity. I would even dare to say that Job became closer to God and entered an even more intimate union with Him when he was in poverty, afflicted by rotting wounds, than when he sat on a majestic throne, surrounded by honor and glory. No dark calamities can steal the joy and happiness of the heart and mind that are committed to the will of God.

The sunflower, according to Pliny, never changes its leaves and the same can be said about a person who gives himself totally to the will of God. "He shall be like a tree planted by the water-side, that will bring forth his fruit in due season; his leaf also shall not fall, and all whatsoever he doeth, it shall prosper" (Psalm 1:3).

II

A certain Persian who boasted about the size of the army he commanded on one of the Greek campaigns said proudly, "Tomorrow we will darken the sun with our arrows."

Immediately, one of the Greeks answered him, "I am very glad of this, for it is easier for us to fight in the shade."

This is how a person truly committed to the will of God speaks. If the hosts of demons attack me, if my enemies are multiplied against me, darkening the sun with the number of their arrows, my heart will still not fear, for it is better for me to fight in the shade (see Psalm 26:3). I will fight, but the outcome of the battle depends on the will of heaven. So let it be (see 1 Maccabees 3:60).

St John Cassian tells of the following event. One time, an old man from Alexandria, a Christian, was surrounded by many pagans, like a lamb surrounded by ravening wolves. All of the pagans with one voice decided to tear apart this old man, to beat him, to rob him, and to make him the object of their mockery and insults. Finally one of them asked the old man, "What miracles has Christ accomplished that you are so proud of?"

The old man wisely answered him with humility,

This is the miracle of Christ: I can patiently endure your insults and ridicule without it changing my knowledge of Christ's greatness. I am ready even to endure greater mockery for the sake of my love for Him. Truly great miracles are accomplished even in our times by people who are committed to the Lord's will. They themselves know what power makes them so fearless even in the midst of storms and waves, preserves them whole and untouched even in surrounding destruction. All human attacks they consider to be as nothing. Truly, even today the ancient miracles are repeated—the burning bush that was not consumed, the three youths in the fire who remained untouched by the flames.

Similar sorrows are experiences now as in the past, both deservedly and innocently, but often the pain of sorrow arises not from an inciting event but from the lack of patience of the sufferer. Those people who accept all unfortunate events as permitted by God as a witness of their courage and endurance are not afraid of any discomfort. They do not murmur at God for their afflictions; they do not even complain. They accept everything that happens to them with gratitude and transform it to their own benefit, ascribing everything to God's will and God's direction of the world.

It was said in ancient times that Mount Olympus (which is found on the border of Greece with Macedonia) is the tallest of mountains, so high above sea level that neither wind, nor rain, nor snow ever reaches its summit. The poet Lucian expressed himself thus: "Olympus is higher than the clouds, its summit is surrounded by pure sky beyond the limits of all atmospheric changes. There you will find no birds or other animals. The air is so thin and rarified, that it is not enough for human breath."

Natural philosophers only proved all this much later, when people began to invent various ways of breathing at high altitudes. For example, they took wet sponges with them and inhaled through the nose. They also used other means of thickening the air during their ascent to the mountain. When they reached the summit, they left markings in the sand. When they returned a year later, they found the markings undisturbed, as though they had just scribbled them in the sand a few moments before. This was proof that at the heights of Olympus there is neither wind, nor rain, nor snowfall, nor storms of any kind.

Mount Olympus is an effective symbol of the life of a Christian who has reached the heights of self-rejection, that is, who has completely abandoned his own will to God's will. As on Olympus there is no place for storms or attacks by beasts or other dangers, so a person who has reached the heights of God's omnipotence will always remain calm and at peace. The clouds of sorrows are beneath him; his heart is always filled with quiet and sweet repose in the single will of God.

Blessed Augustine said that in this agreement (a state of total lack of conflict) is found total perfection. This is why the peacemakers are called the sons of God in the Gospels, for they have nothing within them that would resist God and in any case sons must have the likeness of their father (God). Such a peace is given to men of goodwill (those who are blessed by God). Such people are truly wise and righteous.

Abba Dorotheos said,

Those who wholeheartedly fulfill the Gospel's commandment regarding self-rejection and complete commitment to God's will walk the road of life as though they were being borne on a carriage along with all their daily troubles (crosses). On the contrary, those who do not

know the power of complete self-rejection plod along on foot and carry
their heavy crosses on their own backs along the many crossroads of life
with difficulty, complaining the whole time.

III

True submission of the heart to God's will in all circumstances in life truly
gives us a sense of being in heaven, though we are still earthbound. This is
the first and most profound foundation of the love that reasoning creation
has for its Creator and God. Whoever you may be, dear reader, if you accept
everything—pleasant or unpleasant—as God's will or permission, as though it
came from God's own right hand, then you will be "blessed ... and it shall be
well with thee" (Psalm 127: 2). With your love you become part of God, with
whom the blessedness of heaven is always present: "And His place hath been at
Salem [that is, 'in peace'] and His tabernacle in Zion" (Psalm 75:3).

The sunflower, according to Pliny, is poisonous for ants. Likewise, the
agreement of man's will with God's destroys many calamities, sorrows, and
ill news. St Benedict of Nursia[43] said, "Whoever desires true joy and a serene
life in God must confirm himself in all cases in the immutable foundation of
agreement of his own will with the will of God. He must attach himself to
it constantly, he must follow it constantly, according to Christ's own teaching
concerning selflessness."

There can also be such a situation in the life of a person (this is especially
true of a person who is prone to sadness or lack of faith) when he is attacked
by opposition (a force that fights against his desires), spiritual paralysis (i.e.,
despair), or laziness in prayer; when his mind complains about his lot in life;
when his heart is not ready to submit to all that God's will determined for him.
When this happens, he must take the highest point of view and accept even
this lack of self-rejection as God's will. If a person is also attacked by a great
doubt concerning the course of action he must take, then he must reject even
his own doubt. Finally, if his despair is so deep that he cannot force himself
to choose any of the contradictory paths before him, then he must accept his
lack of resoluteness also as God's will, and to accept his weakness humbly from
God's hands.

Meanwhile, he must deflect from himself everything that might hinder his
self-rejection, so that the will of God can be like a fire that burns away all his
impurities and leaves only that which is for his benefit. This is the kind of lack
of selflessness that is done reasonably and supersedes everything by its fruits

and actions, and more directly brings us to true unity with God, to true humility, to true rejection and abandonment of things for the sake of God.

O Christians! If only we concerned ourselves exclusively with making our will agree with God's will in all cases, so that God's will would become our own! This is a truly great work and deserves our greatest diligence, so that we would desire nothing other than what God desires, so that we would reject everything that God rejects, everything He, the Merciful One, turns away from.

Believe me, brothers in Christ, it is the greatest benefit for us to be so close to God and to lay our hopes on the Lord (Psalm 72:28). This is true blessedness; this is heaven on earth.

PART IV

HOW TO TURN ASIDE ALL OBSTACLES THAT HINDER FASHIONING THE HUMAN WILL TO THE WILL OF GOD

 CHAPTER 17

What Prevents Us from Living According to God's Will

Let us imagine that some person acquires the keys to a city fortress or to a house, giving him the ability to enter and leave at his own will and to arrange all things according to his own pleasure. Christ God often desires the keys that open our inner heart, in order to have free entry. However, we are rarely eager to allow our merciful and generous Lord to have these keys.

Louis de Blois (1506–1566)[44] tells an interesting story that is worth contemplating. A certain virtuous maiden saw a vision of Christ, Who said to her, "My daughter! In this hand I hold health, and in this other, disease. Choose one or the other as you wish." What could the maiden do? To choose health might seem shameless and suspicious. But to prefer a life of sickness might seem falsely humble. If we offer someone two possible objects to choose from, the chooser usually takes the lesser gift. Therefore, it would seem to be more proper to choose sickness for the sake of avoiding eternal suffering and torture. Generally speaking, it would seem the wiser choice, especially if we consider how the Great Martyr Catherine chose a crown of thorns instead of a golden diadem.

However, this wise maiden in Louis de Blois's tale acted even more wisely and virtuously. She made no choice, but, folding her arms across her chest and bowing to her knees, she said, "O my Lord, I only ask one thing of You. Let it be according to Your will, not mine. Therefore, I choose neither health nor sickness, but I am ready to accept everything that Your will decrees. For only You, O Lord, can rightly and properly decide what to give me."

The Saviour answered her, "Whoever desires to have Me as a frequent visitor must give Me the key of his own will, and never require Me to return it."

The maiden, thus instructed by the Lord Himself, uttered with compunction in her heart and with great humility, "Not my will, but Yours be done, O most beloved Jesus!" From that time, she gave an oath to repeat that prayer three hundred and sixty five times a day. It is a short prayer, but (if uttered from the whole heart) is more pleasing to God than thousands of other prayers. It is very wise to repeat, day and night, this prayer: "Not my will, but Yours be done, O most beloved Jesus." It is especially useful to repeat this prayer when you find yourself in difficulties, surrounded on all sides by various problems.

However, weak human nature finds it very difficult to bend its own will to the eager endurance of heavy sufferings, hardships, deprivations, and other problems that afflict people for unknown reasons or by the permission of God. The human will naturally turn away with disgust from such afflictions. Therefore, it is imperative for anyone who wishes to conform his will to God's to be ready to reject self-will and to force his unruly will to do that which it hates.

I

A person who follows God's will must first of all decide to be ready for everything that may happen to him by either the will or permission of God. He should pray to God often:

> O Lord, my God! I am ready to serve You equally in poverty as in prosperity. I will not reject even the poverty that deprives me of all pleasant comforts and so makes me sorrowful. This sorrow is my salvation, and if Your will desires it, make my heart like dried-out earth. If You give me a cup full of bitterness, wine mixed with gall, I will accept it eagerly from You. I know, Lord, that You have a bottomless wealth of sweet, superior wine, but You, in order to test the faithfulness of Your servants, occasionally give them wine mixed with vinegar. I accept it from You and eagerly, joyfully drink the bitter cup to the dregs. Punish me, Lord, in any way You see fit. I only ask one thing of You. Make me wise concerning those things that are pleasing to You. Your divine will is the greatest joy for me. I seek nothing but Your will. Whether I am sick or healthy, rich or poor, it does not matter. I only ask You for one thing, O God—let me always do Your will.

St John Chrysostom greatly praised Joseph, the betrothed of the Virgin Mary, for his virtuous ability to always do the will of God, even if the commands of God seemed to contradict each other. When Joseph received a command in his dreams from an angel to leave his land and to flee to Egypt, he did not fall prey to doubts. He did not say, "This is not a true saying, for just recently you told me that He will save His people (see Matthew 1:21), and now you are telling me that He cannot save *Himself* from persecution? You are telling me to flee, to become a pariah, to move to a different country? This is contrary to God's promise!"

No, Joseph said nothing like this to the angel, for he was a faithful man. He did not even ask the angel about the time of their return, even though the angel indicated that their travels would be for some indeterminate time. Joseph was not upset by this vagueness; instead, he eagerly believed the words of the angel, ready to accept any sorrow or discomfort along the way. He did not reject flight; he did not refuse to leave his own country. He went to Egypt together with the Child and His Mother.[45]

Fulfilling the will of God lightens every difficulty. Having committed ourselves with all our weaknesses to the will of God, and having acknowledged our spiritual poverty, let us continue with our discussion.

II

Having sacrificed our self-will, let us sentence ourselves to the willing endurance of slander and vilification. Let us heed the Apostle Paul's words: "In all things we commend ourselves as ministers of God: in much patience, in tribulations, in needs, in distresses … by honor and dishonor, by evil report and good report; as deceivers, and yet true" (2 Corinthians 6:4, 8). Whoever has given himself over completely to the will of God must repeat these words often:

> Lord! For Your sake I eagerly condemn myself to any vilification, dishonor, or rebuke, especially when I am innocent. For You I will not refuse to be despised, abased, and disregarded. Such food is bitter and unpleasant; however, I joyfully accept it, for it belongs on the table of Christ's saving economy. Christ God Himself not only willingly subjected Himself to all kinds of insults and mockery, but He endured everything for our sins, having become a curse for our sake, as it is written, "Cursed is everyone who hangs on a tree." (Galatians 3:13)

The greatest of God's righteous ones, during the times of persecution at the hands of the pagans, were vilified as the worst criminals. They heard these accusations and knew about them, yet they endured it all patiently. However, there is a big difference between being a true criminal and being considered one by popular opinion as a result of certain religious convictions. The first state requires no explanation; it is clear even to children. The difficulty of the second is only understood fully by those who (having been completely innocent) did not oppose being vilified publicly, following the Gospel's teaching and accepting reproach as the greatest honor and glory, as God's will, as God's good gift, given by His own hand.

Take the example of the Mother of God, the Most Blessed Virgin Mary, who committed her soul and heart entirely to the will of God. Joseph, her betrothed, seeing her with child, was horrified and intended to secretly divorce her. What did she do? She remained silent. Any public opinion concerning herself she left to God's disposal. Many saints followed her example. Though they were falsely accused of terrible crimes, they remained silent and endured dishonor and much reproach, relying solely on the will of God in all things.

St Macarius the Great of Egypt endured dishonor, vilification, and reproach silently, with great long-suffering and humility. A certain young woman (who had secretly sinned with a young man and became pregnant) accused this saint—an angelic man in his life of sinlessness—of being the one responsible for her situation. She said to her parents, "I sinned with this ascetic of yours, this man you consider a saint. When I once walked outside the town, near the place where he lives, he met me on the road and raped me. Because of my shame and fear I said nothing until this day."

Her parents and their neighbors, enraged by her words, rushed to the house of the innocent holy man, and with great shouts and angry words they pulled him out of his cell, beat him for a long time without mercy, then led him into the town. They collected all sorts of rubbish and filth—rotted skulls, chamber pots, and the like—tied them around his neck and led him through the town, screaming at him all the while. They pushed him around, beat him, pulled his beard and hair, and kicked him. They said, "This monk has defiled our maiden. Let every person beat him!" This continued for many hours, until their anger dissipated, but even then they did not release him, though he was barely alive, not until he promised to take financial care of the child and its mother, as though he truly had raped her. All this the holy man did after he recovered from his wounds, raising money by weaving baskets and selling them through his cell attendant. He sent all his money to support the girl who had slandered him.

This meek, kind, gentle, humble man, worthy of all praise, innocently endured much dishonor, reproach, and cruel beatings, and yet he generously forgave his persecutors. What should we draw from this? We, who are guilty of so many countless sins and falsehoods, rail at those who offend us even the smallest bit. We do not endure anything; instead, we seek revenge and restitution. Is this pleasing to God's will? Without the will or permission of God nothing can happen to us, and if the will of God is pleasing to us, then nothing, not even the worst reproaches, will upset us or force us to counterattack those who offend us.

Our Saviour Christ left us a perfect image of humility during His earthly life, but even after His glorification (i.e., after His resurrection) He refused the worship of Mary Magdalene, until His humanity would be presented to His Heavenly Father:

> Now on the first day of the week Mary Magdalene went to the tomb early, while it was still dark, and saw that the stone had been taken away from the tomb. Then she ran and came to Simon Peter, and to the other disciple, whom Jesus loved, and said to them, "They have taken away the Lord out of the tomb, and we do not know where they have laid Him." Peter therefore went out, and the other disciple, and were going to the tomb. So they both ran together, and the other disciple outran Peter and came to the tomb first. And he, stooping down and looking in, saw the linen cloths lying there; yet he did not go in. Then Simon Peter came, following him, and went into the tomb; and he saw the linen cloths lying there, and the handkerchief that had been around His head, not lying with the linen cloths, but folded together in a place by itself. Then the other disciple, who came to the tomb first, went in also; and he saw and believed. For as yet they did not know the Scripture, that He must rise again from the dead. Then the disciples went away again to their own homes. But Mary stood outside by the tomb weeping, and as she wept she stooped down and looked into the tomb. And she saw two angels in white sitting, one at the head and the other at the feet, where the body of Jesus had lain. Then they said to her, "Woman, why are you weeping?" She said to them, "Because they have taken away my Lord, and I do not know where they have laid Him." Now when she had said this, she turned around and saw Jesus standing there, and did not know that it was Jesus. Jesus said to her, "Woman, why are you weeping? Whom are you seeking?" She, supposing Him to be the gardener, said to Him, "Sir, if You have carried Him away, tell me where You have laid Him, and I will take Him away." Jesus said to her, "Mary!" She turned and said to Him, "Rabboni!" (which is to say, Teacher). Jesus said to her, "Do not cling to Me, for I have not yet ascended to My Father; but go to My brethren and say to them, 'I

am ascending to My Father and your Father, and to My God and your God.'" Mary Magdalene came and told the disciples that she had seen the Lord, and that He had spoken these things to her. (John 20:1–18)

This bright image of the Lord Jesus's appearance in the first moments after His resurrection to Mary Magdalene shows the profound depth of His humility and love for mankind. Let us emulate Him in these virtues. Christ God could have refused us communion with Him after the terrible way we tortured and abused Him; however, He, the Merciful One, refused Mary Magdalene's touch only temporarily, until He ascended to His Father in heaven, paving the way to Heaven for all humanity. But we, sinful people—unrighteous mortals, still in the sinful flesh, guilty of many crimes—dare to say to each other with anger, "Do not touch me! Who are you to dishonor me? Who are you to rebuke me, to personally insult me, to drag my name in the mud?" Wake up, Christians! How far are we from knowing God's will, and yet we demand respect from everyone, even when we dishonor ourselves with our actions and ignorance of God's will.

Everyone who understands that nothing occurs without the will or permission of God (neither praise nor reproach) must condemn himself before God, saying, "O Lord! I am completely worthy of all these insults and disdain. For what reason should I rail at my enemies? I know, Lord, that unless You will it, no one can insult or offend me."

"And I will again uncover myself in this manner and will thus remain vile in your sight" (King David's words in 2 Kingdoms 6:22).

III

Having prepared our hearts to the patient endurance of poverty, reproaches, and vilification, let us continue to speak about the patient endurance of physical illness.

This life is like lamp oil. The burning of an oil lamp depends entirely on the person who cares for the lamp. In the same way, our health or illnesses are directed by the will or permission of God exclusively. Therefore, whoever truly commits himself to the will of God will cheerfully submit to its precepts. Such a person, like a flame that always strives heaven-ward, turns with hope in all situations to God, the Creator of all, with prayer:

Lord! I thank You with my whole heart for all that You send me. If it pleases You to preserve me in health, I thank You. If You desire to cover me with sores, to live many years in the throes of illness, to nail me to the bed of sickness, let Your will be done. I eagerly agree with everything You send me. If it pleases You, then it must also be pleasing to me.

Louis de Blois tells a story concerning a certain holy maiden. She was asked how she was able to achieve such a level of perfection, even in this life. She said, "Never was I ever so burdened with diseases that I did not ask of God even more diseases for the sake of His love."

Another chaste maiden endured hellish pain for the sake of preserving her virginity and never hoped to be relieved of it quickly. Instead, she prayed to God in her heart, saying, "O sweetest, beloved God! Remember that You are my Lord and Creator. Here I stand before You. Judge me righteously. I am ready to bear this hellish pain for as long as it is pleasing to You. Let Your will be done in me." By thus completely submitting herself to the will of God, she spent her entire life in the love of God and in good deeds.

These examples show that one must incite the will in order that the heart—whether in health or in sickness—might always abide in love for God and neighbor.

IV

A person who is committed to God does not live for himself, but to serve God and his neighbors. Therefore, he does not give himself the right to choose between life and death but leaves that to God. He is not passionately attached to a long life nor is he intent on quickly leaving this life for the next. Presenting himself to God's will completely, he prays to God silently:

O Good Jesus! You know better than I do what is more beneficial for me—to live or to die. Do with me as You will. I would only like to beg You, my Lord, that You, in Your mercy, save me from sudden death, for my sins frighten me. Remember me, O Lord, when You come to judge the living and the dead. But even as I ask this, I leave everything to Your decision, and I will not oppose Your holy will. I know that if a righteous man dies unexpectedly, he will be at rest (Wisdom of Solomon 4:7). Forgive me, Lord, and cleanse me, for I have sinned before You. Therefore, I will not run away from an untimely death, nor will I fear a terrible and frightening death. The truly faithful know that many die in peace, but are then cast into hell, while many who die horrifying deaths are immediately transferred to heaven. Inscrutable to us are the judgments of God. Therefore, I eagerly offer myself to Your good will concerning my own passage from this temporary life into life eternal. "For none of us lives to himself, and no one dies to himself. For if we live, we live to the Lord; and if we die, we die to the Lord. Therefore, whether we live or die, we are the Lord's." (Romans 14:7–8)

St Martin of Tours said on his deathbed, "Lord! If I am useful to Your flock of reasonable sheep, then I do not refuse to do further work for them, but let Your will be done in me." The Church remembers him saying, "O wondrous man, untiring in work, unconquered by death, unafraid of it even on the deathbed, when you refused to lay down the burden of your work and your life, committing everything concerning yourself to the will of God."

This is an example worthy of emulation! A certain ancient writer-moralist said, "All brave men are quicker to disdain death than to hate life. The lazy are demeaned by their laziness, the assiduous are only held back from their work by death itself. Death is the last inescapable limit to which all must walk without fear, leaving themselves fully to God's disposal."

Our life and death are equally in God's all-wise and all-good authority. God alone knows which is most beneficial for us: to continue living or to die. Therefore, we must gratefully and eagerly accept from Him both our life and our death. Does God desire us to live? Let us continue living with joy, thanking God in any circumstance, both positive and negative, working only to acquire blessedness in the future life. Does God desire us to die? Let us die with an eager heart, as another ancient writer teaches, "Let us not walk lazily to death, which bring us to the endless life."

Alas! Is this how the majority of us live and die today? Rarely does anyone die without a strong desire to live on; rarely does anyone die without sighs and tears. All this is repugnant to God's will, for He declares our insufficiency through the limits placed on our life. We must, each one of us, be ready at every moment for our death, for that hour is hidden from us by the wisdom of God. It is not fair for the debtor to rebuke his creditor when the creditor asks to be repaid by a certain deadline. For us sinners, there will never be enough days in our life if we begin to count them.

In addition, think carefully, reminding yourself that simply prolonging life, without reference to our manner of life, is not a good thing. It will never lead us to salvation. Therefore, be content with that limit on your life declared by God and hurry to avail yourself of your allotted time to do good deeds, to reach the blessed repose of the righteous. Remember the words of the wise man: "But though a righteous man may die before his time, he shall be at rest. For old age is not honored for its length of existence, nor measured by its number of years; but discernment is gray hair for mankind, and a spotless life is the maturity of old age" (Wisdom of Solomon 4:7–9).

V

Finally, as a conclusion to this chapter, I offer the reader a few vivid examples of how the saints, those eagles of virtue, looked unstintingly at the light of the noetic sun, the will of God, the will of the loving Father and almighty Creator, the protector and director of the cosmos. They completely and perfectly subjected their own will to His with love and reverence, and never resting their gaze at any obstacles along their way, they followed God's will.

Who was more courageous in this respect than the holy Apostle Paul? Neither the sharp edge of a sword, nor the shine of spears, nor stoning, nor storms at sea, nor riots, nor dangerous and impassable roads could prevent him from continuing on the path of God's will. In the fulfillment of God's will, no obstacles could hinder him. As he said concerning himself, "For we who live are always delivered to death for Jesus' sake, that the life of Jesus also may be manifested in our mortal flesh" (2 Corinthians 4:11). St Paul, on fire with the Holy Spirit, would not refuse to go into the fire if the will of God demanded it. "For I could wish that I myself were accursed from Christ for my brethren, my countrymen according to the flesh, who are Israelites" (Romans 9:3–4). "What are you saying, O Paul?" declared St John Chrysostom. "Did you not say that nothing can separate us from the love of Christ?" Do not doubt Paul's words, O Holy Golden-mouthed, for they show Paul's love for Christ in the highest degree. Through them, Paul expresses his ardent desire for the greatest number of his countrymen to come to love Christ, and in return he was even ready to share with them the excess of blessedness and glory with Christ that he had already known. He did not mean that he rejected the love of Christ.

Look, for Paul is like an eagle that directs his gaze directly at the righteous sun of God's will. Such firm agreement with the will of God can be defeated by nothing, even if many hosts were to stand in the way, with all possible weapons of flattery, mockery, or persecution.

Many holy martyrs eagerly ran to their tortures for the sake of Christ, considering it nothing to shed their blood for His sake, for even in the midst of horrifying tortures they were greatly strengthened by divine consolation, and so they eagerly despised their tortures and even their own death. St Laurence

(225–258 A.D.), while lying on a red-hot metal grate, rested like a pilgrim lying on a soft bed. St Andrew the First-Called kissed the cross that was considered accursed by the Romans, as though it were the bridal chamber of a king. St Stephen, the first martyr, considered the hailstorm of stones to be like pleasant dew. Anyone who accepted these tortures and death willingly, because all this occurred according to God's will and command, truly labored greatly for the sake of Christ. For we have received everything from God, both physical and spiritual gifts, and so which of these gifts, even life itself, will we not return to God if He asks?

Consequently, the old adage—"there is no rule without exceptions"—has no place here. The rule of the lordship of God's will has no exceptions. Everyone who desires to live by God's will must conform himself, all his actions, desires, and thoughts to the will of God. A certain teacher had this to say to his students: "Remember the teaching of the one whom God chose as a man after His own heart, King David, who said to God concerning himself, 'My heart is ready, O God, my heart is ready; I will chant and sing in my glory'" (Psalm 107:2).

My heart is ready to thank You in times of plenty as well as in times of want. Do You wish to make me a pastor of Your reasonable sheep? My heart is ready, God. If You, O Lord, say to me, "I have no delight in you" (2 Kingdoms 15:26), then do with me as You will. Here I am. This is the most profound humility of the heart, worthy of a pious king, a full rejection of one's own will. For what do these words mean: "I have no delight in you"? This means that God does not wish you to be king, or even to continue to live. I am ready to submit to You, Lord, said David. David endured many heavy trials, permitted by God's will, with profound humility. He was persecuted by Saul, he was hounded by an angry son-in-law, he was nearly killed by his own son, he hid from his enemies in caves and lairs of beasts, he meekly endured mockery, vilification, and even the casting of stones. In all this, David humbly submitted to God's will, saying, "Let the Lord do with me according to His good disposition."

This is true virtue, worthy of the greatest of kings. For its sake alone David was beloved by God, and much more so when he raised his gratitude to God in song with tears for all that He sent, both good and painful. He considered God's mercy so precious—this man according to God's own heart—that he was willing to buy it with any possible suffering—the loss of freedom, children, riches, glory, even his own health. But never would he oppose God's will. He abandoned himself and all his surroundings completely to God, saying at all times, "My heart is ready, O God!"

 CHAPTER 18

The Dangers of Irrational, Unrestrained, and Deeply Rooted Self-Will

A certain eloquent teacher said, "Our irrational will *destroys God*. We would like for God not to punish us for our sins either by His lack of existence or by His lack of desire to intrude into human affairs or by His lack of knowledge of the human heart." Consequently, our irrational will either completely denies the existence of God or, acknowledging it, considers God powerless or not all-knowing or unjust. In order to resolve these confusions of a childish mind or of someone who has taken leave of their senses, it would be very instructive to pay attention to the following story.

I

Some time ago certain monsters masquerading as human beings— thieves, plunderers, and robbers—gathered in great numbers and wrote a petition. They sent it to the judges of a city, asking them to make a new law: to remove all instruments of torture and death standing outside the gates of the city—such as the gallows, gibbet,[46] or hedman's block— which were unpleasant for the eyes and offensive to the smell of those people passing by.

The judges answered their petition: "If you desire to destroy this ancient custom, then at first you must cease all your evil deeds, robbery, and plunder, and then we will immediately destroy these instruments of torture. Only order all your fellows to stop robbing and raping!" One of the bravest robbers then dared to raise his voice at the judges, "Lord Judges! We were not the first to begin robbing, plundering, and attacking others. Since we did not invent these evildoings, we cannot reject them."

The judges answered, "We also did not invent these gallows, and so we do not desire, nor are we able, to destroy them."

The forefathers of mankind, having sinned against God's commandment (by eating the fruit of the tree), fell into self-will. In other words, they appropriated to themselves the unlimited use of God's gift of freedom, which had been limited by one well-known condition, and immediately they were changed by this self-willed action (i.e., they saw their own nakedness). This transgression against God's will turned into self-will, a sin that cannot be healed by human agency, a sin that was then passed on to every other human being. The consequence of this fall included terrible punishments: exile from Eden and the loss of intimate communion with God.

We, the last of Adam's descendants, are upset that hell exists, and we often turn to God with our requests, begging him, "Lord! Do not send us into the fires of hell. O Lord, if only You would destroy hell, then we would be calm and fearless."

But the word of God answers us, "If you remove the cause of hell (that is, your sins), then the fires of hell will immediately be put out."

But we cry out all the more loudly, "O Lord! We were not the first to sin! Why must we be held responsible for the sins of others, for ancestral sin? This is the sin of our forefathers, not our own sin."

But the Lord corrects us,

I also am not responsible for the abysses of hell. Hell is a consequence of pride and transgression. Its source is older than man; this is an eternal fire, "prepared for the devil and his angels" (Matthew 25:41). Lest you continue complaining that you are paying someone else's penalty, I will give you, through the words of my servants, a joyful good news (the preaching of the Gospel), whom no one can contradict.

What is this good news? One of these last of God's servants expressed it beautifully: "Let human self-will cease, and hell will cease to exist." This statement is based on the following conclusions: (1) There is nothing more repugnant to God, nothing more worthy of punishment, than our self-will, since it contradicts our very Creator. (2) The fires of hell burn one thing more violently than all others—our desires. So, if we endure cold or hunger or anything else contrary to our own will, then the only thing that suffers is the will of our ego. But if we accept all that gratefully, then we are already guided by a higher will (i.e., the will of God) that allows us to bear undesirable things for the sake of salvific goals.

Here are some of the damaging effects of self-will on a person (let all who are in its thrall listen and beware). Self-will estranges and separates a person from God, his Creator, Whom every person is obliged to serve and obey. But this estrangement is not the only consequence of self-will. Self-will also assumes and then irrationally wastes all the gifts God has given to mankind freely, for human desires know no limits. An extortionist is never content with a rate of return on a loan; if possible, he would claim for himself all the riches of the world. But even this would hardly sate his self-will, which would not even stop, in its horrifying madness, to attack his own Creator: "The fool hath said in his heart, There is no God" (Psalm 13:1).

Self-will is the cruelest of beasts—a ferocious lion, a ravenous wolf. It is a disgusting leprosy of the soul, requiring purification in the Jordan and a strict emulation of the life of the One Who came *not to do His own will*, the One who prayed to His Heavenly Father with the following words, "Not My will, but Yours, be done" (Luke 22:42). Let self-will cease, and the fires of hell will be put out.

Question: Will this hellish fire truly be put out, and in what manner can it be put out?

Answer: This is not a childish or vain question. That the fire can be put out is without doubt: God does not reject our prayer about the extinguishing of hell, and He is ready to put it out. All He requires from us is the rejection of our own self-will. Once self-will ceases, hell is abolished. But who will force all of mankind to reject self-will? Every one of us can do this individually, but only if each person wisely realizes that as soon as he ceases following his own will and begins to live in agreement with God's will, he has already destroyed his assigned place in hell, as though hell were actually destroyed for him, its flames extinguished.

May our self-will be destroyed, and hell with it! Other teachers have expressed this same teaching in other words: "The eye is the door and window of the heart. Close the window, and the desire to possess will disappear."

II

How sad! So many people in this world suffer a great deal, endure many difficulties, discomforts, and deprivations, but they do not receive any benefit or consolation from them, for they do not pay any attention to the true source of these difficulties. Instead, they blame each other and often even blame God. God allows these temptations (tests) for their correction. It is as if He is indicating His will in these difficulties with a heavenly voice, saying, "I want you to feel these blows." But the people, as though sticking their fingers in their ears, are not content with this, and if they could, they would happily avoid these blows. This is the essence of self-will, because there is no agreement with the will of God.

We know many parents who expend great energy and care to correct their children's behavior when stubbornness and self-will were not tamed from the earliest years. Every day they must hold back their children's self-will: "Be quiet! Stop that! Don't do that! Don't touch that!" Sometimes the children explode into such hysterics that the caring mother, assuming a strict face, even takes a switch to threaten them with a spanking, saying with anger, "You are not my children, I do not know you, you are not like me or your father. You are real troublemakers! Get out of this house, you ungrateful brats, and go wherever you like. Neither your father nor I want you any more."

As horrible as this sounds, our self-will can become so deeply rooted that we provoke a similar reaction from God Himself. How often does God warn the drunkard or the debaucher! He reveals their sins to their consciences in all their exposed horror, and their consciences rebuke and torture them. It is as if God says,

> Stop, you foolish children, you are harming yourselves! You are destroying your own soul. You are wasting and infecting your body. You are losing your health and throwing about your money as though it were rags. And, finally, you are removing yourselves from My good will for you, from My mercy, for you know that I do not condone any of these human abominations and I despise any will that resists Mine.

After such fatherly instruction, God, our merciful Father, seeing our continued incorrigibility, begins to employ physical measures for the correction of the prodigal son (i.e., every transgressor against the will of God). He sends us tangible chastisements, such as loss of money, disease, or the death of a beloved child. If even this does not improve us, and we continue our insubordination to His will again and again, then the Heavenly Father, grieved by our sins, speaks to all the people through the mouth of the prophets: "Alas, sinful nation, a people full of sins, an evil seed, lawless children. They forsook the Lord; they have provoked to anger the Holy One of Israel. Why should you still be struck as you continue in lawlessness? The whole head is in pain, and the whole heart in sadness" (Isaiah 1:4–5). "But the prolific multitude of the ungodly are useful to no one, and none of their illegitimate seedlings will grow a deep root or establish a sure footing" (Wisdom of Solomon 4:3). "So I gave them up unto their hearts' lusts; they shall walk in their own imaginations" (Psalm 80:13).

How terrible is this anger of the Heavenly Father! Separation from God is more horrifying and torturous than hell itself, according to the words of Christ at His dread judgment: "Depart from Me, you cursed, into the everlasting fire prepared for the devil and his angels" (Matthew 25:41). God acts in the same way toward all proud and arrogant people. Rebuking them, He says,

> You are useless for God and for mankind, for you have despised Me, seeking to receive human praise for your pride. In your stupidity, you are mistaken, and instead of praise, you remain despised by them. You knew My will, you knew that I do not endure proud men, that I did not even spare the angel who grew arrogant. Still less will I spare a proud man. Who does not know that I do not endure proud men? Yet you remain constantly in your pride.

But still God, through invisible inducements, also draws the covetous, the irritable, and the envious from a life of sin to a life of self-correction. He offers them many means of according their wills with the will of God. God instructs every person to strive toward salvation by the best possible path. Thus, Samuel said to King Saul,

> Were you not small before Him, you who with a sceptre lead all the families of the tribes of Israel? Even so, the Lord still anointed you king over Israel. Now the Lord sent you off on a mission and said, "Go and utterly destroy the sinners for me, the Amalekites, and fight against them until you consume them." Why did you not heed the voice of the Lord, but rushed down on the spoils and did evil before the Lord? That sin is one and the same as divination. Idols bring grief and pain. Because you rejected the word of the Lord, the Lord rejects you from remaining king over Israel. (1 Kingdoms 15: 17–19, 23)

III

What was the meaning of God's command to the ravens to feed Elijah when he hid in the desert from the wrath of Jezebel?[47] These birds, though they love to eat meat, eagerly brought the desert dweller his lunch and dinner. Why? God commanded this in order to teach us that even the irrational beasts submit to God's holy will, though it be contrary to their natural instinct. What is even more amazing is that the command was given to a raven, a bird that is ravenous for all kinds of meat.

You may say, "For God, anything is possible; it is within His power to force the raven to bring meat to a prophet, but this is done not by the bird's desire, but merely by blind necessity. The raven could not do otherwise."

Yes, your words are true. However, that only means that man, a rational creature, has all the more responsibility to freely submit to the will of God, for God gave him this freedom. He does not force us, desiring that we freely submit to Him, and by doing so we deserve the greatest blessedness both now and in eternity.

Let us leave behind the lesson of the raven and let us consider the weather. You will see that even the wind is obedient to the will of God: Jesus "rebuked the winds and the sea, and there was a great calm" (Matthew 8:26). The Apostles were amazed, saying, "Who can this be, that even the winds and the sea obey Him?" (Matthew 8:27). Even the stones witnessed to nature's grief and terror at the sight of the dying Lord;[48] only man sometimes turns into a stone, becoming hardened by repeated sinfulness. "The heart is deceitful above all things, and desperately wicked; who can know it?" (Jeremiah 17:9 NKJV).

If you only begin to plumb the depths of this abyss, you will find there, hidden in the darkest corners, hidden thoughts that resist God:

> Lord! Do You want me to love my enemies? Do You want me to reject all these pleasant things that I love? This heavy, unbearable command extends to all the other movements of my will; You would deprive me of my will in all things! What is there left for me to do? No, I will not do this. I will not bother my self-will. I will only submit to Your will in moderation.

This is how a wicked, obstinate heart thinks, to its own detriment.

Trebellius Pollio tells that the seventh tyrant of Rome was a man named Marcus Aurelius Marius.[49] One day he was declared ruler, the next day he ruled, the third day he was killed by one of his useless soldiers, who, as he stabbed Marius in the heart, said with a sneer, "This sword was made by you," for the short-lived tyrant was a former smith. In the same way, every person who opposes God will be mocked and profaned. He will be mocked by others who will say, "This sword that you kill yourself with was made by your own hands," the sword being insubordination before God.

Why is human will so inclined to resist God's will? St Caesarius offers a possible answer:

> The devil has two servants—the flesh and the world. The flesh defiles itself, its desires inflamed by the devil, and in order to prevent the desires from fading, the world covers them with its sanction and its manners. Much sin comes from the flesh, and the world offers many different immoral enticements and pleasures, inspired by the cunning of the evil spirit. Thus, everything is ready to entice our will and desires, as the Lord once revealed to the Prophet Jeremiah, saying, 'Run to and fro through the streets of Jerusalem, and you will see and know; and seek in her streets if you can find a man, if there is anyone who does judgment and seeks faithfulness; and I shall be merciful to them... You chastised them, but they have not grieved; You consumed them, but they were unwilling to receive correction' (Jeremiah 5:1, 3), They lied to their own Lord, and said, 'These things are not so. Evil will not come upon us, nor shall we see sword or famine' (5:12). 'The children gather wood, the fathers kindle the fire, and the women knead dough, to make cakes for the queen of heaven; and they pour out drink offerings to other gods, that they may provoke Me to anger' (7:18 NKJV). All take part in this; both parents and children help each other. For whom are these breads prepared? For the queen of heaven is the moon and the sun is the king of heaven. The will of man is much like the moon, for it constantly changes, and to this queen are sacrifices and gifts brought. The flesh, like a beloved daughter, prepares the wood, that is, its desires. The father of pride, the devil, lights the wood. The cares of the world prepare the dough, decorated in many ways, with the caresses of oratory, the luxury of adornments and sensuality, and other such gifts. Thus are fine sacrifices prepared, not to God, but to self-will.

IV

Such insubordination, or better yet, opposition to the will of God is described very well by St Augustine in his interpretation of Psalm 100[50]. St Augustine contrasts a *straight heart* with *a crooked heart* and examines the actions arising from each. He says,

> The heart of a man, who wishes not anything contrary to any that God wishes, is called straight. If therefore the righteous heart follows God,

the crooked heart resists God. Suppose something untoward happens to him, he cries out, "God, what have I done unto You? What sin have I committed?" He wishes himself to appear just, God unjust. What is so crooked as this? It is not enough that you are crooked yourself: you must think your rule crooked also. Reform yourself, and you find Him straight, in departing from whom you have made yourself crooked. He does justly, thou unjustly; and for this reason you are perverse, since you call man just, and God unjust. What man do you call just? Yourself. For when you say, "What have I done unto You?" you think yourself just. But let God answer you: "You speak truth: you have done nothing to Me: you have done all things unto yourself; for if you had done anything for Me, you would have done good. For whatever is done well, is done unto Me; because it is done according to My commandment; but whatever of evil is done, is done unto you, not unto Me; for the wicked man does nothing except for his own sake, since it is not what I command." When ye see such men, brethren, reprove them, convince and correct them: and if you cannot reprove or correct them, consent not to them.

This same Father expands his discourse concerning those who are straight of heart in a different commentary. In describing those who are straight of heart, he describes them as those who conform their will to God's, but do not try to force God's will to accommodate their own. In short, man must strive toward God. Do you wish to have a straight heart? Do what is pleasing to God. Do not desire or try to force God to act in all things according to your own wishes. This is how those with straight hearts think. They do not strive to walk ahead of God, but try to walk in God's wake, following Him, and in this way, walking in His steps, they do not wander, but in every place they receive gifts from Him. They receive moral correction, spiritual consolation, instruction, and the illumination of their mind. Finally, they receive the crowning of all their labors in this life, according to the words of the Apostle: "All things work together for good to those who love God" (Romans 8:28). Such people are truly the sons of the Eagle, who are able to look directly at the sun without blinking, careful to conform their will in all circumstances to the will of God.

Those who have secretly turned away from God and quietly resist Him act quite differently. They often do not like bad weather: they complain at prolonged rain, they become bored of long winters, and yet they also complain at excessive heat. Sometimes they raise their voices against God in discontent. They complain that He does not send enough for their daily needs, that He allows the attacks of wicked robbers and persecutors, that He does not destroy all their enemies who are worthy (according to them) of all possible punishments. They always complain and slander God's wisdom, because the world is not made according to their own desires. This is a truly crooked heart.

V

All evil, both mundane and extraordinary, sprouts from a single root—self-will, which has inside itself two insatiable leeches that constantly demand more and more. No gratification is ever enough for it. The heart is never sated with vanity nor is the body ever sated by sensuality, according to the Scriptures: "Neither will the eye be satisfied with seeing, nor will the ear be filled with hearing" (Ecclesiastes 1:8). Run from these bloodsuckers, and you will find true freedom from all evil, for self-will attracts only evil to itself. If you reject self-will, you will cast from yourself a terrible yoke. Self-will corrupts the hearts of men and darkens their reason. It is an unrestrained evil, intrinsic to our fallen nature. It dares even touch objects that should not even be considered. From where do temptations come? Why are we troubled? Only because we are directed by our own irrational self-will and we give full freedom to our harmful desires. If we are hindered in any way in the striving after our own desires, we immediately grieve, complain, and despise the one obstructing us, not understanding that "we know that all things work together for good to those who love God, to those who are the called according to His purpose" (Romans 8:28). And yet, it seems to us that everything is accidental in this world, and there is no need to reject all that our desires want, as long as the circumstances are favorable. This frightful delusion of our deceived reason and our debauched will is witnessed by the word of God, which declares to us the will of God. Let us preserve ourselves from self-will as from a poisonous snake, for our unbridled will alone can destroy our souls!

Abba John, one of the Desert Fathers, while lying on his deathbed, was asked by his disciples to give a short instruction as a memorial, instead of an inheritance. He answered them, sighing deeply, "I never followed the dictates of my own will, and I never taught anything before I had fulfilled it in action."[51] There are not many such teachers, hardly one in a thousand. On the contrary, it is easy to find many who would say the opposite on their deathbed: "What I could, I did according to my own will; I pampered all my own desires; I taught others much, and more than that I ordered others to do all that which I never wanted to do."

St Pimen (ca. 340–450 A.D.), another Desert Fathers, was asked, "How do the devils battle against us?"

He answered, "They do not battle against us very often, because we do their will without even entering the fray against them. More often, our own desires are our demons, and they trouble and defeat us."

St Achillius of Larissa (fourth century) said,

> Once the trees on the slopes of Lebanon's mountains were speaking to each other in sorrow, saying, "How tall and great we are, but still we are cut down by seemingly insignificant pieces of metal. Then we are made into tools that are used to further destroy other trees. We become the handles of axes!" If applied to people, this parable is explained thus. The trees are people. The metal is the temptation of the evil one; the handle of the axe is the human will.

The much-suffering Job, sitting on the dung heap, is a much more convincing preacher of the greatness, goodness, and omnipotence of God than Adam in Eden. The first said, "As the Lord willed, so it became." Adam said, "I heard Your voice as You were walking in the garden, and I was afraid because I was naked; so I hid myself" (Genesis 3:10).

Tertullian[52] speaks beautifully about Job: "Job with mighty equanimity kept scraping off the unclean overflow of his own ulcer, while he sportively replaced the vermin that broke out thence, in the same caves and feeding-places of his pitted flesh!"[53] It is as if he jokingly said to the worms feeding on his flesh, "Go ahead, satisfy yourselves!" This great man knew that all this was done by God's will, and so he humbled himself before God. This is why he replaced the worms on his wounds, saying,

> Why are you running away? You were sent to eat my flesh; do what you were commanded to do, eat my body! For none other than the One God, Who gave me so many thousands of sheep, donkeys, and other beasts, is the One Who mercifully sent these worms to gnaw at me. Both the first and the second is sent by the right hand of God, and so I must accept both with a grateful heart.[54]

St Simeon the Stylite (ca. 390–459 A.D.) also spoke to the worms that were falling off his rotting flesh, "Eat what God gave you." But Herod (11 B.C.–44 A.D.), eaten from within by worms, had a completely different disposition of spirit. Angrily scraping off the worms, he said, "Go to hell, you horrible insects, find some corpse hanging on a gibbet. It is your work to decompose dead bodies, but I am still alive. Why are you eating a living man?"[55] These are the words of one's self-will opposing the will of God. Here it becomes obvious, according to the words of St John Chrysostom, that our self-will is truly the source of all evils:

> May no one dare to deplore the beauty of virtue. Let no one say, "This man was killed by his goodness." No, our perverted self-will was, is, and will always be the source of all evil. Therefore, even in the Old Testament, God warned His people against self-will and rebuked them for their lack of obedience to His will: "I will deliver you to the sword, and all of you shall fall in the slaughter; because I called you, but you did not obey; I spoke, but you refused to listen. You did evil in might sight, and did not choose the things I willed." (Isaiah 65:12)

Here is the source of all evil—our self-will. "You did not choose the things I willed."

 Chapter 19

How Our Will Can Become Obedient to the Will of God in All Things, Even in That Which We Do Not Desire

Neither the will of an angel or human being can ever be a *goodwill* if it is not conformed to God's will. The more our will aligns with the will of God, the better and more complete it is. The opposite is also true: the less our will conforms to God's, the worse and more evil it is. Only the divine will is a model and guide for the activity of all the heavenly and earthly wills. Not one of these wills ever becomes good if it does not first approach God's will in all its desires and actions.

I

The kingly Prophet David praised those who are "true of heart" (Psalm 31:11). Blessed Augustine describes this "trueness" in detail in several of his interpretations of the Psalms. See how many contradict God, how His works are abhorrent to so many people? If God does something contrary to man's will, He is the Lord and knows what He is doing. He pays more attention to our benefit than our desires. Those who desire to follow their own will rather than God's often try to force God's will to accommodate their own, instead of correcting their own will according to the model of God's will. "Praise becometh well the upright" (Psalm 32:1). Who are these "upright," people with true hearts? They are those who commit their will, their heart, to the divine will, and if their human weakness troubles them, they seek support and encouragement in divine Truth. Sometimes their mortal heart conceals hidden desires that accord more to their own comfort and convenience, but as soon as they understand that God wishes otherwise, they immediately prefer the most high will to their own, the almighty and perfect will to their weak and erroneous one. Then they follow God all the more eagerly.

As much as God exceeds man in goodness, so does His will exceed human will. Though you desire something pleasant, instead you receive sorrow from an unfulfilled desire. If that happens, immediately remember God Who is greater than you. You are of the lower orders; He is the commander in chief. He is the Creator, you the creature. He is the Lord, you the slave. He is almighty; you are weak. Therefore, correct yourself, submit to His will and cry out to Him with humility, "My Father! Do not what I desire, but what is pleasing to You."

If this is how you live, your heart is straight, and you will be deserving of praise. This is not how lazy and self-loving people act. They praise God only when they are happy, and they complain when nothing goes according to their will. Wake up, you fools! You are like an irrational boy in the house of the father. The boy loves his father when he caresses him, but he expresses his disapproval when his father is strict with him and punishes him. The boy does not understand that both the caressing and the punishing father acts in order to prepare the best possible future for his son.

Why do the true-hearted deserve praise? Because their life pleases God. Listen to the righteous David's confession before God: "I will bless the Lord at all times, His praise is ever in my mouth" (Psalm 33:1). We praise God everywhere and always, whether in prosperity or in poverty, for if we praise God only when we are joyful and never in sorrow, how can it be "at all times?" They say that people rejoice at pleasures and then they sing praises to God. There is nothing terrible in this. However, these same people must acknowledge God as their chastising Father as well and never murmur against him, but instead must strive to correct themselves, in order not to be deprived of the blessing of God and the inheritance of the eternal heavenly kingdom.

Who are the upright? They are those who accept with pleasure all that God sends them. They are those who praise God even in the heaviest trials, saying together with much-suffering Job: "The Lord gave, and the Lord has taken away ... Blessed be the name of the Lord" (Job 1:21).

Such righteous ones are deserving of praise, not those who at first praise God, then rail at Him. Learn, instead, to thank God both in joys and in sorrows. Learn to genuinely feel in your heart the words that you should speak— "as it pleases God." There is even a secular proverb that says that punishment is often for the benefit of the sufferer. Remembering this instruction, who will not repeat these words to God? "As it was pleasing to God, so it was done. Blessed be the name of the Lord!"

II

The preceding instruction, taken largely from Blessed Augustine's works, explains and proves that human happiness depends entirely on obeying the will of God. All virtuous and righteous people in human history knew this to be true. Truly, submission in all things to the will of God serves as a foundation for all virtue, the beginning of a truly Christian life, and the pledge of a blessed passage into eternal life. However, the previous section only covered about a half of Augustine's words concerning the subject. It would be unfair to deprive all truly faithful Christians of the witness of this inspired writer and teacher.

This God-inspired hierarch insists that even in troubles and calamities, we must not take even a single step outside the circle of God's will. He again reminds us that those of a "true heart" are those who have never opposed the will of God that decrees occasional health, but occasional sickness as well. When you are healthy, the will of God pleases you, but when you are sick, the will of God is bitter. You are wrong. Why? Because you do not want to obey God's will. Instead, you want God's will to agree with your own. God's will is right, but you are not, for your will is required to follow God's, not the other way around. Only by doing this will you acquire a straight heart. Then, if you are asked, "Are you happy in your life?" You may answer, "Blessed be God who consoles me." If you are asked, "Is your life difficult?" You may answer, "Blessed be God Who tests and corrects me." If you do this, you will have a true heart and together with David you can sing in the secret chamber of your heart, "I will bless the Lord at all times."

St Augustine is not the only one to give us this teaching, but David himself left us an instructive example. When he fled from his rebellious son Absalom with the priests bearing the Ark of the Covenant, David ordered the Ark to be returned to its previous place, saying, "If I find favor in the eyes of the Lord, He will bring me back and show me both it and it's majesty. But if He says thus, 'I have no delight in you,' behold, here I am, let Him do to me as seems good to Him" (2 Kingdoms 15:25–26). These are the words of a powerful king who found himself in flight and the worst humiliation, yet he understood the true significance of the will of the Most High. With his whole heart, he entrusted himself to the will of God.

Pious Christians! If we had such wisdom, then truly we could achieve anything. There would be nothing uncomfortable for us even in the most difficult troubles, nothing would weigh us down, and we would accept everything with joy, as decreed by God's will. Christ in the garden of Gethsemane gave us the only true instruction concerning long-suffering in any sorrow, showing that it is better above all to entrust ourselves up completely to the will of the Heavenly Father, saying, "My sorrow is great, save me, O Father. But not my will, but Yours, be done!"[56]

What else does the example of the God-Man teach us? Notice how before His prayer, Christ was sorrowful, even to death, afraid of the coming Passion. However, after His prayer, having recommitted Himself completely to the Father's will, He received new strength and even encouraged the disciples to stay strong in the face of their coming enemies.

Blessed Augustine wrote lengthy interpretations of this Scriptural account. How can one explain that Christ the Lord, revealing His humanity, teaching us the God-pleasing life, giving us life, finds within Himself a certain human free will, the same will as we have? The answer is simple. Christ is our head, and we are the members of His body. He declared to God the Father as a man, "O My Father, if it is possible, let this cup pass from Me; [in this exclamation he revealed His human will, but this is a Man who desires to have a true heart, a Man Who asks to be corrected if there is anything sinful in His heart] nevertheless, not as I will, but as You will" (Matthew 26:39). By this, Christ desired to show us that in Him there was a personal human desire that desired something other than what God desired.

III

The union of the human will with the divine creates a home in the heart. What sort of home is this? It is the union of human will with the divine. This home, when one first moves into it, seems to be small, but whoever desires to become accustomed to it soon finds it to be more expansive than heaven itself and more impenetrable than the securest prison. All confusion is refused entry at the door, for this union is a fortress unassailable even by heavenly hosts, much less by physical enemies. Whoever keeps his will in all things obedient and inseparable from God's will makes all of his actions subject to one law: "Whatever God wants, let Him do with me." True are the words of Blessed Augustine: "My sickness will come, and it will bring consolation. Sorrow will be followed by joy." Gold does not shine when it is still ore; it receives its shine after it has been made into a coin or an adornment. However, it must first pass through fire, or the crucible, to be purified of any dirt and only then will it shine.

This crucible is an image of the whole world. There are impurities, there is gold, there is the fire, there the artist does his work. In the crucible, the impurities burn away, and the gold is purified. Let us speak more directly: the crucible is the world, the impurities are the wicked, the gold is the righteous, the fire is sorrows, and the artist is God. Thus, whatever the artist desires and commands, that is what I do. Has He commanded me to endure? It is because He knows my sins and purifies me of their foulness. If the impurities burn up and try to burn me with them in an attempt to destroy me, they still become ash, while I am purified of filth. Why? Because my soul obeys the Lord.

This is the true submission of human will to the divine. It is the beginning of every good deed. There is no greater or more pleasing sacrifice to God than committing oneself in the midst of any sorrow or trouble to the dispensation of God.

In antiquity, Abraham obeyed God and received great praise. God, in order to show the whole world that Abraham was ready to eagerly and unconditionally fulfill the most difficult and painful of His commands, constantly switched one command with another, each more difficult and painful for Abraham and his household, testing his faithfulness. Abraham was ready to diligently do — with all the powers of his spirit—everything that God's will commanded, committing himself completely to God's disposition. The Old Testament speaks of ten difficult trials of Abraham's obedience and love of God.

1. God commanded Abraham to leave his homeland of Mesopotamia, along with his family and possessions, and to go into an unknown land (Genesis 12:1).
2. Abraham came to Canaan as an outsider and wanderer, suffering from lack of food, then temporarily settled in Egypt (Genesis 12:10).
3. In Egypt, Abraham was in despair of losing his life, and Sarah feared to lose her virtue (Genesis 12:10–20).
4. When the shepherds of Abraham and Lot began to argue concerning cattle, Abraham was forced to part with Lot, whom he loved like a son (Genesis 13:7–18).
5. In order to free Lot from captivity, Abraham was forced to battle four kings with only his household (about 318 people) (Genesis 14:11–24).
6. Abraham, incited by Sarah, was forced to expel his faithful servant who had become his wife (Genesis 16:5–16).
7. In old age, Abraham accepted the covenant of circumcision according to God's command (Genesis 17:9–11).
8. Abimelech, the king of Gerar, took away Sarah, intending to marry her, but in a dream an angel of God threatened him, and he returned Sarah to Abraham, rebuking him for calling her his sister (Genesis 20:1–18).

9. By God's command, Abraham threw out Hagar, his servant and wife, a second time, this time with her son Ishmael (Genesis 21:8–21).
10. The last and most horrifying test of Abraham's loyalty was the command from God to offer his only beloved son Isaac, the source of God's promised prosperity, as a sacrifice to God (Genesis 22:2–18).

There were many other temptations in Abraham's life that are common to all people. However, Abraham remained the same Abraham, never changing, always himself, a true and complete fulfiller of the will of God. He understood well that only in complete devotion to God does one find protection against all calamities.

All you who are sorrowful and heavy-laden! Ascend this mountain for your own joy. Let it be known to all sufferers that God before the ages foresaw all that now happens to them, and He also determined what would happen and when. Therefore, the foreknowledge of God directs each event for the benefit of each of us.

IV

God allows all catastrophes and calamities. This is made obvious from the following example. It is well known to all that governments are not able to simply turn aside the armies of an invader nor can they ensure that an epidemic (such as the plague or cholera) will never strike the people. Neither can any person prevent disease from striking when it does. Some people will be afflicted in their legs, others in their stomach, others will hallucinate, afflicted by brain fever. All these calamities depend on the will or the permission of God. How can a government not allow the coming of war when the country is already in the thick of it? What can people do to prevent a disease when it has already infected them? Can they oppose God's will? No, they cannot.

Does that mean there are no means for their salvation? There are, but with the condition that God allows it and wills it. How did Abraham act in Moriah when he, obeying God's will, was about to plunge the sacrificial knife into the heart of his son Isaac? Hearing from the angel the voice of God telling him of the previous command's cancellation, Abraham found a ram stuck in a thicket by its horns, and he sacrificed the ram instead of his son Isaac (see Genesis 22:10–13).

In a similar way, the kingdom plunged into unwilling war, the country afflicted with an epidemic, the person tortured with a painful disease—all these must seek means that are most appropriate to stop the calamity. If it pleases God to put a stop to the troubles or to lessen them, then He will send a sacrificial ram (i.e., a way out of the problem). If nothing seems to help, then it becomes obvious that God desires that you bring Isaac as a sacrifice. In other words, the kingdom will lose the war, the country will be decimated by the epidemic, or the person will die from his disease. The same light must judge all other troubles. Wherever God sends help, there Isaac is spared. Where God's help is absent, there Isaac will be slaughtered on the altar. Thus, a person must in all situations of his life obey God's will eagerly. The best means for him to overcome any evil is to always think of God, to always pray to God, to always submit to God, and in all cases to subject his own mind to the Reason of the Most High.

Saint Remigius (ca. 437–533), foreseeing a terrible failed harvest and famine in the coming year, gathered reserves of wheat to feed the poor. But among the poor for whom he cared were some wicked people—drunkards, debauchers—who said to each other, "What is our cheerful old man planning? Does he perhaps plan to build himself a new city? Why did he stock up so much extra wheat? Does he perhaps plan on increasing taxes on us? Let us gather together and plan how to stop his projects."

They chose an appropriate time and decided to burn down the archbishop's granaries. As one of them prepared to burn it down, he said, "Let us see how in a moment these riches will turn to ash!" Then he set them on fire. The archbishop got wind of their evil deed. Not wasting a single moment, he rode on his horse to stop them. However, he saw that the fire was already too widely spread and could not be stopped, no matter how hard anyone would try. The archbishop, though pained by the loss, was even more pained at the spiritual state of his flock. However, he did not utter a single sorrowful or rash word nor did he rebuke the arsonists. Having dismounted, he approached the fire closer than seemed possible, as though he wanted to get warm, and said, "Warmth is always pleasant, especially for such an old man as I am."

Here is a truly kind heart, a person who has given himself completely to the will of God. Therefore, he was not troubled by any confusion. He would have greatly liked to put out the fire, but since no reason or power was sufficient to do this, he left everything to the will of God, uttering the words of Job, "The Lord gave, and the Lord has taken away ... Blessed be the name of the Lord" (Job 1:21). This is how we must act during any misfortune when we are unable to do anything to accomplish our goals. Instead, let us commit our work to God, saying with our whole heart, "Let God's will be done. Let Isaac be sacrificed when there is no ram to be sacrificed, if the Lord so wills. Let this house be destroyed, let my lands be destroyed, if only that is Your will, O Lord, for us."

V

When a harpist tunes his harp, he tightens or loosens the strings until they all agree with each other harmonically, so to speak. In the same way, every person who desires to submit himself to the direction of God's will must learn, force, submit, and teach his own will to align to God's for as long as it is necessary until the two are in harmony. As King David said, "Doth not my soul wait still upon God? For of Him cometh my salvation" (Psalm 61:1). In the Hebrew text, these words have the following meaning: "Thus my soul will not begin to contradict God, it will remain silent, for He is my salvation." This fully accords both with our theme and with the disposition of David's own heart, which says,

> Whatever happens to me, both good or evil, I will not oppose God's will. I will accept God's statutes, and even if all the misfortunes in the world were to fall on my head, I will not complain. I will not let slip a single word against God's dispositions. I will always be content with God's commandments. Everything that is difficult or bitter I will bear with courageous patience, and this will make my burden lighter.

CHAPTER 20

An Instructive Example for People Who Refuse to Follow God's Direction

This instructive story concerns not just any self-willed or proud person but the man of God, the Old Testament Prophet Jonah, who—seemingly for a good reason—refused to fulfill the command of God, and because of that suffered various troubles and sorrows until he submitted his own will to the will of God.

I

The will of God was declared to Jonah clearly, definitively, in the following words: "Arise and go to Nineveh, the great city" (Jonah 1:1). This was the first part of the command and the second was to "preach in it." Jonah arose and went, but not to Nineveh: "Jonah rose up to flee to Tarshish from the presence of the Lord" (Jonah 1:3). Here there was a double transgression: not only did Jonah not preach in Nineveh, but he did not even go there. Therefore, the righteous punishment of God immediately followed him. "The Lord raised up a great wind upon the sea, and there came about a mighty tempest, and the ship was in danger of breaking up" (Jonah 1:4). But Jonah still did not understand that the storm was raised against him. "Jonah had gone below into the hold of the ship, had gone to sleep, and was snoring" (Jonah 1:5). There is nothing bitterer or more dangerous than such inexcusable carelessness.

The storm continued and grew worse. The mariners ran back and forth in fear and trembling. They lowered the sails to protect them from the winds, they cast out all the heavy cargo, but nothing seemed to help. The storm only worsened, and soon all hope was lost. They had only one hope left—hope in God. Every one of them directed their personal prayers to God. They woke Jonah, saying, "Get up, and call upon your God" (Jonah 1:6). In a general council, the sailors decided to cast lots to find out who was responsible for God's punishment, the storm. The lot fell to Jonah and when asked who he was, he answered, "I am a servant of the Lord, and I worship the Lord God of heaven, who made the sea and the dry land" (Jonah 1:9).

Is this how you worship the Lord God? Is this how you respect and fear Him? Why then did you not listen to His command? Like Jonah, many say, "I fear only God" and immediately break His commandments, taking and stealing from their neighbors. Beloved brothers! To say that you fear God and to act in opposition to His will means that you do not fear Him or respect Him. No, you disregard His holy will, you do not submit, but rather you brazenly oppose your own Creator and Saviour. This is confirmed by the actions of Jonah himself. His confession—that he worships and fears the Lord God—was not enough to stop the storm. Instead, it continued to get worse. Finally, Jonah was cast into the sea in order to calm the waves.

However, before this was done, Jonah admitted his fault, saying, "Take me up and cast me into the sea, and the sea will grow calm for you, for I know this great tempest is upon you because of me" (Jonah 1:12). And now the Instructor of the seas awaits you; He will soon teach you the truth that every person must desire what God desires, and desire only that which God desires. "So they took up Jonah and threw him into the sea, and the sea ceased from its raging" (Jonah 1:15).

"Now the Lord commanded a huge sea creature to swallow Jonah" (Jonah 2:1). These are the consequences of stubborn self-will. Let this be for us a study in how to accept on our own shoulders the good and light burden of God's will. Listen on, and learn how Jonah was corrected, and how easily and quickly he submitted to the command of God. Imprisoned in the belly of a living sea creature as in a dark cell, plunged into the very abyss of hell, he wondered if he were still alive or not. And, as though in a dream, he called out to the Lord. When his soul was very near its end, he remembered God. Truly, this is how we sinners act as well. We are not quick to act. Only extreme necessity forces us to awaken and only then do we begin to desire what we wickedly refused before.

Well, Jonah, will you go to Nineveh? I will. Will you preach to the Ninevites? I will. Do you desire to fulfill the promise you made Me in the belly of the sea beast? I will fulfill it all to the last detail. "Then the Lord commanded the sea creature, and it cast up Jonah onto the dry land" (Jonah 2:11).

"Now the word of the Lord came to Jonah a second time, saying, 'Arise and go to Nineveh, the great city, and preach there according to the message I previously spoke to you.' So Jonah arose and went to Nineveh, just as the Lord spoke" (Jonah 3:2). Now Jonah rejected his own will and wanted that which God wanted. He hurried to preach to the great city, working with his feet, hands, and voice, saying, "Yet three days and Nineveh shall be overthrown" (Jonah 3:4). Now Jonah became transformed into action. He spoke with a voice of thunder; he corrected and instructed the city-folk, inciting them to repentance. If only he had continued acting thus and did not return to his previous self-will!

II

Alas, how afflicted we are by weakness and inconstancy of will! One moment our will is God's and suddenly it separates from him into self-will. "Jonah was deeply grieved and was troubled" (Jonah 4:1). These are the evil signs of a human will entering into battle with the will of God. Whoever is submissive and obedient to the will of God will never be grieved or irritated; he will never weaken under the weight of his own sorrows until he becomes angry with the Most High Himself. What is this, Jonah? What brings your will, in nearly all other aspects obedient to the will of God, into such confusion? Here is the reason for his new opposition to God:

"O Lord, were these not my words when I was yet in my land? ... because I knew You to be compassionate and merciful, long-suffering and abundant in mercy, and willing to change Your heart concerning evils" (Jonah 4:2). The opposition between Jonah's and God's will is found in that God decided, because of Nineveh's repentance, to spare the city. Jonah wanted the Ninevites to be actually punished, thinking in his mind that it is pointless to threaten when there is no strength behind the threat, knowing God's proclivity to be merciful. After this, Jonah could find no other consolation than these words, "And now, Master, Lord, take my life from me, for it is better for me to die than to live" (Jonah 4:3). Perhaps this is better for you, Jonah, but it is not pleasing to God. Self-will cares and pays attention only to those things that are safe and pleasant for it, and it never thinks about what is pleasing or abhorrent to God.

"Then Jonah went out of the city and seated himself opposite it. There he made for himself a tent and sat under its shade, until he might observe what would happen to the city" (Jonah 4:5). His self-will was not yet satisfied. He left the city, awaiting its destruction with pleasure. Why did Jonah leave the city? Why did he not continue to exhort the people to repent? What necessity forced him to build himself a new dwelling, shaded by a gourd? Thousands of residents would have gratefully accepted this prophet of repentance into their own homes. But this is not pleasing to self-will, which is not content even in the largest cities, even feeling itself constrained by the whole world. Jonah was sure that as soon as he left the city, thunder would strike and fire from heaven would rain down upon the city, for God had commanded the prophet with the following words: "Yet three days and Nineveh shall be overthrown" (Jonah 3:4). Therefore, Jonah built himself a temporary dwelling in a safe place, to watch how God would put His threat into action. It is as if he said to himself, "He will not be merciful to these people and He will destroy them from the face of the earth."

Jonah awaited this destruction for a long time, and he saw that the sky remained clear, with not a single cloud or lightning bolt or thunderclap. No punishment came from the heavens. Not only that, but as soon as day dawned, a worm ate away at the gourd shading Jonah, and Jonah was left exposed to the scorching sun. Jonah was exhausted and even more grieved, saying, "I am exceedingly grieved, even unto death" (Jonah 4:9).

What was the reason for his anger and grief? The desire of his heart did not come to pass. Jonah, how impatient is your will, especially in its own dispositions and conclusions. Why are you so angry with God's mercy and long-suffering? Or do you not know that it is in God's nature to forgive and be merciful? Do you desire to ascribe to God man's lack of patience? If someone offended you, you would immediately strike him down. If someone grieved you, you would immediately throw lightning bolts at him. You would do this, but not God. We humans are ready to quickly avenge our wrongs, giving back much more than we received. But God is not like us: "The Lord is merciful and gracious, longsuffering, and of great kindness. The Lord is good unto all, and His mercies are upon all His works" (Psalm 144:8–9).

Why, Jonah, are you grieved about a gourd eaten by a worm? You did not plant it, you did not care for it, and you did not call the worm to eat its roots. The Lord gave it, and the Lord took it away. Why do you murmur at God? If you are sorry for the gourd, why do you wish God to destroy an entire city, as large as a small kingdom (Nineveh had more than one hundred and twenty thousand inhabitants)? You grieve for the lost shade of a gourd, but not the people of Nineveh? O great prophet! Correct your own will (as much as this is possible for man) in all its movements, so that it becomes one with God's. The gourd has withered, but you should not grieve for it. Nineveh is saved, and you should desire it to be prosperous in a God-pleasing way. Grieve only that you did not immediately obey the will of God.

III

Do you understand, brother-Christians, what sort of harvest self-willed people reap for themselves? Notice the terrible delusions that befall even righteous men when they obstinately insist on their own opinions. Until we reject our passionate attachment to self-love and self-will, opposing all events occurring by God's will, we will never be able to do anything good and pleasing to God. Not a single gift, oath, prayer, or sacrifice to God will be accepted when offered by an enemy of God's will. God is pleased by fasting; God loves alms; prayers inspire His mercy, but only when all this is done not pharisaically (hypocritically), that is, not in order to achieve any external goal that flatters our vanity, avarice, lust for power, and other sins contrary to God's will. This is frightening even to say!—although fasts, prayer, and almsgiving are pleasing to God, He rejects all of them when they are done hypocritically, in opposition to God's will, to please ourselves. To such hypocrites God speaks through the mouth of Isaiah:

> If you fast for condemnations and quarrels, and strike a humble man with your fists, why do you fast to Me as you do today, so your voice may be heard in crying? I did not choose this fast … Rather, loose every bond of wrong-doing; untie the knots of violent dealings; cancel the debts of the oppressed; and tear apart every unjust contract. Break your bread for the hungry, and bring the homeless poor into your house. If you see a naked man, clothe him, nor shall you disregard your offspring in your own household. (Isaiah 58:4–7)

Why does God reject an unrighteous fast? Because in the days of the fast, the hypocrite caters to his own will first of all instead of rejecting himself. He uses the fast in order to achieve his self-will's most fervent desires. But God says, "I love fasting, but I hate and reject flattery that defiles fasting."

If a person who cannot endure the smell of onions or garlic is given food seasoned with them, not only does this not please him, but it forces him to remain hungry, for his hatred of the smell takes away his appetite. It is the same with fasting. The sweetest spiritual food—praised by the angel in his words to Tobit: "Prayer is good with fasting, almsgiving, and righteousness" (Tobit 12:8)—seasoned with the onion and garlic of self-will becomes repugnant to God. Its sweetness turns into the food foul, unworthy of the heavenly feast.

St John Chrysostom said, "Whoever fasts and sins does not fast for the glory of God, and he does not humble himself before God, instead contenting his own vanity." A disobedient self-will ruins everything, befouls everything. It becomes the extreme, inexorable calamity of all who fall away from God and are cast into the abyss of hell. The obstinacy and disobedience of these people is so strong that they become more and more cruel with time, and eventually their wills cannot eternally unite with God's will, being eternally opposed to it. Never will the sinful desire what God desires. They will not even be able to desire it.

Blessed Augustine describes their conditions eloquently, saying, "Their will is such that they desire the perdition of others and they are never capable of changing to a desire for others' good." Since those who will rule with Christ will find no trace of evil will within themselves, so the condemned, those cast out with the devil and his angels into the eternal fire, cannot have a good will. How terrible! What is more horrible to the imagination than hell, even if hell is nothing more than the necessity to remain always separate from, and irreconcilable with, God's all-holy will. O my God, help me, that I may reject my own will, and teach me always to do Your will (see Psalm 142:10).

 CHAPTER 21

Factors That Incline Us to Disobey God

Among the heavy sins with which the Lord rebuked Jerusalem, we find the following: "O Jerusalem, Jerusalem, the one who kills the prophets and stones those who are sent to her! How often I wanted to gather your children together, as a hen gathers her chicks under *her* wings, but you were not willing" (Matthew 23:37). The obstinacy of self-will is the source of all lawlessness. I wanted this, said the Lord, but you did not want it. Blessed Augustine once said, "I sighed so many times, being tied not by the iron of another hand, but by my own iron will. My enemy has seized my desire, and from it has wrought a chain with which he has bound me." Three evil qualities of our human will greatly contribute to our resistance to God. They are (1) bad habits, (2) a lack of patience (long-suffering), and (3) the inconstancy and fickleness of the desires of our self-will.

I

Blessed Augustine describes bad habits thus: "From evil will grows evil desire, and when a person frequently fulfills his desires, then the habit unnoticeably turns into a necessity to constantly feed that desire, and so the person becomes a slave to his passions." It is true that sometimes in this person a better-directed will awakens, as though the will is re-newed. This feeling occurs when a person turns to God in repentance for his sins, full of the desire to be at peace with his own conscience and God's will. However, this "new" will is powerless to defeat the old will by itself, because the old will has long become hardened, even petrified, by repetition.

Thus, I have within me two wills (every person does). One is old, the other new. One is carnal, the other spiritual, and they battle each other, cleaving my soul into two. More often the old takes the upper hand, since the new is still not habitual to me. So, when sin roots within me and becomes a typical occurrence, then I have no time to heal it and I find no place for repentance. Sin becomes incurable if I do not quickly heal myself with repentance, and then it will take a great deal of effort and discomfort to cut out the scars of the sin completely. Sometimes the sinner is not able to do this.

St Gregory the Great writes,

> When self-will turns into habit, then even though the soul wants to oppose it, it has no power to do so. For it falls again and again into the same sins, and they become as though bound to the heart with heavy chains. In our youth, it is easier for us to improve than in mature years, when we become dirty and the dirt turns to rust, like a bloody cauldron that has not been cleaned for a long time. To clean such a cauldron, we must work very hard until the hardened dirt and blood can be scoured and burned off. (cf. Ezekiel 24:11–12)

Truly, our old, habitual sins are hard to root out, becoming obstacles in our path to correction. As St John Chrysostom said, "There is nothing more difficult in the works of man than the torment of a years-long habit of sin." Therefore, Blessed Augustine counsels, "Sinner! Do not put off your repentance, lest your sins follow you into the next life and burden you eternally with an unbearable heaviness." Plato,[57] having noticed a youth often losing himself in gambling, sternly rebuked him. But the youth complained, "Why should I beware of such an insignificant thing?" Plato answered, "A bad habit is no insignificant thing."

II

The second quality that strengthens our self-will is a lack of patience. When we passionately desire to acquire something, and our desire does not come to fruition as quickly as we would like, we are immediately beside ourselves with anger, we complain, and we even become like the beasts. Often we hear the yelling of such impatient people: "I want this to happen immediately, and if it does not, then all hope is lost!"

King Saul was such a man. He did not want to wait for the coming of Samuel in order to bring his offering to God, and so he took on the role of the priest himself. Therefore, Samuel said to his face, "You have rendered it vain because you did not keep my commandments which the Lord commanded you. For now the Lord would have established your kingdom over Israel forever. But now your kingdom shall not stand" (1 Kingdoms 13:12–13). Often we act likewise before God, when our prayers or petitions are not answered quickly enough. Immediately, our minds weaken, we fall into despair, even if our petitions are as mad as the request to receive John the Baptist's head on a plate (Mark 6:24–25).

We lose all patience and fall into despair, but the Prophet Baruch encourages us, saying, "O my children, take courage, cry out to God, and He will deliver you from the power and the hand of the enemies" (Baruch 4:21). King Jehoiachin though he was in bondage for thirty-seven years received his freedom and his kingship.[58] He is a good example for us of the wisdom of waiting as long as necessary for God's help. Patient endurance is a great virtue, and it has a wondrous power to give us our desired gift, even after a very long time. Wise and wonderful are the words of Sirach:

> Accept whatever is brought upon you, and in exchange for your humiliation, be patient … Consider the ancient generations and see: Who believed in the Lord and was put to shame? Or who stood fast in His fear and was forsaken? Or who called upon Him and was overlooked? … Woe to you who have lost your patient endurance! What will you do when the Lord visits you? Those who fear the Lord will not disobey His words, and those who love Him will keep his ways." (Sirach 2:4, 10, 14–15)

The enemies of the Lord Jesus Christ mocked Him on the Cross in many different ways with the intention of dragging out his tortures without end. "If you are the Son of God, come down from the Cross." St John Chrysostom answers them: "He is the Son of God, and so He will not come down from the Cross" (Matthew 27:40). The long-suffering of Christ waited for the moment when His patience finally said, "It is finished!" (John 19:30). This is how our head—Christ—acted, and so we must do likewise, since we are the members of His body.

The will of the Heavenly Father must be accomplished in us continually, until our last breath. Truly blessed is he who, though troubled by many persecutions and afflictions, does not seek to be delivered from them, but endures everything to the bitter end, not desiring to come down from his Cross if it is not God's will to take him down from the Cross. Truly blessed is he who, casting himself into the abyss of God's goodwill, commits himself to the awesome and mysterious judgments of God with such faith that he is ready to endure sufferings willed by God not merely one week, not one month, but even until the day of judgment, or even unto the endless ages. Such a person is even ready to endure the torments of hell for the sake of God's will.

Such complete self-abnegation and faithfulness to the will of God supersedes any evil deed. Compared to it, rejecting dominion over a thousand worlds will seem insignificant. However, anyone who does not entrust himself completely to the will of God will never find peace within himself and will suffer internally. When God visits him through some kind of sorrow, he thinks his life is over, and this thought plunges him into the depths of grief. Such thoughts can lead even to suicide. Then he says to himself, "Now I have perished; there is no salvation in me. I am rejected by God and man."

No one desires to reach such a state, naturally. But in order to avoid it, to find peace in your heart and conscience, you must seek to acknowledge your own insignificance with a courageous and free heart. You must seek to reject yourself and the insignificant world, entrusting yourself wholeheartedly to God, your Creator and Saviour. This will preserve true peace in your soul. And since everything in our life depends exclusively on the will or permission of God for our benefit, it must be true that the hand of God sends both gifts and grief. Thus, we must accept both with a joyful and grateful heart. God is already on the path, He walks toward you, and He will not linger along the way. All you must do is wait patiently, for He will come.

III

The third sin that hardens us in opposition to God is our will's fickleness, the transitory nature of its desires. In our changeability, we rival even the moon. We change our desires every hour. In the morning we desire one thing, but by the evening we want something completely different, sometimes even the opposite of our earlier desire. We hardly ever resemble ourselves. This is natural for our will when it does not desire to submit to the wise, immutable, and all-encompassing law of the will of God, and so it worries constantly, attracted by quickly fading and transient things. And we foolishly think that this inconstancy of our will can banish our sorrow and depression, while in actual fact we only become ever more sorrowful and depressed.

We often labor in vain, receiving no benefit from it; we often contradict ourselves, even absurdly desiring an object and abhorring it at the same time. Our will and everything that comes of it—the "holiness of our life," so to speak—is not an unbreakable pillar standing on top of a high mountain, built on a firm foundation. No, rather our will is a house built on sand, which will fall apart at the slightest wind (see Matthew 7:26–27). Are you virtuous? That is good; continue to be virtuous. Do you make the right choices in difficult situations? I applaud you. But will you act thus for a long time, or for all time? Alas! How quickly we change, faster than any changes in weather, falling often into a pit of foulness and impurity. We shake like a leaf at the slightest wind; we are torn from the Tree of Life and we flutter about "winnowing with every wind and following every road, like a double-tongued sinner" (Sirach 5:9).

We are not the same person at any given moment. We contain within ourselves many people, each quite different from the next. It was said of Job that he was a "true" man. Blessed Jerome interprets this to mean that Job did not vacillate between the right and the left, appearing always inconstant, but he was a firm and unassailable man. We, on the other hand, are not "true men," but rather cease to be men at all, shedding all virtuous human acts like clothing. We are weak and inconstant in good deeds (I will speak more of this inconstancy of will in a later section).

Our free will is what makes us belong to ourselves. However, the perversion of our free will makes us belong to the devil, while the proper use of our free will makes us belong to God. However, those who would like to belong only to themselves—as gods who know good and evil—inevitably belong not only to themselves but also to the devil. This is simply a fact. Our own will makes us slaves of the demons, for it does not actually belong to itself. Our will cannot be fully independent until it submits completely to its Creator. This is a true saying, though terrifying: it would be better for us not to have been born if we insist on following our own will exclusively.

Louis de Blois wrote that Christ the Lord, having appeared to an ascetic maiden, said to her,

Know that all punishments that people meet in life depend on their own will. If their will was directed toward virtue and was truly obedient and harmonious with My will, then their labors, illnesses, sorrows, and other troubles were not punishments at all, for they bore them all with joy and a generous heart. These virtuous people were full of love for Me and firmly believed My will or My permission decreed all their trials for an unknown, but beneficial, reason.

The mind of such a person remains free during any physical suffering, and these sufferings are lessened by the thought that his will remains in all things obedient and consonant with God's will. Thus, the human spirit, having rejected its own will, finds peace and calm, though the person still remains in this world.

 CHAPTER 22

We Must Be Ready to Reject Ourselves and Submit Our Will to God Both during Times of Trouble and in the Hour of Our Death

During times of relative ease and minimal labor, we submit to the will of God often without a second thought. However, when it comes to matters of heavier importance—the loss of money, honor, health—here we see do-nothingness, contradictions, and a great insubordination of the human will. In such situations, we encounter our true desires or lack of desires. Why do we, weak ones, vainly battle against our circumstances? The will of God abides forever and will abide forever, like a high mountain. We cannot pull it to ourselves, but it will rather pull us to itself. Would we not laugh if someone were to tie a ship to a cliff, expecting the ship to move it? Instead, the ship would merely come closer to the cliff. Our foolishness is no less laughable if we, being dependent on God's will, try obstinately to pull God's will toward ourselves, wanting it to submit to us, and not the other way around.

I

There are some people who fulfill the law of God and instruct others to do likewise, and by doing so they consecrate their wisdom to the service of God. But there are also those who study the Law of God and instruct others with words, but when it comes to *acting* in the spirit of the Law, they prefer their own will over everything else. They coddle their own will and never renounce it for the sake of actually doing the commands of God.

In old times, God-fearing people greeted each other thus: "May God do good to you, and may He remember His covenant with Abraham,

Isaac, and Jacob, His faithful servants. May He give all of you a heart to worship Him and do His will with a strong heart and willing soul" (2 Maccabees 1:2–3).

Truly, those who prefer God's will only in situations where it does not contradict their own do not worship Him with a strong heart and willing soul. Wherever a situation arises that demands action to preserve riches, glory, honor, or life itself, such people stick to their own will obstinately. In these situations they show their true colors.

In ancient times, willing soldiers eagerly entered the army, promising to fight for the honor and health of their commanders, their kings, and their homeland. For this they were given honors, freedom, and lands of their own. If we, obstinate antagonists of God's will, would submit without complaint to His most high will, then we would receive God's mercy, authority, and the total freedom to eternally praise our Creator and God in heaven. Among the men of ancient times, such an obedient servant of God was King David, a pious, meek man always ready to set aside his own will. Even while living on this earth, King David praised the Lord and was grateful to Him for all misfortunes, saying, "In God have I put my trust; I will not fear what man can do unto me. In me, O God, are vows, which I will pay in Thy praise" (Psalm 55:12–13).

There is nothing more self-willed under the sun than the will of man. All the creatures of God wondrously submit and obey their Creator. Man alone freely acts according to his own will in all things. Whatever he wants, that he does, even if it contradicts the will of God and the hosts of heaven and earth combined. Human will that allows itself such contradiction with the will of God is the beginning and root of all troubles in all human organizations, whether familial, societal, or governmental.

This is how human will, perverted by obstinacy, acts. God says, "I want this to be done in the following way." But man answers brazenly, "Well, I don't want to do it that way." God says, "This is My will." Man answers, through his actions, "But my will does not agree with Yours!" And man does things as he pleases (this occurs whenever we act contrary to the Law of God). Then God says, "My Spirit will not be opposed by men forever; in their delusion they are carnal, and 'to be carnally minded is death …. Because the carnal mind *is* enmity against God; for it is not subject to the law of God, nor indeed can be' (Romans 8:6–7)."

Therefore, God said, "So their days shall be one hundred and twenty years" (Genesis 6:3), the time given by God for human repentance. Thus, if we abandon our resistance to God's will—this wicked *I want* or *I do not want*—sin and evil will simply cease to exist. In order to destroy sin already committed, there exists a single medicine—true repentance, that is, admission of guilt before God with a firm resolution never to repeat the sin. Repentance can be the best medicine, but only when a person, having stopped sinning, subjects his will to the will of God.

The action most appropriate for the human will is love, just like the eye is made to see and the ears to hear. Anyone who truly loves something or someone will eagerly dedicate himself completely to the object of his love with his whole soul and body. No heavy labor, no prolonged disease, nothing horrifying can tear him away from the object of his love. In the same way, a person truly dedicated to God accepts everything that pleases God—whether it is pleasant or difficult—because God gifts it to him. This is how our will must act during any difficulties that lie in our path, whether willed or permitted by God, including poverty, sickness, insults against our honor, or even death. King David was such a man, a man after God's own heart (1 Kingdoms 13:13).

II

In around 439 A.D., a certain bishop named Quodvultdeus (Latin for "what God wills") attended a local ecclesiastical council. By order of King Genseric[59], he was placed in an old boat with his clergy and left to die. But somehow, beyond all hope, the boat reached Naples successfully, where the bishop peacefully ended his life. Let all Christians have such a name!

A wicked person accedes to God's will when everything in life goes his way, with no troubles or sorrows. On the other hand, a person who constantly says with his whole heart, "Let it be with me as God wishes"—in poverty, sickness, dishonor, or even on the deathbed—accepts everything from God with gratitude. He does not refuse to accept losses of estates, loss of health, slander, or even the loss of his own life. He always says, "Let it be with me as God wishes," without asking, "Why this? Why now? Why must *this* be my death?" Instead, he is ready for anything.

Seneca once asked a question: "What is necessary to become a kind man?" He answered, "You must desire to be a kind man, and what can be kinder or better than what the wisdom of God desires and demands of us?" For whoever thinks otherwise, preferring to resist the will of God, I offer the following instructive words of the same Seneca:

You may be angry and aggrieved at your troubles, but you do not understand that there is nothing evil in these troubles except for the evil of your own anger and lack of patience. You say, "I am exhausted in that day when I sorrow, when some affliction attacks me. My family is sick; I lost my riches; my house burned down; troubles and cares abound from the fear of various calamities, epidemics, wars, and so on." Why do you grieve? All this is not new. It has always been thus, all this comes by itself and is soon forgotten. Truly, such things are inevitable, for everything occurs by the will and counsel of God, not by some blind chance or fate. If you believe me, I will reveal to you the secret of my own heart. In all troubles and unpleasant circumstances, I prepare myself not only to believe and submit without doubts to God, but also to be in agreement with Him at all times. I know that it must be thus, and I follow His holy and wise will not by necessity, but willingly. [Shame on us Christians, before this pagan, shame!] I have never encountered troubles that would excessively grieve or confuse me. There is no offering that I would ever give by necessity. All that you regret, all that you fear—these are our sacrificial offerings to life, from which we should not hope to be freed. We should not even pray to be freed from these things. Our heart must become well-inclined toward them. Everything that exists in the world exists by the will of God, and the same is true of the moral world. Everything in it is either willed or allowed by God; consequently, it must be so, and we must not contradict God in this, but we must submit to Him, and not dare to condemn the divine Essence.

It is a great thing not to oppose the order established by God in the general currents of human history, and better still to always do His commandments without complaining, eagerly obeying His will in all things. An incapable and despised coward is that soldier who reluctantly, fearfully enters the battle, sighing all the while. Therefore, we must also eagerly go to war with our desires and the aspirations of our perverted will that are contrary to God's. Whoever has completely committed himself to God is truly brave; conversely, cowardly is the one who wants to oppose the current of his own life, considering it evil or uncomfortable, desiring to improve the works of divine providence instead of improving himself. He despises the works of the Most High and His divine providence, and prefers everything to be done other than in God's way, rather than laboring to become wise and to correct his weakness. All this has placed us in an abnormal position. We do not want to live, but neither do we want to die. We are bored with life, but we fear death. Everything in our desires is inconstant and changeable. Even the most prosperous life is incapable of satisfying us.

III

It is absolutely necessary for our eternal blessedness to align our will with God's, as we have said numerous times before. A certain theologian goes further, saying that anyone who approaching his own death will find the mercy of God more by the works and merits of Christ the Lord, our Saviour, than by his own good deeds. Let him, therefore, place his hope in Christ's goodness and the intercession of the most blessed Theotokos Mary, and let him pray to the holy chosen ones of God. Let him call to mind the terrible tortures, open wounds, and shameful, bitter death of Christ. Let him remember Christ's unutterable Love for us sinners, for whom He gave Himself in sacrifice to the justice of God. Let the sick man plunge himself completely, together with his sins and his carelessness, into the immeasurable depths of Christ's inscrutable mercy. By doing this, he will bring himself as a living sacrifice for the honor and glory of God. Then he can ask God's help to strengthen his weakness, both in the hour of his death and after his passage into eternal life.

The person who has truly come to love God without hypocrisy, completely rejecting his self-will, will endure everything for the sake of God's honor and righteousness. He will not be cast after death into the fiery Gehenna, even if he bore the sins of the entire world on his shoulders. There is no more beneficial instruction for those preparing for death than this: let them commit themselves with their whole hearts to the will of God, with profound repentance for their sins, and with undoubting trust in God's mercy and Christ's saving sacrifice. For since no torture can touch God, the same can be said of the person who has entrusted his will to the will of God and has united with God in sincere love.

The best example of this was the Wise Thief, who was crucified together with Christ. With his whole heart he regretted his sins; he believed in the divinity of the crucified Christ, to Whom he entrusted his eternal fate completely, not asking for anything other than mercy and grace: "Lord, remember me when You come into Your kingdom" (Luke 23:42). If your weak nature is horrified and full of trepidation before the face of death, then lay all your sorrow and terror on the Lord, and immediately you will receive reliable support. The death of Christ will give you consolation in your own death. He, and many of His chosen, came before you, and you should not be slow to follow in their footsteps. The perishable body that you are now leaving is a poor garment. Why do you care if it is temporarily covered by earth and decomposes? At the end of time, this same body will come back to life, arise, and will be made immortal, imperishable, glorified, and illumined.

Also, you must not forget how ready for death were the ancient righteous men—Abraham, Isaac, Moses, David, and others like them—even though in their time the door to the heavenly kingdom was still shut. We read of this in the Pentateuch: God told Moses to climb Mount Nebo, where He showed him all the lands He had promised to the sons of Israel. Then "Moses the servant of the Lord died there in the land of Moab by the word of the Lord. Then He buried him in a valley in the land of Moab, opposite Beth Peor, but no one knows his grave to this day" (Deuteronomy 34:5–6). See how eagerly, by God's command, Moses, the friend of the Most High, accepted his death, even though he never entered the Promised Land. Instead he was carried away into a better, invisible land, the bosom of Abraham, where the souls of the righteous awaited the coming of Christ in peace and calm.

Jesus Christ threw open the doors to the heavenly kingdom for the faithful. Therefore, beloved Christian, seeing your imminent death, or even better far before that moment comes, overcome your own will completely and submit it to God's, giving yourself completely to God's direction. In any situation, repeat these words, "Let it be as pleases God."

IV

The desire to continue one's life and the opposite desire to quickly pass into the future life often exist simultaneously in people, leading to great confusion. The fear of death is present in nearly all people. Let us discuss this fear in order to calm ourselves and pacify our contradictory desires.

Everyone knows that all will die. No one disputes this. People agree they must die, but not now. They want to pay their due to nature, but not now. They have a desire to pass into the heavenly mansions, but later. How unfortunate and foolish of us! We madly say that we desire to be freed of our poverty, but not yet; we desire to be blessed and glorified, but we have yet to reach the place we think we should. Why do we create for ourselves such a high ladder to heaven, why do we add rungs to it, thinking we have plenty of time to climb slowly and lazily as we approach our death? Why do we desire a long life, thinking erroneously that many years of life will prepare for us a painless death? We must be ready to die now or tomorrow.

I know what deludes many people—when death knocks on the door, they think that a stupid creditor has come to collect payment before the day it is due. What a foolish comparison! The Lord of death determines our "due date." Why do you think an early death ever comes "before its time"? You were prepared long ago for death's coming by the knowledge of its inexorability, and you were already given a great deal of time to correct yourself. You will not be able to correct yourself any more than you already have, because you will always put off your improvement, and the more years you live, the more you will be unprepared for death. A long life has made a great many people greater sinners. The desire to avoid death for the sake of future repentance is its own kind of sin, for this repentance is never actualized in deed. The point is that the only kind of person who is able to improve himself is the one who is ready to die when it pleases God. God never wants anything evil, and He can even transform evil into good. Therefore, when God decides it is time for your death, He is doing you the greatest of favors, because He is limiting your ability to sin further. Let everyone abandon all doubts concerning a so-called "death before its time." Instead, let us say with our whole soul, "Let my death occur at the time and in the manner that most pleases God."

It will not be excessive to add the wonderful words of Seneca:

If you, having cast aside your delusion, will desire to know the truth, then you must come to admit that not everything you love and desire is beneficial to you, if you first do not train yourself to properly react to all misfortunes in your life, if you do not become convinced of the necessity of misfortunes, and if you do not admit that God's desires do not accord with yours. If you admit all this, you will come to say, "I used to think that a long life is a good thing, but God willed otherwise and it is better than it seemed to me." If you thus accord your will with the divine, you will do very well, and you will accept everything that happens with equanimity. An ill-natured man turns everything into evil, even when it appears to be good. A righteous man, one with an unblemished heart, has the power to ameliorate life's evils, lessening all that is unpleasant and heavy by the wisdom of his endurance. He accepts everything and endures everything in life. The good he accepts with gratitude and meekness, while the evil he endures calmly and bravely. Never, no matter what the calamity, does he speak evil. All unexpected sorrows he accepts with equanimity, considering himself a citizen and a warrior, and he does not refuse the labors and sacrifices that are proper to those callings. No matter what happens to him, whatever circumstances fate places before him, he does not despise his difficulties, but considers them to be appropriate and proper to himself, saying, "This situation is my own."

Are you cast into grief or have many troubles? May you bear them without complaint and murmuring against the providence of God and the goodwill of the Most High. As God wills, so let it be.

V

Even idol-worshipers understood all this! Yet we Christians either do not know this or do not act according to our knowledge. This is very sad! It is sad that we ignore something that is the foundation of all our hope and consolation. There is no greater consolation, no more reliable hope anywhere or in anyone, than in the almighty and unerring will of God. In all situations that test our will, we can only find a lessening of our burden and sure salvation if we run to God with a contrite heart and a living faith, with firm hope in His almighty aid.

The righteous Job, according to St John Chrysostom, was more pleasing to God and received a greater honor and reward for his meek endurance and his spare utterances than for all his great almsgiving. Job, deprived by Satan of all his riches and children, struck down by leprosy, said, "The Lord gave, and the Lord has taken away. As it seemed good to the Lord, so also it came to pass. Blessed be the name of the Lord" (Job 1:21). By these words Job was more pleasing to God than by his previous generosity to all and his great almsgiving.

Many other teachers say the same thing. It is more beneficial to endure insults and ridicule than even to do good deeds, for God does not require our good works, but only our obedience to His holy will (see Psalm 15:2).

Anyone who desires to diligently follow the will of God, whether he be healthy or sick, must thank God for everything and endure all trials patiently. The will of God that abides in us and for us is our only true good, our only happiness, our only salvation. When we are sick we should call a doctor and take whatever medicines he prescribes; however, we do this only with the hope that our improvement accords with the foresight of God and His will.

King Asa did not do this, and he was justly punished for that reason, for in his sickness he only turned to physicians and not to God, putting all his hope in their skill.[60] King Hezekiah acted more wisely, because he ascribed his healing not to medicine but to the help of God.[61] In our case, if the help of doctors comes to naught, or if the doctor incorrectly diagnoses our illness and we do not get better, then we should not hurry to foolishly cast about blame. Do not seek other reasons for your continued illness except this—it was not pleasing to God for you to get better. It pleased Him to prolong your illness.

St Lydia, a God-pleasing virgin, was tormented by so many sicknesses that it was difficult to look at her. She was a heaping mass of all possible diseases. However, she had such firm hope in God that she did not speak, act, or even think anything in opposition to God. She endured everything bravely, saying with Job, "Would that my request would come about, and the Lord would grant my hope. Let the Lord begin and wound me, but let Him not utterly destroy me"(Job 6:8–10). O Lord, let Thy will be my comfort.

In all trials, sorrows, and tribulations, complete submission of our will to the direction and disposition of the divine will give us the greatest joy.

PART V

THE MEANS BY WHICH A HUMAN WILL CAN LEARN TO ACT IN ACCORDANCE WITH THE DIVINE WILL

 CHAPTER 23

The Agreement between Human and Divine Will Cannot Occur without Complete Trust in God

Self-rejection, or our free submission to God's will, cannot occur if our faith in God is weak, if we do not have unflagging hope in Him. Consequently, we cannot follow God's will if we do not truly love Him. How can I ever act in agreement with another person if I do not trust him? And how can I trust a person if I am not absolutely sure that he will diligently and faithfully care for me? Therefore, it is appropriate to speak of our trust in God.

I

What is written in the Scriptures concerning trust in God? A certain sixteenth-century writer answered this question: "There is hardly a single chapter in the Scriptures where God does not promise all His faithful His grace-filled help and His providence over all."

The blessed King David, the best teacher concerning trust in God, praises it over all other virtues, saying from the fullness of his heart, "I will lay me down in peace, and also take my rest, for it is Thou, Lord, only, who has made me to dwell in hope" (Psalm 4:9). "The Lord is my firm foundation, and my fortress, and my deliverer; my God is my helper, and I will trust in Him, my defender, the horn also of my salvation, and my protector" (Psalm 17:3). "The Lord is my light, and my Saviour; whom then shall I fear? The Lord is the defender of my life; of whom then shall I be afraid? Though a legion were laid against me, yet shall not my heart be afraid; and though there rise up war against me, yet will I put my trust in Him" (Psalm 26:1, 3). "Whoso dwelleth in the help of the Most High shall abide in the shelter of the God of heaven" (Psalm 90:1).

"They that trust in the Lord are as mount Zion; he that liveth in Jerusalem shall never be shaken" (Psalm 124:1). "In Thee, O Lord, have I put my trust; let me never be confounded, but rescue me in Thy righteousness, and deliver me" (Psalm 30:1). How expansive was David's heart, full of love for God and hope in Him! He often drew inspiration from the divine source and reflected that treasure in his Psalms.

Like David, all wise and sagacious men zealously glorified the virtue of trust in God. Solomon, the inimitable model of wisdom, said, "Trust in God with all your heart, and do not exalt your own wisdom" (Proverbs 3:5). He does not praise all wisdom, but only wisdom that comes from the whole heart. The most zealous of the Apostles wrote, "Therefore humble yourselves under the mighty hand of God, that He may exalt you in due time, casting all your care upon Him, for He cares for you" (1 Peter 5:6–7). King David added, "O cast thy care upon the Lord, and He shall nourish thee; He shall never suffer the righteous to stumble" (Psalm 54:23). Solomon said, "In all your ways know wisdom [that is, God's wisdom] that she may cut a straight path for you" (Proverbs 3:6), and David added, "It is better to trust in the Lord, than to put any confidence in man" (Psalm 117:8).

Later in the Old Testament, the Prophet Jeremiah said,

Blessed is the man who puts his trust in the Lord, for the Lord shall be his hope. He shall be like a flourishing tree alongside the waters which spreads its roots toward the moisture. He will not fear when the burning heat comes, for He shall be like the root in a grove in the year of drought. He shall not fear, for he shall be like a tree that does not cease yielding its fruit. (Jeremiah 17:3–4)

Judas Maccabeus charged his fellow countrymen, "Understand from generation to generation that all who hope in the Lord will not be weak" (1 Maccabees 2:61)."Blessed are all they that put their trust in Him" (Psalm 2:12). "Stand by your covenant and attend to it, and grow old in your work ... trust in the Lord and remain at your work" (Sirach 11:18, 19). "Therefore let him who thinks he stands take heed lest he fall ... but God is faithful, who will not allow you to be tempted beyond what you are able" (1 Corinthians 10:12, 13). Remember, "Man shall not live by bread alone, but by every word that proceeds from the mouth of God" (Matthew 4:4), and "God is able to raise up children to Abraham from these stones" (Matthew 3:9). Everything is possible to God. He can save us equally well in serious and in insignificant dangers.

II

Amaziah, the king of Judah, borrowed one hundred thousand brave warriors and one hundred talents of silver from Israel. But a man of God came to him and said, "King, the army of Israel will not go with you, for the Lord is not with Israel, nor with any of the sons of Ephraim; and if you try to be strong in battle, the Lord will cast you down before the enemy, for the Lord has power to strengthen and to overthrow." Amaziah then asked the man of God, "'What shall we do about the hundred talents I gave the army of Israel?' And the man of God answered, 'The Lord can give you more than this.'" Amaziah trusted God and listened to the man of God, and with God's help destroyed twenty thousand men of his enemy without help from Israel. This is what it means to trust God and not human strength (see 2 Chronicles 25).

Thomas More,[62] a pious and enlightened man, was imprisoned for refusing to assent to King Henry VIII's marriage to Anne Boleyn. To his daughter Margaret's many questions addressed to him in prison, he answered,

> Nothing can occur if it is not pleasing to God. Everything that God wants must be very good, even if it seems to us unpleasant. Margaret, I do not doubt God's goodness, even though I feel myself weak and powerless. Even if in utter fear I would find myself rejected and ready to cast myself into the abyss, I will remember holy Peter, who was already sinking in the sea by his own lack of faith, and like him I will call to Christ the Saviour: Lord! Save me, and command me to walk on the water toward You. I believe and hope that He will not despise me, that He will give me His hand and will not let me drown. If He does let me go, to make me an even closer intimate of St Peter in his rejection [that is, his denial of Christ], then I will truly say that I would still not lose hope in God's mercy to the repentant. I would cry bitterly concerning my fall and He would look at me and say, "Peter, do you love Me?" I love You, I love You, I love You with all my heart, Christ, Lord! I will cleanse my conscience and I will wash away the sin of my fall. This earthly life I offer in sacrifice to the glory of Your holy name. In this I am fully sure. God will not abandon me. Amen.

What a truly Christian, wise reflection this is! For in all man's actions, the providence of God is present: "Such as bless him shall possess the land, but such as curse him shall be rooted out. By the Lord are a man's steps directed, and he shall well like His way; though he fall, he shall not be harmed, for the Lord upholdeth him with His hand" (Psalm 36:22–24). Thus, before all else, we must have firm hope in God.

III

Jesus Christ often remembered and praised this single unwavering trust in God. The divine Teacher offered many examples taken from nature: the birds, the lilies, our hair, and even his unfaithful servants, in order to confirm in us the undoubting trust in Him in all things:

> Consider the ravens, for they neither sow nor reap, which have neither storehouse nor barn; and God feeds them. Of how much more value are you than the birds? And which of you by worrying can add one cubit to his stature? If you then are not able to do the least, why are you anxious for the rest? Consider the lilies, how they grow: they neither toil nor spin; and yet I say to you, even Solomon in all his glory was not arrayed like one of these. If then God so clothes the grass, which today is in the field and tomorrow is thrown into the oven, how much more will He clothe you, O you of little faith? ... For all these things the nations of the world seek after, and your Father knows that you need these things. (Luke 12:24–28, 30)

What a variety of images the Lord used to instruct His disciples, teaching them to trust in God always! Thus, desiring to feed five thousand people gathered around him in the desert, he said to Philip, "'Where shall we buy bread, that these may eat?' But this He said to test him, for He Himself knew what He would do" (John 6:5–6). In a similar manner He, desiring to strengthen four thousand people with food, called His disciples to Him and asked them how much bread they had. The disciples, still so weak in faith, doubted they would be able to find the sufficient number to feed everyone.[63]

O wondrous disciples! God can do anything. He Who commands us to have complete and constant trust in Him will not fail us in this. The providence of God is unerring, and He does not desire to leave us who trust in Him in need. God will fulfill all His promises, and there are many historical examples from all ages that prove this. Let none of us fall into despair, but instead let us raise our hope to the Almighty One, laying on Him all our desires and sorrows! He will arrange everything for our benefit.

IV

King David prayed to the Lord God, "O Lord, my Lord, who am I and what is my house, that You have loved me even until now? O Lord, my Lord, this is very insignificant before You, yet You spoke on behalf of the house of Your servant, even this for the distant future" (2 Kingdoms 7:18–19). A certain writer explains these words in the following way. God always takes care of the humble and meek by an unchangeable law, while the proud He opposes. This law is as eternal as God Himself, and for the human race it has been in effect beginning with Adam. Every person must keep this covenant with God—to love and revere Him with your whole heart, soul, and thought. And the Lord will always take care and preserve you. For to Whom do we cry out, "Our Father, Who art in the heavens"? Truly, this almighty, endlessly rich, and generous Father will illumine us greatly with His grace.

Blessed Jerome said that if even the smallest animals do not die without God the Creator's will, and if His forethought encompasses all of creation, then of course we who are immortal should not fear that the providence of God will leave us. Why do we not have complete trust in him? Why do we not have courageous hearts, worthy of such a Father? Do not despair. What does it matter if our home is frightfully poor? We have a Lord Who is extremely wealthy; He will never let us die from hunger. Are countless hosts of enemies arrayed against us? We have the indomitable Commander Who can send all the forces of heaven and earth against our enemies. Are we cursed and slandered by everyone around us? Let us direct our gaze to heaven, and God, the most just Judge, is ready to justify us, so that we never need fear earthly slanderers and judges. For no human power can defeat God, and no earthly power can overcome His unutterable mercy.

Does someone believe unconditionally in God? God will give him even more. Does someone trust without any doubt that God will listen to his petitions? God will give him more from his endless treasuries and will bless him in all things, for it is enough merely to entrust God with all our hope, and to not vacillate with doubts, and He will give us the greatest gifts and riches. The more we trust in Him, the more heavenly gifts we will receive. We often see that not only can our trust not compare with God's goodness, but His goodness exceeds and supersedes our trust greatly.

V

Blessed Augustine speaks more expansively of what we mentioned in a previous section in his explanation of Psalm 145. "Blessed is he that hath the God of Jacob for his helper, whose hope is in the Lord his God; Who made heaven and earth, the sea, and all that therein is" (Psalm 145:5–6). If God created not only the heavens and the earth, but everything in them, then He also created you, and not only you, but the birds, the grasshoppers, and the worms. All these God created, and He cares for them all. Do not say, "I do not belong to God." Your soul and your body belong to Him, for God created both. Perhaps you say that the word of God did not notice you in this countless multitude of created beings? How did He not, since He has counted all the hairs on your head?

Instead, you say, "Too often we are so bowed down by troubles and deprived of all joy and help that it is not strange that our faith is weak." Blessed Augustine also has an answer to this (and please pay great attention to his words). If you want nothing to occur contrary to your own will, then admit that everything occurs by God's will, by His providence, by His direction, by His command. If we do not understand why and for what reason something happened, then let us trust ourselves to His providence, for nothing happens for no reason. The providence of God teaches us not to disdain events that seem to happen for no reason, but instead we should search for the benefit in every such event. Whenever our reason fails to do this, our faith must help us understand that nothing happens without a reason, even if that reason is hidden from us.

Even in times past there have been events inscrutable for contemporaries that only became understandable later. But even this hiddenness is for our benefit, because it teaches us humility or it shows us the insignificance of our arrogance. As an example of this, Blessed Augustine offers the ant and the bee:

Who so wisely designed the members of the ant and the bee's body, that they each have their own behavior, their manner of life, and their work? Investigate and examine only one of these smallest of living creatures. Every one of them has everything that is necessary for life: a wise arrangement of limbs, an awakening to life that moves it, a desire to avoid death, a love for its own life, a desire for sweet things, an ability to avoid dangers. Each acts in fully developed behaviors and protects itself in whatever way it can. Who gave the mosquito its sharp nose, by which it sucks out our blood and poisons it? How thin it is, that small dagger! Who arranged it and created it thus? If you examine the smallest things, you come to the greatest wonder and fear, and so you praise the Most High. Thus also you must come to fear your own falls into sin and the righteous Judge Who gives to each according to his deeds. Do not attach your heart to anything earthly, but raise it up instead, laying all your hope on God alone, and be sure that every event and trouble will help you improve, for who trusted in the Lord and was ashamed? (See Sirach 2:10) "Blessed are all they who put their trust in Him."(Psalm 2:12)

 CHAPTER 24

The Essence of Trust in God

How pathetic and pitiful are we all! How little we know of God! We receive hardly any of God's light, little more than a ray peeking through a crack. We only know that God is the greatest good, so immeasurably great that everything that it is possible to ask of Him (without transgressing His law), we can receive from Him through humble prayer, but only in His own good time and only if we will be patient and hopeful. With an exalted love from the heart for Him, we must trust without doubting in Him, and then we will instill in ourselves the habit of hoping and silently awaiting the salvation of God. Patient waiting (during all offences or while awaiting God's help) is a precious stone for the hopeful. Wherever they turn, they will succeed (see Proverbs 17:9). "The Lord is good to those who wait for Him, to the soul who will seek Him" (Lamentations of Jeremiah 3:22). What is the essence of this trust in the Lord? On what it is founded?

I

At first, let us note that trust is greater than mere hope, and it supersedes it, for trust is firmer than hope; it is a complete hope that is unassailable by any doubts. Seneca expressed the difference between these two in the following words: "I have hope in you, but not trust; trust is a quality that encompasses the entire activity of man." The one who trusts in God will wisely preserve this trust within himself in situations of both great or little importance. In every moment of his life, he believes genuinely, with his entire soul, that God in His time will not abandon His beloved servant. Here is an example.

King David established a school to instruct warriors, and he commanded that the Jews be taught archery, as we see in the Scriptures. Before this military school was ever built, Jonathan was already greatly skilled in the art of war, as we hear in David's own praise of his friend: "From the blood of the slain, from the fat of the mighty, the bow of Jonathan did not return in vain" (2 Kingdoms 1:22). It is not easy to wound a man who is covered in a helmet and mail, but the arrows of Jonathan could even pierce armor.

Trust in God is like the bow of Jonathan. It reaches the heart of God and pierces it, never returning without God's mercy for those who trust in Him. Counted together, there were thirty-nine kings of Judah and Israel; but how many of them deserved to pierce the heart of God by their trust? No more than three or four out of thirty-nine: David, Hezekiah, Josiah, and perhaps Jehoshaphat, if only he had completely destroyed the altars in the high places.[64] The hearts of these kings were truly righteous before God and filled with undoubting, firm trust in God.

When a great multitude of Moabites and Ammonites united in war against Jehoshaphat, he was unable to muster a sufficient force to repel the enemy. He turned with great trust to God and gave himself completely to prayer. He declared a general fast in all Judea and a service at the Temple to beg God's mercy and to ask the counsel of the people. He concluded his prayer with the following words: "Lord God, will you not judge them? For we have no power against this great multitude coming against us. We do not know what to do to them, but our eyes are upon You" (2 Chronicles 20:12). And the help of God was immediately revealed. In this very congregation was found a pious man named Jahaziel, on whom the Spirit of God descended, and he said, "Listen, King Jehoshaphat, all Judah and inhabitants of Jerusalem! Thus says the Lord to you: 'Do not be afraid nor dismayed because of this great multitude, for the battle is not yours but God's … You will not need to fight in this battle. Understand that the salvation of the Lord is with you'" (2 Chronicles 20:15,17).

Encouraged by these words, the king led his armies against the enemy, and in order to prevent his people from running away in fear from such a mighty host of enemies, he, a brave and unbeatable commander, encouraged the hearts of his warriors through his own trust in God, saying, "Hear me, Judah and inhabitants of Jerusalem: trust in the Lord your God, and you shall be established; trust His prophet and you shall prosper" (2 Chronicles 20:20). Immediately, an incredible thing happened in the field of battle. He commanded the choirs of Temple chanters to be placed on the front lines, so that they could walk out before the armed warriors and glorify the Lord, singing the Psalm, "Give thanks to the Lord, for His mercy endures forever" (2 Chronicles 20:21).

What a marvelous thing! A king with his army enters the battle like a bishop entering the church with his clergy. Truly this was an incredible event, even laughable in terms of military strategy. Who would place the most vulnerable, the unarmed, before the armed warriors in battle? But God was with Jehoshaphat, walking with him, since he armed himself with the unbeatable armor of trust in God. While the singers praised God, the Lord invisibly incited a quarrel among the Ammonites and the Moabites. The enemies began to kill each other, until the last man lay dead. When the army of Jehoshaphat arrived at an elevated place, they saw only the bodies of their enemies lying on the earth. There was not a single Ammonite or Moabite who escaped death (2 Chronicles 20:23–24).

On the place of this miraculous victory, Jehoshaphat found a great deal of rich booty—expensive clothing and precious vessels—and he ordered his people to take all of it. For three days they gathered it, so great were the spoils (2 Chronicles 20:25). Do you see how mighty and strong genuine trust in God is? In all situations in life, it is mightier than all other weapons. In a word, it is undefeatable.

II

If in all our actions we must trust completely in God, then of course this is especially necessary when we pray or when we endure some kind of trouble. I will speak more of enduring troubles in the next chapter, but concerning prayer I will speak here.

A certain eloquent orator once said,

> The prayer of many people is either frightened, lazy, or foolish. Frightened prayer never reaches heaven, because fear confuses the mind so much that prayer not only does not ascend, but it should not even be offered. Lazy prayer ascends, but as it rises it loses power due to despair or lassitude, and eventually it fades. Foolish prayer reaches heaven, but falls from there and returns to the petitioner, because it meets an obstruction. Not only does it not receive mercy from God, but it also irritates God with its foolishness. Genuine prayer, which is humble and ardent, rises up without hindrance to heaven and cannot but be answered. Therefore, first of all, our prayer must be genuine.

How many of us, before we even begin praying, already doubt—the Lord will not hear me; I will not ask Him concerning what I need, for my cries will be in vain. Such a prayer is a poor emissary to God. No sooner has it left the lips than it falls back to earth, finding no wings on which to fly. Christ Himself teaches us about the trust we must have for our prayer to be receptive to God:

> There was in a certain city a judge who did not fear God nor regard man. Now there was a widow in that city; and she came to him, saying, "Get justice for me from my adversary." And he would not for a while; but afterward he said within himself, "Though I do not fear God nor regard man, yet because this widow troubles me I will avenge her, lest by her continual coming she weary me." (Luke 18:2–5)

This is what firm trust is. It constantly says, "today the judge will hear me." When the judge did not listen to her, the widow said, "Not today but tomorrow certainly he will defend me, or on the third day, or in a month, or during the course of this year." Thus, the persistent trust of the widow finally triumphed. Christ offered us this parable as proof that constant petition (i.e., prayer) has power even over the actions of an unjust judge. How much more, then, does it have power and efficacy to call down the mercy of the Heavenly Father! Our mind, like the widow, has a great many enemies. Why is it then so slow to seek help? Why does it not turn to the all-righteous Judge, revealing all its needs and obstacles, asking Him to take care of them with complete trust in Him? Will God not protect His chosen, those who call to Him day and night? Will he not immediately punish their persecutors if this is for their benefit?

King David, inciting us to turn to God for help, said, "Open thy way unto the Lord, and put thy trust in Him, and He shall bring it to pass" (Psalm 36:5). What are you afraid of? Why do you wallow in unbelief? Are you subjected to slander or rebuke? Give it to the Lord, and He shall bring it to pass (i.e., he will fix everything for your benefit and protect you). Does your flesh not follow the spirit? Pray with tears, and He shall bring it to pass. Are you attacked by temptations or do the snares of the enemy never leave you at peace? Call on God's help, and He shall bring it to pass. In everything that you do, trust God, and He will bring it to pass.

III

Let us continue speaking about prayer. Jesus Christ offers us yet another example, saying,

Which of you shall have a friend, and go to him at midnight and say to him, "Friend, lend me three loaves; for a friend of mine has come to me on his journey, and I have nothing to set before him"; and he will answer from within and say, "Do not trouble me; the door is now shut, and my children are with me in bed; I cannot rise and give to you"? I say to you, though he will not rise and give to him because he is his friend, yet because of his persistence he will rise and give him as many as he needs. So I say to you, ask, and it will be given to you; seek, and you will find; knock, and it will be opened to you. (Luke 11:5–9)

There is nothing more pleasant to God than when we turn to Him with such trust, asking Him for help, in the same way as our friend does in the parable. No person should ever think that it is too late to call upon God; no one should ever despair of God's salvation. Look at how a poor beggar, in order to receive a crumb or piece of bread, patiently stands at the doors or runs after those who sit on carts and humbly bows before them, asking for alms. What should we then do when we ask for the mercy and forgiveness of the generous, all-merciful God? We must be constant and patient when we do not quickly receive what we asked for, and we must have undoubting trust that God will not abandon our petitions without beneficial consequences for us.

John, the beloved disciple of Christ, writes, "Now this is the confidence that we have in Him, that if we ask anything according to His will, He hears us. And if we know that He hears us, whatever we ask, we know that we have the petitions that we have asked of Him" (1 John 5:14–15).

If a son asks for bread from any father among you, will he give him a stone? Or if he asks for a fish, will he give him a serpent instead of a fish? Or if he asks for an egg, will he offer him a scorpion? If you then, being evil, know how to give good gifts to your children, how much more will your heavenly Father give the Holy Spirit to those who ask Him! (Luke 11:11–13)

However, it often happens that we foolish ones ask neither for bread, nor for fish, nor for an egg, for we often do not know what we should pray for. However, "the Spirit Himself makes intercession for us with groanings which cannot be uttered" (Romans 8:26). If God, protecting us from perdition, does not answer our prayers, sometimes we lose patience and begin to complain.

We say, "He does not see us or hear us!" O, foolish ones! Do not parents often prevent their children from eating an unripe apple or other harmful food, even if children really want it? Do not these same parents also leave many thousands as an inheritance for their children in their will?

The Apostle Paul prayed diligently to God to be spared from a certain temptation of the flesh, thinking that he was asking a wise and beneficial thing. However, God did not fulfill his petition. Instead, God told him, "My grace is sufficient for you, for My strength is made perfect in weakness" (2 Corinthians 12:9). When we do not receive what we asked for, let it be known to us that this is done either because the fulfillment of our petition would be harmful to us, or because it would be more beneficial to us to wait a long time for our prayer to be answered. There is a third possibility: God has already foreseen a far better time for the fulfillment of our petitions, inspiring greater trust in us, encouraging us to constantly pray for His goodness. However, to ask something cruel or inhuman of God (such as the death of one's enemy) is not allowed for two reasons. First of all, God, our merciful Father, will always reject such a petition. Secondly, as the righteous Judge, He will turn our curse against ourselves, and our prayer will be counted as a great sin (see Psalm 108:7).

> Let it be known that every prayer uttered with obedience and submission to God's will is always heard, and we will either receive what we asked for, or God will give us something else that is even better for us. This should greatly strengthen our trust in God. Everything that we ask of God—if it accords with His will—He will hear our petition and give it to us.

 CHAPTER 25

By What Means We Can Confirm within Ourselves a Firm Trust in God, Especially in Times of Trouble?

A helmsman proves his mettle during a storm, a warrior during battle, and an ascetic during temptations. No one knows what he is capable of, if he is not first tested in battle. In order to come to know oneself, one must pass through trials. How can a person do his work as it must be done if he does not first study its theory, then practice it until he becomes proficient? Some even willingly give themselves up to troubles, testing whatever virtues might be hidden within themselves during times of prosperity. Great men rejoice in sorrows and labors, as brave warriors do in battle. All valor desires a time of testing. It travels a straight path, battling whatever troubles lie in the way, and these victories are part of valor's glory.

Therefore, God allows His chosen to labor, even to suffer, and He often gives them an opportunity to accomplish something valorous and generous, requiring self-sacrifice. This also means that any unpleasantness in this life is in some sense inevitable. How can we know how much we have come to trust in God if everything always goes according to our desires? How will we know that we can love poverty if we are always rich? How will we know that we have the courage to endure dishonor and envy if we spend our entire lives in joy with no sorrows? Truly, in order to come to know ourselves, trials are necessary. It is absurd to pray in this way during times of ease and comfort: "The Lord is my firm foundation and my fortress, and my deliverer, etc." (Psalm 17:3), especially when the poor man says at the same moment, "I know I will not die of hunger this week, because I have a bag full of bread." Even when he has no hope, he says this.

Trust in what we already have is not trust at all, for if we see it in our hand, what do we have to hope for? But when we trust in something we do not see, we wait for it with patience (see Romans 8:24–25). Therefore, trust in God becomes all the more evident and vivid when we endure all our troubles bravely.

I

There are two truths I will present as the foundation of our discussion:

1. It is true that everywhere in the world, in all situations and all social circumstances, our life is subject to trials and troubles. It is not possible to live otherwise. Even Christ, our God, predicted this: "In the world you will have tribulation; but be of good cheer, I have overcome the world" (John 16:33). All who desire to live piously in Christ Jesus will be persecuted (see 2 Timothy 3:12).

2. We must not forget the words of St Paul: "God is faithful, who will not allow you to be tempted beyond what you are able, but with the temptation will also make the way of escape, that you may be able to bear it" (1 Corinthians 10:13).

When God punishes you, the punishment is always much less than you deserved. Why then do you not humbly submit to Him? What sort of foolishness do you spread about, saying, "Have I done anything to deserve prison or exile?" When people treat me like this, will I get drunk to drown my worries? Why do I torture myself? Why do I not give myself the consolation of God, since I am burdened with such troubles? This is what it means to betray oneself to one's enemies; why do you not put your trust in the friends of God? Come to your senses and call them to your aid! Trust in God and humbly submit to Him. Wherever there is trust in God, there our will is firmly tied to God's. On the contrary, it is very vile and repugnant when the all-good Lord God desires to correct His errant servant with a light punishment, but the servant answers that he does not want the punishment because he did not deserve even a light blow from his Master. Abandon your madness. Trust in God and live in your proper place, not breaking your oaths and responsibilities. Do not envy the actions of a sinner. Believe in the Lord, and remain in your work (see Sirach 11:19–20).

Blessed Jerome, encouraging us to trust in God, noted that there are a great many flattering attractions in the world, countless snares. But we must cry out to God, "Though a legion were laid up against me, yet shall not my heart be afraid, and though there rise up war against me, yet will I put my trust in Him"

(Psalm 26:3). If, by the inspiration of the evil spirit, thoughts begin to arise in your heart, confusing you, and you begin to be attracted by them, then your reason and conscience will ask, "What must I do?" Elisha answers, "Do not fear, for many witnesses speak for us" (4 Kingdoms 6).

St Ambrose wrote,

> Wherever there is great calamity, there you will also find great help, for God is our most powerful helper in times of plenty and in times of sorrow. God transformed a stone into a container of honey and oil, for God fed the Israelites in the desert with honey from the rock and oil from the solid rock (see Deuteronomy 32:13). Hundreds and thousands of nations have been refreshed and fed by Him from pure sources in places where not even the smallest bird could satisfy its thirst. God has winged servants, very quick, faster than the winds, through whom He sends food to His chosen ones. If we lay our heart's trust on God, He will be with us. He will never leave us.

However, often our inquisitive mind raises many questions like the questions of Gideon, who asked the angel, "If the Lord is with us, why then have these evils come upon us? And where are all His miracles which our fathers told us about? ... But now the Lord has driven us out ..." (Judges 6:13). If God is with us, why do many evils come upon us?

II

A certain wise teacher, having seen his Abba aggrieved by something, wanted to cheer him with the words of the Psalms: "Let not the water-flood drown me [you], neither let the deep swallow me [you] up, and let not the pit shut her mouth upon me [you]" (Psalm 68:16). Let your humble-mindedness become used to being always triumphant over evil, and defeat evil with good, and you will be victorious if you lay a firm hope in God and will patiently endure your troubles to the end. It is better for you to humbly give yourself up to the mighty hand of God and to not in any way oppose the direction of the Most High. Even though the devil attacks you cruelly and is armed mightily against you, without God's command he can do no harm to anyone. He cannot even touch the swine without God's permission (see Luke 8:32).

Why should we fear the serpent of hell, who is tied with iron chains, who is fearful to no one, who can harm no one except the one who freely approaches him? But I have heard some people say this concerning themselves: "I suffer so much that it seems to me that I am already cast into hell." O Christian, is this why you lose your trust in God? Believe me, you are not the only one to suffer thus. There are many who, though they suffer truly hellish pain, come out of this hell unharmed. Tobit, a righteous man of blameless life, found himself in such a bitter situation, but he did not lose trust in God, and having been heard, he praised God in the following words: "For He scourges, and is merciful. He brings down into Hades, and leads up. There is no one who will escape His hand" (Tobit 13:2).

In order to teach the holy Apostles how to be generous and care for others as much as for themselves, Christ the Lord took them with Him into a ship and allowed a storm to strike them. Tossed back and forth among terrible waves, the disciples of Christ thought that they had already perished and were even more afraid when they thought that Christ was deeply asleep. So they began to wake Him, saying, "Save us, for we perish!" Then Christ said to them, "Why are you fearful, O you of little faith?" Where is your faith? What can harm a sleeping person when God is wakeful over him and never sleeps? Here it becomes obvious that trust in God, especially amid the worst calamities, triumphs always, while everyone else trembles in fear (see Matthew 8:24–27).

What terrible calamities struck the righteous Job! His enemies took all his cattle. Whatever was left was destroyed by fire from heaven. All of his children were crushed by a collapsed house. Job himself was not only covered in gangrenous wounds but also was torn apart by rebukes from his wife and friends. Everything was lost. All that remained was his trust in God. He was abandoned on a dung heap amid worms that ate his flesh. His many wounds oozed from his many wounds, but he did not wipe them off with a cloth, but scraped them with a bone. And still, he bravely exclaimed, "Though He slay me, yet will I trust Him" (Job 13:15 NKJV).

And this sorrowful spectacle was soon transformed into the greatest joy and imperturbable calm. How often a grievous beginning is crowned with a good end!

In the same way every person who is buffeted by the waves of sorrows should be brave and magnify his trust in God. How do you act, O person of weak faith, when a strong downpour catches you in an open place? Yes, if this happens in a village or town you have nearby cover from the rain, and in a field you can hide under a tree. But now, during the storm of sorrows, your safest haven is trust in God. You will never find a more pleasant resting place in the desert of the world, or a better haven from the rain, or a warmer steam room during the deep freeze, or a more sure protection in any danger than trust in the Lord. If you trust in Him, you will be like a sailor who prepares everything for a good voyage, but awaits the necessary winds from God. So we should be in our chosen calling, and God will take care of everything. Man proposes, but God disposes, as the wise proverb has it. Thus, you should prepare everything that your work requires, but let God accomplish your work to the best possible end by His holy and just will. And if something difficult occurs, endure it for as long as necessary, and wait, like a farmer, for the good harvest. Trust in God!

III

Some may say that to endure evils from an enemy is not that difficult. But the worst kind of evil one can think of, a kind that is unbearable, is when one has to suffer from people who previously seemed to be kind to you. This is beyond all endurance. It disturbs us and grieves us completely.

But what is so new and unusual in this? It was always thus in the world. In the times of the Apostles, it was a commonplace occurrence to judge unfairly against victims while maintaining the appearance of justice. It was usual to hide flattery in the heart and cover it with a mask of justice. It was just as usual to endure offences and injustices, to suffer from one's friends, family, and benefactors. True are the words of Christ, foretelling the last days of the earth: "For from now on five in one house will be divided: three against two, and two against three. Father will be divided against son and son against father, mother against daughter and daughter against mother, mother-in-law against her daughter-in-law and daughter-in-law against her mother-in-law" (Luke 12:52–53).

Moreover, you will see how good deeds are transformed into evil; you will see criminals who should be hunted at the expense of health and life left in peace. David was persecuted by his closest counselor Ahithophel, and by his father-in-law Saul, and even by his own son Absalom. And who killed the Lord Christ? Not the pagans, but the sons of Israel, beloved of God. As it says in the prophecy of Zechariah, "What are these wounds in the middle of your hands? And he will say, 'Those with which I was wounded in the house of my beloved'" (Zechariah 13:6).

It is even more tragic to consider how much Jesus Christ had to suffer at the hands of His own disciples. Judas Iscariot—whose feet Jesus washed only a few hours before, who Jesus included in the Mystical Supper—betrayed his Lord to His enemies. The beloved Peter rejected Him during His passion. The rest of the disciples abandoned Him and fled. Why are we amazed? "A man's enemies are all the people of his own house" (Micah 7:6). But the one who trusts in God defeats all this handily. How, do you ask, can we have such glorious triumph? Here are six short examples.

1. If you find yourself in a difficult situation, you must immediately turn to God and open up your heart to Him concerning your suffering and your unendurable pain. In this regard, we all sin grievously. When troubles and tribulations begin, we immediately complain and try to win the pity of everyone around us. God alone we forget. He is always the last one we run to for help. By forgetting God, we turn order into chaos. David acted otherwise. He said, "I lifted up mine eyes unto the hills; from whence will my help come? My help cometh even from the Lord, Who hath made heaven and earth" (Psalm 120:1–2). Every person who does not act thus in the beginning of every calamity is immediately disturbed by anger, sickness, or confusion to such a degree that he is completely beside himself. Therefore, at the beginning of even the smallest trouble, immediately call to the Lord, saying, "Lord! What do You command me to do?" Immediately you will hear the answer of the interpreter of God's will: "Wait thou on the Lord; be of good courage, and let thine heart stand firm, and wait thou on the Lord" (Psalm 26:14). Cast away all evil thoughts and resist them with all your strength. Destroy them and constantly keep in mind the words, "Lord, what do You command me to do?"

2. Be silent, and at least rein in your mouth and tongue if you are unable to hold back your thoughts. Follow the good counsel of King David: "I said, I will take heed to my ways, that I sin not with my tongue; I kept my mouth as it were with a bridle, when the sinner stood up against me. I was mute and held my peace; I kept silent, even from good words …" (Psalm 38:1–2). Therefore, be silent, for if in trouble and persecution you will not rein in your tongue, know that more trouble will not be long following, for you will trip over your own words. Therefore, it is always safer to be silent, especially concerning the things that you hate and your enemies. Can you say nothing good about them? At least say nothing evil. Let your conscience be your consolation, and let the righteous God be your judge. Your enemies and their evil intentions are not hidden from Him. Trust God and be silent.

3. When you turn to God and learn to be silent, dedicate yourself completely to God's will and sincerely submit to it. Thank God that He willed to allow you to suffer innocently. If you deserved to suffer, then your guilt will be washed away by your endurance, and you will reveal a lack of malice within yourself. Whoever submits to God's will holds God in his own embrace, as it were, saying together with Jacob as he wrestled with the angel, "I will not let you go unless you bless me" (Genesis 32:26). If two friends grab each other

firmly as their boat capsizes, both must fall into the water. In the same way, it is necessary to intimately unite with God and submit to His all-righteous will in all misfortunes, humbly saying, "Do with me as You will, O my God. I will not let You go. I will take You into the depths of the sea, into the very waves surrounding me. The more I trust in You, the less I hope in myself."

IV

4. When the grievous storm calms somewhat, immediately pray to the Holy Mother of God, the holy angels, and the saints. Tell them your needs and your troubles. It is not enough to do this once. Repeat it again and again for many days, even for many years, if your work demands this. Do not stop opening the right hand of God with your prayers, even if He has closed it shut. After hearing Sennacherib's threat, King Hezekiah immediately went into the Temple and unscrolled Sennacherib's words before the face of the Lord and prayed, having in his mouth and heart constant trust in God. He said,

> Lord God of Israel, enthroned on the cherubim, You alone are God in all the kingdoms of the earth. You made heaven and earth. O Lord, incline Your ear and hear. O Lord, open Your eyes and see. Hear the words Sennacherib sent to reproach the living God ... Now O Lord our God, save us from his hand, so that all the kingdoms of the earth will know that You alone are the Lord God. (4 Kingdoms 19:15–16, 19)

Every person who has been burdened by sorrow should uncover his own scroll before the Lord, and whatever sorrow and unpleasantness he may experience, he should offer them to the gaze of the righteous Judge and merciful Father. If your petitions will not be accepted, think of the inscrutability of God's judgments and of the complete omniscience and providence of the Most High, and completely submit yourself to the will of God. You have done what you must do; leave the rest to God.

5. Ask the advice of a wise man, and, as Sirach counsels, "Do nothing without counsel, and when you have acted, do not regret it" (Sirach 32:19). More than anything, be careful of following your own desires and inclinations, for you will lose all patience, you will destroy all meekness if you listen to your inner counselors, that is, your inclinations and passionate attachments. They are evil counselors. Sorrow is your lot, and not without God's disposition. He knows better than anyone how to free you from your sorrow and destroy it. But

you decide to act before the time is right, saying, "I want it to be this way. This is how I command it to be. I prefer my will in this matter." Even if this makes you feel happy, you are destroying God's disposition concerning you, and later you will regret that you caused yourself such evil. Every evil that comes of our disobedience we lay on ourselves. The Prophet Baruch reflects on this with sorrow, "To the Lord our God belongs righteousness, but for us shame is on our faces … who have sinned before the Lord. We have disobeyed Him and have refused to heed the voice of the Lord our God, to walk in the ordinances of the Lord, which He gave to us openly" (Baruch 1:15, 17–18). Therefore, let every person lay his hope only on God, fulfilling His commandments. The firmer your hope is in God, the mightier you will be against your enemies, and you will remain in safety and calm.

6. If, despite all your attempts and diligence, something still does not go according to your plans, do not become angry with God or with any of His creations. Instead, remember that God knows every detail of your suffering and what suffering still remains for you. He desires to come to know and increase your courage. Therefore, whatever God wants, let that be your desire. "O Israel, we are blessed, for what is pleasing to our God is known to us" (Baruch 4:4).

Let no one dare say, "I see that I labor in vain. I asked God for help with great trust in Him, I committed myself completely to His will, but nothing has happened." "But you say, 'What does the Mighty One know? Will He judge down into the darkness? A cloud is His hiding place, so He cannot see as He travels through the circle of heaven" (Job 22:13–14). These are the words of transgressors. There is nothing useless in a job well done. Do you imagine God has only one treasure, and if someone has not received money from Him, then nothing else is forthcoming? Foolish is the worker who wishes to receive payment only in the form of copper coins. So, let everyone who has not received what he asked from God know that he does not pray in vain. God will inevitably give him something far better.

V

If God does not lessen His anger, punishing us with various misfortunes and sorrows, then He, our merciful Father, treats us as a wise parent. Good parents punish their children, even spanking them sometimes. Then they ask their children, "Will you continue to disobey me?" If the ill-behaved child continues to be stubbornly silent, the punishment may continue until the child comes to his senses and with genuine regret promises to correct their behavior. Then their father says, "Do not forget or repeat your bad behavior."

This is how God punishes us and occasionally asks us, "Do you wish to follow Me in all things, to hope in Me alone?" What usually happens is that we stubbornly say nothing or answer half-heartedly or evasively. And so God often does not cease to send various misfortunes for our chastisement, always waiting a positive answer from us: "Yes, my Father, I want to follow Your will in all things. Tell me, what do You command me to do?"

A certain eloquent teacher beautifully characterized the question—Lord, what do You command me to do?—with the following words: "What a short sentence, but how full, how vivid, how effective, how worthy to be repeated!" There are very few people in the world who have reached such heights of self-rejection, who have given their hearts completely to God. Such people say, "I want what God wants, not what I want." They constantly repeat, "Lord, what do You command me to do?"

The problem of our time is that we find more blind men than newly converted Apostles like Paul, who asked the Lord on the road to Damascus, "Lord! What do You want me to do?" (Acts 9:6). When the blind man asked the Lord to have mercy on Him, Jesus asked Him what he desired (see Luke 18:39–41). How great is Your mercy, O Lord! How great is Your goodness! Is this how a Lord talks to a slave? Truly that man was blind, for he did not tremble in fear at his own words, he did not say humbly,

> No, Lord, I am not worthy of such a question. It is more proper for me to say to my Lord, "Lord, what do You command me to do?" For it is not my will that should be done by You, but rather let Your will be my unchangeable law, so that I may always follow it. Lord, tell me what to do!"

Such trust in God, of which we spoke in this chapter, cannot remain in us constant and unchanging if we do not confirm it with our own long-suffering and submission to the will of God until it becomes habitual. In the portico of Solomon's Temple there were two columns. One of them was called Jachin, the other Boaz. These columns were compared to long-suffering and constancy (see 3 Kingdoms 7). Our trust in God should be established on such columns. Long-suffering swallows up even limitless sorrow. Constancy is not limited by time. He that trusts in the Lord is like Mount Zion. He will never be shaken and will remain forever (Psalm 124:1).

 CHAPTER 26

How the Saints Trusted God

The true nobility of the Christian race is found in the ability to trust in God alone during all doubtful or difficult situations. The mind of such a person is noble and courageous, making the person honorable and glorious, especially if he has the firmest hope in God at the moment of greatest danger. In this chapter, we will examine the lives of holy men and women who have belonged to this noble race.

I

I will not speak much about Abraham, so firm of faith in God. Abraham believed in God and trusted in Him, and though he had no hope of offspring because of his age, he did not doubt God's promise, but was victorious through faith, glorifying God. He knew that God is mighty enough to fulfill His promises. He, along with three hundred eighteen of his men, defeated the armies of four kings. I will also remain brief in my praise of Joseph, whose position in Egypt was second only to Pharaoh, who was many times brought to the greatest sorrow, but never despaired, for he had a heart that trusted in God.

How many wondrous deeds did Moses accomplish, strengthened by God? All of Egypt's forces he drowned in the sea; in battle against the Amalekites, instead of countless weapons, he had only a rod in his hands. Still, he said to his commander Joshua, "Choose for yourself some mighty men and go out, and set the army in array against Amalek. Tomorrow I will stand on the top of a hill with the rod of God in my hand" (Exodus 17:9). What an awesome, wondrous deed! Moses stood, doing nothing, as a spectator, and still he destroyed all the forces of the enemy.

Later, Joshua, having unutterable trust, dared command the sun to remain in place, and it stood still in the middle of the sky, not rushing to the West for nearly the whole day. There was no other day before or after where the Lord was so attentive to the voice of man, and this is because the Lord Himself fought for the Israelites (Joshua 10:12–14). As Joshua stopped the sun, so Hezekiah, by word of the Prophet Isaiah, forced the sun to go backward (see 4 Kingdoms 20:9–11).

Let us remember Caleb. He had such strong trust in God that he was not afraid to enter among the host of Israelites that had rebelled against Moses and Aaron and to rebuke their unrighteousness, saying, "Since the Lord chooses us, He will bring us into this land and give it to us, 'a land that flows with milk and honey.' But do not apostatize from the Lord, nor fear the people of the land, for they are our food; their time has come and gone, but the Lord is with us. Do not fear them" (Numbers 14:8–9).

Gideon had equally great trust in God, though he was sooner born to be a farmer than a warrior. He, trusting in God, dared with three hundred men to attack a countless host of enemies and defeated them.[65]

Let us remember Hezekiah. How wonderful and terrifying it must have been to see the sun move back ten degrees! But, by the will of God, it did so instantaneously, as though someone jerked the sun backward with a string. Hezekiah's trust in God showed itself a second time when King Sennacherib of Assyria surrounded Jerusalem. Hezekiah, encouraging the city of David, focused on increasing the people's trust in God first of all, saying,

"Be strong and courageous. Do not be afraid of the king of Assyria, nor before all the nation with him; for there are more with us than with him. With him are arms of flesh, but with us is the Lord our God, to save us and to fight our battles." And the people were strengthened by the words of Hezekiah king of Judah. And the Lord sent an angel, who cut down every mighty man of valor and leader and captain in the camp of the king of Assyria. So he returned shamefaced to his land. And he went into the temple of his god, where some of his own offspring struck him down with the sword. (2 Chronicles 32:7, 8, 21)

Zedekiah, however, did not follow Hezekiah's example, though he had a greater army. The reason for Zedekiah's failure was that he trusted more in his strength than in God.[66]

II

The same reason led to the downfall of the pious King Asa, who ruled well for thirty-six years and was beloved of God, but afterward lost the grace of God because he put his hopes not in God, but in human strength. Using human logic, Asa's situation seems to be unworthy even of a small punishment. What was his crime? He sent gold and silver to the son of Hadad, the king of Syria, saying, "Let there be a treaty between you and me, as there was between my father and your father. Here, I have sent you silver and gold. Come and drive away Baasha king of Israel so that he will withdraw from me" (2 Chronicles 16:3). However, Hanani the prophet of God said to Asa's face, "Because you relied on the king of Syria and did not rely on the Lord your God, therefore, the army of the king of Syria escaped from your hand ... For the eyes of the Lord look over the whole earth and strengthen every heart that is loyal to Him. In this you did foolishly, and from now on you shall have wars" (2 Chronicles 16:7, 9).

For this same reason, Job did not ascribe virtue to himself, but ascribed everything to God, saying, "Or do I not see the shining sun eclipsed and the moon waning? For this does not depend upon them. If my heart has been secretly deceived, and if I have laid my hand upon my mouth and kissed it, then may this also be reckoned to me as the greatest lawlessness, for I have lied against the Lord most high" (Job 31:26–28). St Gregory the Great confirms the words of Job, saying, "All the good deeds accomplished by Job's hands, he ascribed not to himself, but to God alone. Job did not have the habit of ascribing the work of his hands to his own wisdom. Neither did he find solace in them. He was not puffed up with his own might and power, but put all his trust on God alone."

King Charles V (1500–1558 A.D.), the Holy Roman Emperor, would act the same way after every military victory. He said, "I came, I saw, but God conquered."[67] Trust in God also raised King David to the heights of holiness. In this particular virtue he surpassed all others. Whoever lovingly reads the Psalms cannot help but agree with me in this. How often did he repeat such words, speaking from a sincere heart: "The Lord is my light, and my Saviour; whom then shall I fear?" (Psalm 26:1). "Wherefore should I fear in the evil day, when the wickedness at my heels shall compass me round about?" (Psalm 48:6 and many other psalms).

Jonah, imprisoned in the belly of the sea monster, finding himself at the very threshold of death, did not despair, but as though he were on the safest of ships, he prayerfully cried out to his Lord God. Every place is a good place to pray.

What did Jonah seek? "You cast me into the depths of the heart of the sea, and rivers encompassed me; all Your surging waters and Your waves passed over Me. Yet ... I remembered the Lord. May my prayer be brought to You, into Your holy temple" (Jonah 2:4–8). Here is a model of the greatest trust in God.

Daniel in the den, surrounded by hungry lions, prayed in the same way. The three youths in the Babylonian furnace raised the complete trust of their prayer to the Lord.[68] Tobit showed us an unusual example. He, having lost his riches and homeland—a poor man, a wanderer, struck blind—still did not lose his first trust in God, diligently preserving and nurturing it, though his own family, wife, and friends laughed at him and said, "Where is your hope now, for which reason you gave so generously to the poor? In vain was your hope." But he said to them, "Do not say this, for we are children of the Holy One, and we await that eternal life that God promised and will give to those who are firm in faith and trust in Him."[69] This trust in God returned to Tobit his estate, his fatherland, his sight, and gave him an eternal reward in the future life.

St Paul greatly possessed this virtue, as we see from the following: often when he imagined the end of his earthly life, he would say, "I know whom I have believed and am persuaded that He is able to keep what I have committed to Him until that Day [that is, the day of Judgment]" (2 Timothy 1:12). Armed with such trust, St Paul did not turn aside from a single labor or misfortune. He avoided neither the right nor the left road. He braved the sword, stoning, various fatal dangers, arrows, and fire, all the while strengthened by his trust in God, by Whose power he often escaped prisons and bonds.

III

Judith surpassed all women in this virtue, accomplishing an unheard-of deed. Having given an oath to kill Holofernes, she laid all her trust on God, crying out to Him, "O God, my God, hear me also, a widow. For You did those things and the things that occurred before and those that followed after; and You have planned the ones present, and the ones for the future ... for all Your ways are prepared beforehand, and Your judgment is by foreknowledge" (Judith 9:4–6). "For Your might is not in numbers, nor Your power in men who are strong, but You are the God of the lowly; You are the helper of the oppressed, the defender of the weak, the protector of those who are forsaken, the savior of those without hope. Yes, O God of my fathers and God of the inheritance of Israel, Lord of heaven and earth, Creator of the waters, King of all Your creation, attend to my prayer" (Judith 9:11–12).

With the same trust she spoke to Holofernes, "I will not eat any of this … lest it cause offence. But I will be supplied by the provisions I brought with me … My lord, even as you live, your handmaid will not use up what I brought with me until the Lord completes by my hand what He has purposed" (Judith 12:2, 4). When she stood by the bed of the drunken Holofernes, she secretly shed tears and prayed in her heart, "O Lord God of Israel, at this moment strengthen me" (Judith 13:7), and she accomplished everything she set out to do successfully.

Having returned to Bethulia, her first words were "'Praise God! Praise Him! Praise God! For He has not taken away His mercy from the house of Israel, but by my hand He has shattered our enemies this very night!' Then she took the head [of Holofernes] out of the bag, displaying it to them" (Judith 13:14–15).

Let us also remember the chaste Susanna, that paragon of purity, modesty, and trust in God, who, being led to the place where she was to be stoned, raised her eyes to heaven with tears, for her heart still firmly trusted in the Lord. And it was not in vain. The prophet Daniel rebuked her slanderers in court, accusing them of false witness against her, and she was exonerated, while her slanderers could not escape the fate they had prepared for her (see Daniel chapter 1 in the OSB).

Esther had equally strong faith in God. In the court of Artaxerxes, there was a custom that prevented any man or woman from entering the inner chambers of the king without being called in first. Whoever broke this rule was to be executed, excepting those cases where the king gave the sign of his mercy, a golden staff. When Haman threatened to kill all the Hebrews in all the regions of the kingdom, Mordecai, the mentor of Queen Esther, was warned in advance. Mordecai insisted that Esther must enter the king's inner chamber with a petition to spare the Hebrews from Haman's cruelty, but the king did not summon her to him. Fearing to break the law, she first ordered all the Jews to remain three days in fasting and prayer, and she did the same with her ladies in waiting. After this time passed, she, laying on God the greatest trust, entered the king's chamber without being summoned, begging him to repeal Haman's command to kill all the Hebrews, and everything happened as she hoped (see Esther 3–5).

It is proper and appropriate to remember here the miracle done in old Rus. When the Greek Archbishop Michael, inspired by God, arrived from Constantinople to preach the holy faith to the people of Rus, those of weak faith demanded to see some kind of miracle from him. The archbishop asked them, "What kind of a miracle do you demand?" They answered, "We will throw the book containing the teaching of your Christian faith into the fire, and if it remains unharmed, then we will know that your faith is the true faith, and that your God is great."

Archbishop Michael, raising his hand to heaven, prayed and said, "Christ God, glorify Your name!" And with the greatest faith, he placed the Holy Gospel in the fire, and when the wood was consumed and the fire was quenched, the book was revealed unharmed in the fire. Seeing this miracle, many believed in Christ and were baptized. See what miracles those who trust in God invariably do!

We may find many other miracles in the lives and acts of the saints, whose names He Himself knows, for He counts all the stars and gives them names. He writes the names of all the saints in the book of life. It is right and fair to say concerning all of them: who among them was ashamed by their trust in God? Let every person always call to mind the words of the wise man: "Trust in God with all your heart" (Proverbs 3:5). There are many who do not have such trust, who expect only the help of other people in all situations. Therefore, God often leaves them to their own will and their own vain desires. Look at the history of man, and you will see: who was ever ashamed by trust in God?

 CHAPTER 27

The Many and Diverse Gifts That God Gives to Those Who Trust in Him

In the life of the world, protection from danger comes in many forms—helmets on the head, chain mail on the chest, an anchor at sea—and yet there are many people who are still struck down despite their helmets, who are pierced despite their chain mail, and who fall into the sea despite the anchor. However, in the life of the spirit, "they that trust in the Lord are as mount Zion; he that liveth in Jerusalem shall never be shaken" (Psalm 124:1), for Mount Zion is never moved even by the worst storms or the fiercest waves, not only because it is a mountain but even more so because it is a mountain consecrated to God. In the same way, no force, even the force of calamity, can topple a person who truly trusts in God and eagerly does His holy will in all things. Such trust in God is a helmet impervious to all weapons, chain mail that turns aside all arrows and bullets, an anchor that never allows a ship to sink. This trust is like a firm and trustworthy anchor that enters into our very inner self, into our soul and spirit (see Hebrews 6:19).

I

The Apostle Paul, the preacher to the whole world, noticed some people vacillating in their trust in God, preferring to hope in the vanity of the world. Desiring to turn them from such a calamity, he wrote,

> Let us hold fast the confession of our hope without wavering, for He who promised is faithful ... Therefore do not cast away your confidence, which has great reward. For you have need of endurance, so that after you have done the will of God, you may

receive the promise. "For yet a little while, and He who is coming will come and will not tarry." (Hebrews 10:23, 35–37)

Let us examine each of these rewards in more detail.

The first reward is the promise that trust in God will never cause anyone to be ashamed. Trust in man is fickle; it deludes us a thousand times, but it does not make the deluded any wiser. Plato spoke about this: "Hope in man is sleep for those who are awake or better yet those who desire to be fooled." Trust in man has led many people to dishonor and worthlessness. "The hope of the ungodly man is like dust carried by the wind and like a light frost driven away by a storm, it is dispersed like smoke before the wind, and it passes like the remembrance of a guest who stays only one day" (Wisdom of Solomon 5:14).

Trust in God, on the other hand, never deluded or shamed anyone. "Consider the ancient generations and see: who believed in the Lord and was put to shame? Or who stood fast in His fear and was forsaken? Or who called upon Him and was overlooked?" (Sirach 2:10). The kingly prophet said, boasting in his trust in God, "In thee, O Lord, have I put my trust; let me never be confounded" (Psalm 30:2). Blessed Augustine said,

> Who is most often put to shame? He is the one who admitted to you, saying, "What I hoped in, that I did not receive in deed, for I hoped in you or in another person." Every person who puts his trust in man will be disappointed. You are put to shame, for a false hope has shamed you: every person is false. If you will trust in the Lord your God, you will not be ashamed, for He upon Whom you place your trust is not mocked. This trust puts no one ever to shame.

Remember, moreover, Moses's trust in the God of Israel as the entire nation walked across the Red Sea, even as Pharaoh pursued them with his army. Moses did not despair; he did not lose faith in God. Instead, after praying, he stretched out his hand, struck the water with his staff, and suddenly the sea parted in two, revealing dry passage for the Israelites.[70] Trust in God leaves no man ashamed, and the first reward of those who trust is that their desire is always fulfilled. They will never be put to shame.

II

The second reward for those who trust in God is a peaceful life, free of anxiety. The one who trusts in the Lord does his work sincerely and constantly, even if his labor is always changing or very heavy, with no anxiety, and in any misfortune he does not despair, saying together with King David, "I have put my trust in Thy mercy. My heart shall rejoice in Thy salvation; I will sing unto the Lord Who hath dealt so lovingly with me, and I will chant unto the Name of the Lord Most High" (Psalm 12:7).

The ancients had the habit of writing the following maxim on their walls: "Whoever consecrates his work to God will live peacefully and without cares on earth, and in the eternal life he will be blessed." What does it mean to consecrate our work to God? This means that we must accept that everything we encounter happens by the will or permission of God, and so we must thank God for it. Do we receive good things? We receive them from God's hand. Do we receive evil? This is allowed by God to make us wiser. Let us thank God for the former and the latter! To accept everything as coming from God's hand, or as occurring by His disposal, is a general rule with no exceptions. It is so universal that not only external, societal calamities, troubles, and sorrows but even inner troubles coming from our confusion or sins must be accepted by each person with gratitude, for "we know that all things work together for good to those who love God" (Romans 8:28).

III

The third reward for trust in God is strength in endurance of troubles and indomitability in misfortune. The following words from the Scriptures prove this to us: "The ungodly man is destroyed by the passing storm, but the righteous man turns aside and shall be saved forever" (Proverbs 10:26). The courageous King David said, "trusting in the Lord, I shall not falter" (Psalm 25:1). Blessed Theodoret (ca. 393–458 A.D.) said, "Have God as your teacher and master in all things, so that the manner of your life, your actions, and your circumstances will be arranged by His wise providence. Only then will you be strong and constant in your actions and thoughts." Thousands upon thousands of saints revealed themselves to be such people.

It is an incredible thing to be hanged on an instrument of torture, to be lacerated with metal hooks, to be burned by fire, and yet still remain joyful. It is not strange if many people gather in a place where money is being given out for free. But when heads are chopped off, metal grills are heated up, torture wheels are prepared, when people are crucified on crosses and hanged on trees, when tortures are especially prepared in advance, it is unusual to see crowds assembling to await their turn. And yet, the martyrs of Christ ran to the persecutors, trying to outrun each other to be the first to die for Christ. This is a new phenomenon, unheard-of in the times before Christ.

Eusebius tells of this in his *Ecclesiastical History*:[71]

> I saw with my own eyes how in Egypt a countless multitude of Christians was taken outside the city to the place of execution. Freely, unfettered, each one running ahead of the other, they extended their own necks to the executioner's blade. There were so many being executed that the torturers grew tired and the swords grew dull. Smiths had to constantly sharpen and change the swords, and all this continued not for one day, but several. Not a single one of the martyrs, not even the children, feared death for Christ.

Truly this was an unbeatable army of warriors of Christ, who like Mount Zion did not waver before death for Christ, our Saviour.

St John Chrysostom called trust an unconquerable, firm, and immoveable mountain. Just as a mountain cannot be moved unless it is dug out (an impossible feat), so a person who seeks to subvert a Christian who trusts in God will never succeed unless he kills him, and even then he will not separate him from the Saviour but will only more firmly unite them in the future life. St John also explained the phrase "like mount Zion" by saying that Mount Zion was once uninhabited, but when people began to live on it and applied all their efforts to cultivate the soil, it began to give the best harvest and became a truly beautiful place. In the same way, a pious and constant person, though he be laid low by heavy labors, sickness, or even death, will never waver. The Prophet Isaiah said, "He gives strength to the hungry ... Those who wait on God shall renew their strength; they shall mount up with wings like eagles; they shall run and not be weary; they shall walk and not hunger" (Isaiah 40:29, 31). "Blessed are all they that put their trust in Him" (Psalm 2:12). And so be brave, strengthen your hearts in the Lord, all you who trust in the Lord!

IV

The fourth reward is protection from falling into sin in this life and a special mercy of God to erase the sins we have committed. "The Lord will deliver the souls of His servants, and all they that put their trust in Him shall do no sin" (Psalm 33:23). How can one reach such a state? A certain teacher said,

> Whoever makes it a law never to desire anything that is not permissible, who limits the circle of his desires by what is lawful, will prevent himself

from sinning. Instead, he will only allow himself to act in a way that does not oppose God's will. Such a person will be ruled not by his sinful desires, but will rather oppose them with God's sinless will, accepting it and incorporating it into himself until all his actions are dictated by it.

Such a person truly trusts God in all his deeds, believes in Him, and depends on God's providence and foresight as God has determined what is beneficial for our perfection in every moment of our lives. Such a person is skilled in wisdom and reveals this wisdom in his actions, for by trusting himself to the will of God, he ceases to fear any evil or sin. Genuine trust in God deprives us not only of confusion (restlessness or sorrow) but also of laziness and carelessness.

Another spiritual teacher said that our mind—if it does not trust in itself, but seeks support only in the doing of God's will—can become master of all by preventing any falsehood from entering. No power or delusion or sensuality or any other foul thing can overcome or imprison anyone who stands within the divinely reinforced wall of God's will.

Therefore, let us cultivate the habit of trusting God in all things, without doubting, never paying attention to anything that might seem to contradict our faith. Let us cultivate faith in God even in hopelessness, and the Lord by His will shall take away the disease of lack of faith and will accomplish everything for the good.

V

The fifth reward. Genuine trust in God gives us nearly complete power; it can even make us seem invincible. St Paul said, "I can do all things through Christ who strengthens me" (Philippians 4:13). Of course not many of us can reach the level of St Paul's perfection and may have to limit themselves to bowing down at his feet. However, anyone who trusts in God can bravely say along with Job to the Lord: "Intercede for me, and who then will dare to attack me, who will raise his hand at me?"[72] and with Paul, "If God is for us, who can be against us?" (Romans 8:31).

But why do I cite saints, when Christ the Lord Himself said definitively, "If you can believe, all things are possible to him who believes" (Mark 9:23). Nothing so reveals the omnipotence of God as the fact that He shares His omnipotence with those who trust Him, for is not a person omnipotent if everything is possible for him? St John Chrysostom gave the most definitive statement on this, saying, "Divine grace never leaves those who trust in God."

This grace is the most trustworthy reward to the person who trusts in the One Who can save and actively saves all mankind. "Our fathers hoped in Thee; they trusted, and Thou didst deliver them. They called upon Thee, and were saved; they put their trust in Thee, and were not confounded" (Psalm 21:5–6). Trust in God, you people of God, for "every place the sole of your foot treads shall be yours. No man shall be able to stand against your face" (Deuteronomy 11:24, 25). Our hope will always come true, if only it is founded completely in God. Then it will be always firm and invincible.

The Apostles asked Jesus Christ when they were alone with Him why they could not heal the young lunatic possessed by a demon. Jesus Christ answered them, "Because of your unbelief; for assuredly, I say to you, if you have faith as a mustard seed, you will say to this mountain, 'Move from here to there,' and it will move; and nothing will be impossible for you" (Matthew 17:20). Here omnipotence is ascribed not only to the Christian faith but merely to trust in God, which is invested with God's almighty power to even do miracles. Thus Christ did not say, "Do miracles!" Instead, he said, "Have faith in God" (Mark 11:22).

And so, do not complain at His benevolence; rather cast aside inconstancy and cowardice when faced with God's inscrutable dispositions, and refuse all unbelief. If you are afraid to step on a scorpion, adder, or dragon, then at the very least put down pride, conceit, and disdain of others. If you cannot order fire to dissipate at your command, at the very least quench the fire of your passions. If you cannot tame lions, tigers, or other wild animals, then at least tame your anger and destroy your envy. If you cannot transform a dead tree into one covered with fresh growth, at least fill the hand of a poor man with generous alms. Christ demands only one thing from us: "Have faith in God," for the one who has such faith will transform all evil into good. From any metal ore he will be able to mine out silver and gold. As Boethius said, "Only God's power can turn useless materials into beautiful things in His wisdom."

 CHAPTER 28

Trust in God Weakens and Dies without Acknowledgment of His Providence

During Abraham's sorrowful journey to the place of Isaac's sacrifice, on the third day, as they already approach Mount Moriah, Isaac, who carried wood on his shoulders, seeing his father with a sacrificial knife and fire, asked, "Look, the fire and the firewood, but where is the sheep for a whole burnt offering?" Abraham answered, "My son, God will provide for Himself the sheep for a whole burnt offering" (Genesis 22:7–8). Then they continued on their journey together.

Oh, if only we would repeat these words in our heart during times of need and especially in doubtful situations when we have no joy: "God will take care and provide. God will send us the needed consolation in our sorrows." Let us give some examples. The father of a large family labors and cares for one thing more than all others—to feed, clothe, instruct his children and equip them for their future lives. This good man freely afflicts himself for the sake of his family, knowing that God will see his labors and take care of them. Another man is perhaps strong of body, but not of mind, and tortures himself with thoughts of how to find himself a safe haven after the loss of a benefactor. Truly such self-torture, such despair is pointless. God will not leave him; God will take care of him.

Another, a lover of money and not of virtue, fears and tortures himself with his thoughts. What will happen to me, he thinks, if my desire will not be fulfilled, if my hope is found to be false? O, timorous man of little faith! God will remedy everything, for He has foreseen all ends. "Those who trust in Him will understand truth, and the faithful shall continue with Him in love" (Wisdom of Solomon 3:9). Let us take the example of Maximilian, the Caesar of Rome.[73] Whenever he would be troubled by any difficult event, he would always say, "God will attend, foresee, and send aid." We should always constantly turn our mind to God, for He will not allow us to be deluded nor will He lead into temptation those who trust in Him.

Abraham, the father of the faithful, never doubted God, even when His command to sacrifice Isaac seemed to contradict His previous promises. Instead, he hurried to do God's bidding. Imagine what great trust he must have had to travel for three days to the appointed place. During the entire journey, he prepared himself, repeating, "God sees everything; He will see." Truly He foresaw, and something miraculous and unexpected happened. The father brought his own son to be sacrificed, and Isaac by his willing submission brought himself as a sacrifice. God accepted both offerings, and yet "the victim remains alive," as St John Chrysostom says with amazement. The sacrifice was truly accomplished, for Abraham, who trusted in God, came to the very mountain, the very altar, and he had already taken the knife and raised his hands to slaughter his own son. If the angel of the Lord had not stopped him, telling him that the sacrifices of both the father and the son were already acceptable to God, he would have sacrificed Isaac.

We can develop trust in God by constantly reminding ourselves about divine providence, which has guided us and many others countless times in the past. As we carefully examine our own past life and the lives of people who have already passed through life, we will see how in countless situations of discomfort or grief, divine providence was present and mercifully delivered God's people from terrible misfortunes or unexpectedly indicated a straight path when none was there before. Truly, each of us will be inspired to say wholeheartedly together with David, "He sent from the height and took me, He drew me out of many waters. He delivered me from my strong enemies, from those who hated me; for they were stronger than I. They confronted me in the day of my tribulation, but the Lord was my support. He brought me to a broad place; he delivered me because He delighted in me" (2 Kingdoms 22:17–20).

How many troubles and inconveniences have I encountered in this life, but every time I have been saved! God foresees everything. Let us trust in God! However, no one will have the courage to trust in God until he will be convinced that providence keeps watch over every one of us. The question "Does providence exist?" is the question of a madman, and we must avoid it. Clement of Alexandria (ca. 150–215) said, "Some questions are not worthy of being answered (because of their absurdity)." One such question is the question about the existence of divine providence, for even a simple glance at the created world and its reasonable natural laws proves that everything was created by a reasoning and wise Artist. The world lives and is sustained by His divine foreknowledge and providence.

I

What is Providence? It is one of the essential characteristics of God—to see all that is, was, and will be in the future as though it were the present, to have all-powerful care for the preservation of all creation, and to wisely manage all natural phenomena as governed by the laws of cause and effect. St John of Damascus (675/676–749 A.D.) describes it thus: "Providence is the divine will by which everything is maintained and wisely directed."

Let us examine this idea in greater detail. From before the ages, God foresees in what manner every object or person is created and for what purpose. At the same time, He also anticipates what obstacles or inconveniences can arise in the process. In order to avoid these obstacles, the all-good God wills to choose and indicate those means that are most appropriate for each individual person to achieve his goal or calling. God disposed this all from the beginning of the creation of the world, and He brought it all into action by His illimitable power. Thus, according to Abba Dorotheos, God's foreknowledge comprises the inception of every good thing. This is obvious and well known to every wise person and from this came the folk sayings: "Follow after God" and "Do not fight against God."

In other words, leave God room to take care of you; remember that God foresees all. All these truths are contained in the Holy Scriptures; moreover, many ancient peoples expressed these eternal truths in daily customs, sayings, and traditions. God revealed His providence to us from the beginning of the world in the events of the Flood, the destruction of Sodom, the plagues of Egypt, the manna from heaven that fed so many thousands of Israelites in the desert, and the giving of the Law to Moses, by which He revealed His personal presence before the congregation of the people. God Himself led the people out of Egypt; the Lord walked before them during the day as a pillar of cloud and at night as a pillar of fire, showing them the way, so they could travel both day and night. Then God sent them quail to eat and ensured many victories over their enemies.[74]

There can be no doubt that God cares and provides for His entire creation. Wisdom herself said, "For the Master of all will not shrink back from anyone's presence, nor respect greatness; because He Himself made both small and great, and cares for all alike" (Wisdom of Solomon 6:7). In order to help us more fully instill into our hearts the knowledge of God's providence concerning us, I offer this essential truth: nothing in the world occurs by accident or blind chance.

Many phenomena, if examined cursorily, without delving deeply into caus-es and effects, may seem to be accidental. However, if we look at them again with the proper point of view, that is, if we judge by God's reasoning, we will see that in the world there is nothing that happens by accident. Nothing oc-curs without the will and the providence of God. The Reason of God (i.e., His providence) is limitless and encompasses everything that our mind can com-prehend. Almighty God, in a single moment, with an unchanging movement of the eye pierces through and sees all places: the heights of heaven, the breadth of earth, the depth of the sea, and the hidden things in the abyss. Nothing ever happens without a reason.

As Job said, "I will beseech the Lord, and call upon the Lord and Master of all, Who does great, incomprehensible, and marvelous things without num-ber" (Job 5:8–9). "You have ordered all things by measure, number, and weight" (Wisdom of Solomon 11:20). Thus in all the manifestations of God's rule over the cosmos, His providence and care shine through wondrously. This providence not only rules over all creatures, but it is also intrinsic to them and abides in them always. But we, blind ones, think that much in the world occurs by blind chance. Upon examination, everything, without exception, occurs by the won-drous counsel of God, by His goodwill and providence.

II

Blessed Augustine said, "Everything that we, not understanding fully, consider to have occurred by chance, irrationally, and without any divine providence, actually occurs by God's dispensation." Let us explain this further with an example. A master sends his two servants to the same place, but by different roads, without telling either one of them about the other. Their meeting in that place is a chance meeting as far as they are concerned, for they did not expect to meet each other. However, it is obvious that from the point of view of the master, their meeting was not accidental.

Consider a different example: a poor man finds buried treasure by chance. However, for God Who willed that the treasure be buried in that precise place, to be found by that particular poor man at that moment, is not a chance event. It was not an accident, but God's fatherly foresight that enriched the poor man. There is no blind chance with God. This is true without exception. Therefore, one should not think that anything having to do with earthly affairs is committed unwisely or by chance, for everything occurs by the eternal law that the omniscient Creator established before the ages.

Often we delude ourselves when we consider events that reveal the most exalted divine wisdom and providence to be merely accidental. It was not by chance that the thieves threw the body of the man they killed into the tomb of Elisha. As soon as the body touched the bones of Elisha, he immediately came back to life.[75] It was not by chance that Moses was placed into a basket brushed with tar and sent downriver, where the daughter of Pharaoh found him and adopted him as her own son.[76] It was not by chance that Ahab, king of Israel, was struck down by an arrow in the gap between his breastplate and chest, though the archer did not know he struck Ahab.[77] Truly, God directed the arrow with His hand, in the same way as He directed an arrow to kill Julian the apostate.[78] It was only an accidental event from the point of view of the archer.

It was not by accident that the sparrow flew into the house of Tobit and blinded him with its excrement (Tobit 2:10). This occurred by the dispensation of God in order to show in Tobit a model of patient endurance for all future generations to emulate. This is made obvious by the angel Raphael, who told Tobias that this event was pleasing to God in order to test his father's patience. Nothing happens by blind chance. It was not accidental that Caesar Augustus ordered a census at the time of Christ's Nativity (see Luke 2:1). It was not by accident that Christ met the Samaritan woman.[79] All this was foreseen and written down in the books of divine providence before the ages.

III

When the holy martyrs Cyprian and Justina (ca. third century A.D.; commemorated on October 2/15) were condemned to be beheaded for their faith, they were led to the place of execution. A certain Theoctistus, who rode by them on a horse, said, "These people are unjustly condemned." Felix the judge immediately ordered him pulled from his horse and taken to the place of execution together with the martyrs. "Thy judgments are as the bottomless deep" (Psalm 35:7). This meeting between the martyrs and the sympathetic man seems to be a chance encounter, but it occurred by God's providence.

Abba Paphnutius's (fourth century A.D.) monks asked him, "For what reason do many succeed neither in virtue nor in study, while others who have the same teacher succeed in both?" St Paphnutius answered,

Everything that happens on earth happens by God's will or permission. However, both His will and permission are closely linked with His justice and providence. So, deeds of virtue and piety are accomplished by those people who please God with their submission (that is, they acknowledge themselves as nothing but dust and ashes before God), their utter humility, and ardent love for Him. Deeds of iniquity are committed by those prideful ones who do not trust in God and do not even believe in His providence, trusting in their own reason and human strength. They create all misfortunes, offences, calamities, and falsehoods in the world, even though God allows it.

Why does God allow so much iniquity in the world? Even the pagan Plato advises silence in answer to this question, for the judgments of God are unfathomably deep. Whoever says that nothing occurs in the world without God's counsel and providence speaks the truth. Blessed Augustine said,

The sea of life blusters, and You, Lord, see how the evil prosper and the good are oppressed. What a temptation; what a storm! Lord God! Is it Your truth for the evil to prosper and the good to suffer? And God answers you: Is this your faith? Is this what I promised you [that is, flourishing prosperity]? Or is this the reason you are called Christian— to enjoy earthly success?

Let us humble ourselves before God and calm our hearts. Let us content our hearts with faith in God's providence when we see the unjust in power, the pious persecuted, reverence mocked, and truth destroyed. None of this would occur if God did not allow it. And truly He would not have allowed it if there were not many good reasons for it, reasons for which He considered it better to allow it and not to hinder it. You say that this permission results in many misfortunes and great confusion. It is good to lament this, but within reason, for God had very compelling reasons to allow even these calamities. Do not forget that He can create the greatest good from the worst evil as easily as I can pull a sword from its scabbard. Do not be amazed that the judgments of God are mysterious and inscrutable. In the second coming of Christ, in the terrifying day of judgment, the entire life of every person will be revealed as in a mirror. Every reason for God's direction of this or that event in all kingdoms, cities, families, and individual people will become obvious.

In that day, we will see how merciful God was to the sinners, and how each of them will have nothing to say to justify themselves. We will also see how much God's rule over the cosmos accorded with His glory and righteousness, how beneficial and generous all of His created gifts were to us. Let us not forget that God created some good out of every evil. What is more saddening than the fall of Adam and Eve, along with all their subsequent generations? However, God restored them so greatly that today's Christian is more blessed than Adam ever was in Eden. For although Christ's death on the Cross is "to the Jews a stumbling block and to the Greeks foolishness" (1 Corinthians 1:23), it still became the salvation for the whole world, for all who are called to the glory, honor, and gift of the eternal blessed life.

IV

Once, a certain Theodore came to St Pachomius. This Theodore suffered from terrible headaches, and he asked St Pachomius to pray that these pains would stop. The saint answered his request thus: "Do you think that this pain or other such sufferings occur without the will and permission of God? Endure it, and when God blesses, He will help you and heal you." It is good to be moderate in food and drink; it is very helpful to give alms; but a sick person receives the most benefit from patiently and gratefully enduring a sickness sent by God's goodwill. Here it becomes obvious that whoever is not firm in his belief in God's universal providence will not be able to endure sickness patiently.

The contrary is also true. Whoever has understood—through ardent faith—the mystery of God's all-encompassing providence will not suffer for long, no matter how serious the illness. David said, "Many are the troubles of the righteous, but the Lord delivereth them out of them all. The Lord keepeth all their bones; not one of them shall be broken" (Psalm 33:20–21).

A certain wise man said, "God so arranges the lives of the saints that every moment of time and every thing serves to their spiritual benefit." And why not? For we know that "all things work together for good to those who love God, to those who are the called according to His purpose" (Romans 8:28). This is how God looks after His chosen with His unsleeping eye, how He favors them. This is why there is a kind of mutual loving labor between the Lord and His chosen: there is nothing more pleasant for God's chosen than to desire and do everything that is pleasing and favored by God. God, on His part, always helps them and fulfills all their needs. Righteous people are beloved of the King of Heaven, and whatever they ask of Him, they receive. St John the Theologian assures us of this: "If our heart does not condemn us, we have confidence toward God. And whatever we ask we receive from Him, because we keep His commandments and do those things that are pleasing in His sight" (1 John 3:21–22). He repeats this same thought in chapter 5, verse 14, in order to remove any doubt from our unbelieving hearts.

God commanded Prophet Ezekiel: "Take for yourself wheat, barley, beans, lentils, millet, and spelt; put them into one vessel made of earth, and make loaves of bread for yourself. You shall eat them as barley cakes baked in ashes. You shall bake them in their sight in the filth of human dung" (Ezekiel 4:9, 12). The prophet was justly appalled at eating such bread, saying, "Not so, O Lord God of Israel. Behold, my soul has not defiled itself with uncleanness, nor from my youth up until now have I eaten what died of itself or was torn by beasts, nor has day-old meat entered my mouth." Then God immediately canceled His command (Ezekiel 4:14).

Jacob fought God and said, "I will not let You go unless you bless me" (Genesis 32:26), and he was blessed for it. When St Bessarion[80] went with his disciple to visit another desert dweller, the sun was already far in the west, and the distance to travel was still great. The elder prayed to God, "I beg You, Lord, command that the sun stop until I reach your servant." And it was so. The sun did not set until they arrived.

The lesson is clear: "He will fulfill the desire of them that fear Him, and He will hear their prayer, and save them" (Psalm 144:19). Moreover, God reveals to His saints the greatest of mysteries. "Shall I hide from Abraham, My servant, what I am about to do?" And immediately God repeated His promise to the father of all faithful and told him of the coming destruction of Sodom and Go-morrah (Genesis 18:17). In a similar fashion, Christ says to His chosen ones: "I have called you friends, for all things that I heard from My Father I have made known to you" (John 15:15).

V

When a teacher instructs his pupils how to write, sometimes he takes special pains to teach one student how to best and most beautifully write letters and words, while he ignores another student completely. What is the reason for this? The first student shows promise. He is well behaved, honest, intelligent, and assiduous. The other is an exasperating rascal. He is disobedient, rude, badly mannered, and as lazy as a donkey in completing every assignment.

Sometimes God acts with us like this teacher. He fulfills the petitions of those who do His will and protects them at all times, directing their actions to good ends. On the contrary, to those who oppose His commandments and persist in iniquity He says, "Even when you increase your prayers, I will still not hear you." They answer in indignation, "Why, God, do You not protect us or make our work succeed, as You do other people?" They have only themselves to blame, for "the countenance of the Lord is against them that do evil, to root out the remembrance of them from the earth" (Psalm 33:16–17).

To the obedient, this is God's promise: "If you pass through the water, I am with you; and the rivers shall not overflow you. If you pass through fire, you shall not be burned up, nor shall the flames consume you" (Isaiah 43:2). If you call to Him, He will say, "Here I am!" "I [The Lord] will be for her a wall of fire all around and I will be in glory in the midst of her" (Zechariah 2:9). The human reason that accords itself with the will of God becomes like an altar to God, on which God, the King of kings, sits as on a throne. No one will dare touch such a person without God's will or permission.

St Ambrose of Milan said, "For the lazy, the Lord is asleep. For the righteous, He is awake. This is not because He forgets the lazy. No, He merely instructs, rebukes, arouses, punishes so that all will understand in the clearest possible way how He cares and provides for His chosen." When Esau asked Jacob who were the people he brought back with him, Jacob said, "The children God mercifully gave your servant" (Genesis 33:5). With this meek answer, according to St John Chrysostom, Jacob helped Esau understand how great was God's providence and care for him.

God cares for all virtuous people as His friends and children, but He cares for the wicked as His prisoners and slaves. And if God, as if by compulsion, changed even the laws of nature for the worst because of our sins, He will still restore them to the better one thousand times more for the sake of the prayers of His friends (the saints) and for the sake of our repentance and sincere self-correction.

This is God's wondrous providence, symbolized by the ladder that Jacob saw in his dream. Its foundation is on earth but its top reaches the heavens.[81] Providence is an essential quality of God that directs the universe. God clearly sees everything that occurs in heaven or on earth, for the wisdom of God quickly stretches from one end of the universe to the other and arranges everything for the best (Wisdom of Solomon 8:1). "He who lives forever created everything" (Sirach 18:1), and He alone is righteous, Who arranged everything and cares for all. "But Your providence, O Father, governs its [a ship's] course, because You have given it a path in the sea and a safe track in the waves" (Wisdom of Solomon 14:3). Many other such places in the Scriptures prove that God provides for His creation.

Truly there is One God, and no other God other than He, Who rejoices over all His creation. God was, is, and will always be life. His omniscience always foresees His creatures' tendency to fall from good to evil, and—without compromising human free will—He strives to make that tendency in us harmless for other people, societies, and the whole human race. This, for us, is the most inscrutable of God's actions, consisting in the correction and reestablishment of the law of morality and virtue that we have broken. He does this through His foresight (for God sees) and His providence (for God cares and provides). This action is all-powerful, unchangeable, unconquerable by anyone or anything, as is God Himself. Although we do not often doubt God's foresight and providence and may even acknowledge it, we still complain, as though our free will were constrained. In this we are like children who hate their strict father's punishment.

We ought to abandon all such complaints and follow the will of the Most High in all our thoughts, intentions, and actions, for He is our loving Father. We should prefer His will to our freedom, which is inclined to sin. If we do this, we will change our will from one tending to fall to one that never errs. We will change our will from an evil will to a virtuous will. And so, let us place before ourselves this commandment, never to break it: let us act in all things not as it pleases us, but as it pleases God.

Let us not emulate those madmen who say in their hearts that there is no God, for "they are corrupt, and become abominable in their doings; there is none that doeth good, no not one" (Psalm 13:1). They have become blind and do not see their inevitable, evil end, both in this life and in the future life (if they do not repent). As for us, turning away our gaze from the world lying in the filth of evil, let us enter the inner house of our soul and conscience and examine ourselves. Who are we? Mortal men, powerless. How do we live? By the mercy and gifts of God. Who protects us in trials and sicknesses? The foresight and providence of God. If we do this, then we will be convinced that "not a hair of your head shall be lost" (Luke 21:18). Truly wise are the words of Blessed Augustine: "If the physician will incise all the members of my body, does that mean I will lose them? No, for God has counted all the hairs of my head, not merely my members."

 CHAPTER 29

How Greatly God Provides for All Our Needs in Life

God is a generous master. In His own hands He holds all great and rich necessities and treasures. A certain teacher spoke figuratively concerning God, saying that He has three keys that He entrusts to no one else. One key opens the treasure house of rains, snows, winds, and all atmospheric changes. Another key unlocks the tombs to call forth the dead into renewed life. The third key opens the granaries and storehouses of food. If God closes these houses of treasure, then who can open them, save for God Himself? God alone is the keeper and owner of all life's necessities; therefore, our fervent prayers concerning our needs in life should be directed to God alone.

I

St Mark the Ascetic[82] often said that whoever does not trust in God to provide all temporary necessities can, all the same, trust in God to provide the things necessary to lead a person to the eternal life, such as faith, hope, and love. Jesus Christ anticipated the most common reason for our lack of faith when He said, "Life is more than food, and the body is more than clothing" (Luke 12:23). His firm, true, and salvific exhortations banish from our hearts all fallen, excessive concern for food and clothing. His words teach us to put all our hope in His most high providence. If God is such a kind provider and such a generous giver of gifts—gifts that seem impossibly great, such as the salvation of our souls and admittance into the heavenly kingdom—then for what reason do we foolishly blame God, ascribing forgetfulness to Him in matters largely insignificant, requiring little labor from us?

If He gave us a body, will He not clothe it? The one who graciously gifts a horse will also not spare a bridle. Is not our life (i.e., our soul) greater than food? Is not our body more important than clothing? Since He gave us life (without our merits, before we even existed), which is greater than food, and a body, which is greater than clothing, He will doubtless give and provide everything for the maintenance and preservation of life and nourishment of the body. All the more so will He not refuse us in everything that He Himself desires, by His great goodness, to give us.

If He gives us everything we need freely and eagerly, then He can also give us those things that are not as important for life and nourishment. But He gives them with a condition that we not remain lazy, for He created and called us to tend to the land and to keep it in good order (Genesis 2:15). He does not give us gifts for us to enjoy them lazily.

God rebuked Job, symbolically asking about the preparation of food for ravens that cannot cook for themselves: "Who provides food for the raven? For its young ones wander and cry to the Lord in search of food" (Job 38:41). Christ, taking the model of the birds, teaches us, saying, "Look at the birds of the air, for they neither sow nor reap nor gather into barns; yet your heavenly Father feeds them. Are you not of more value than they?" (Matthew 6:26). Our Heavenly Teacher, repeatedly reminding us of our need for trust, says, "Are not two sparrows sold for a copper coin? And not one of them falls to the ground apart from your Father's will. But the very hairs of your head are all numbered. Do not fear therefore; you are of more value than many sparrows" (Matthew 10:29–31).

This first example of God's providence, taken from the natural world, is intended to teach us wisdom even from the animals. May we learn how to come to know the omnipotence of God's providence, because only then can we ever find consolation and inner peace.

The second proof that Christ gives is the lily of the field. After showing us God's providence for small birds and the hairs on our head, Christ says, "So why do you worry about clothing? Consider the lilies of the field, how they grow: they neither toil nor spin; and yet I say to you that even Solomon in all his glory was not arrayed like one of these" (Matthew 6:28–29). Christ then summarizes, "Now if God so clothes the grass of the field, which today is, and tomorrow is thrown into the oven, will He not much more clothe you, O you of little faith?" (Matthew 6:30). The Lord Saviour adds a third reason for the uselessness of worrying about our daily needs, saying, "Which of you by worrying can add one cubit to his stature?" (6:27). Any worries about our personal needs that are not united with our trust in God are pointless and futile. The Lord says the same: "If you then are not able to do the least, why are you anxious for the rest?" (Luke 12:26).

Vain, vacuous, and harmful is any labor that is not aided or blessed by God. When beginning any work, you must always lay on the Lord your entire and complete trust, and He (without any pains on your part) will arrange everything to the best by His unutterable mercy: "Thou openest Thine hand, and fillest every living thing with benevolence" (Psalm 144:16).

II

Thus, if the Lord God cares for the gratification of our everyday necessities—"Because He Himself made both small and great, and cares for all alike" (Wisdom of Solomon 6:7)—then why are there so many poor people in the world? It would seem that God blessed every man to reap the fruit of his labors. Wondrous, brothers, is the Lord's providence for the poor. Truly, St John Chrysostom spoke about this, saying that not only do the poor need the rich, but the rich need the poor much more so.

If we imagine two villages or cities, one of which is inhabited only by rich people, the other only by poor people, then there would be no connection between the people of both towns, no chance for trade of any kind. In the first city there would be not a single artisan, hired worker, smith, silversmith, goldsmith, seamstress, haberdasher, or any other worker. Rich people do not bother with such activities. There would be no servants in that city; what sort of a city is this, when you cannot find any help, any comfort in it?

The second city would be filled with workers who get, by the sweat of their brow, meager food, clothing, and other necessities that barely cover their basic needs. But if all of them were made suddenly rich and lived in luxury, what would be the consequences? All virtues would disappear and be forgotten. The general activity of the populace would be the following: drunkenness, overeating, dancing at all hours of the day and night, and constant gambling. Social life would be so deprived of virtue that the city would resemble Sodom and Gomorrah, or the world before the Flood. We all know the end of such a way of life—the punishment of God.

Everything good and God-pleasing in the world—whether in the past or the present—is arranged by the labors and activity not of the rich but by work-loving and God-fearing people who, being deprived of excess money, work in the sweat of their brow and sell their work to the rich. They never forget God; they pray to their Creator and Provider, Who in their very poverty is their Benefactor.

Many saints of God, abiding in abject poverty, loved it more than all riches, and as a result they felt God's providence actively in their lives. Having nothing, they seemed to have everything for free, and in constant spiritual joy, they exclaimed, "Our Father, Who art in the Heavens ..." They repeated with their lips and their hearts the words of the Psalmist: "O cast thy care upon the Lord, and He shall nourish thee" (Psalm 54:23).

Truly the Heavenly Father has such great providence for those who have dedicated their hearts to Him that when they are deprived of all human help, He sends them His heavenly aid. An example is His feeding of the Prophet Elijah. First, He commanded the ravens to bring him food, and the ravens brought him bread and meat both in the morning and in the evening, while a stream was his source of drinking water, until it dried up.[83] Then, God commanded Elijah to go into Zarephath of Sidon to a poor widow to be fed by her, though all of her possessions consisted of a handful of flour and a cupful of oil. By God's providence, during the time of the prophet's visit, the flour did not run out and the amount of oil did not lessen.[84] Finally, when Elijah slept, an angel of God brought him food and woke him with a touch, saying, "Stand up, eat, and drink." When Elijah awoke, he saw the food and drink, ate, and fell asleep again.[85]

God revealed the same wondrous grace to many other saints when they found themselves in need. We also often receive the same grace in our needs and insufficiencies, but many of us are weak in our faith, fearing to be deprived of necessities and comforts in our lives. We continue to say, together with the Jews, "Shall God be able to prepare a table in the wilderness?" (Psalm 77:19). We echo the words of the Apostles Philip and Andrew: "Two hundred denarii worth of bread is not sufficient for them, that every one of them may have a little ... There is a lad here who has five barley loaves and two small fish, but what are they among so many?" (John 6:7, 9). How faithless are we! Our Heavenly Father knows everything that we need. Do you think that God's goodness is less than it was in the past?

III

St Paul of Thebes (ca. 227–341 A.D.), the first desert dweller, received a half-loaf of bread for sixty days from a raven. When St Anthony the Great came to him, the raven brought a whole loaf. St John the hut-dweller (fifth century) drank the milk of a hind[86] for fourteen years, during which time he did not see a single human being. Many other ascetics of the desert had both food and clothing from fig trees.

In 653 A.D., Judoc, son of the king of Brittany,[87] renounced his claim to the throne and became a hermit-monk. He built a church on an island and established a monastery around it. He was so generous to the poor that one day the monastery was left with a single loaf of bread. Judoc ordered that even this one loaf be divided in four, to give the first quarter to a poor man. This unscrupulous poor man changed his clothing four times during the day, and each time he received a quarter of the last bread, and so nothing was left for the sustenance of the brotherhood. One of the monks began to complain and to rebuke the abbot for his excessive generosity. But Judoc, consoling him, told him to wait for divine help. After a few hours had passed, four boats filled with stores of food arrived near the monastery, and the monks ate their fill.

Blessed Augustine said, "Do you think that the one who feeds Christ (that is, the poor) will not himself be fed by Christ?" The abbot of another monastery sent two of the brothers on some business for the monastery. When the traveling monks arrived in an unfamiliar village as darkness fell, they began to complain, thinking that since they knew no one in this village, they would have neither food nor shelter. However, one of the villagers met them and asked them why they were grieving. When they told him, he said to them, "You have left everything for the sake of God, trusting in Him greatly, and now you sorrow as though deprived of all hope? God feeds even the swine; will He then leave His own sons to die of exposure and hunger?"

Having said this, the man became invisible. When the monks entered the village church to pray, the village elder invited them to his home for dinner, but immediately another villager, by no means poor, invited them also to dine and stay with him. A third, seeing the two villagers arguing about who would have the honor of feeding and housing the monks, resolved their argument by maintaining the village elder's right to house any visitors. Everyone agreed and all together went to the elder's house for dinner, and he fed everyone well.

Christ entertained His own disciples similarly after His resurrection, after they had fished all night with no results. He said, "'Come and eat breakfast.' … Jesus then came and took the bread and gave it to them, and likewise the fish" (John 21:12, 13). However, none of these examples fully eliminates our lack of faith. Despite everything that God sends us, we are terrified of being poor, and even if we have excess of everything, we are still troubled. Irrational and torturous thoughts begin to burden us: "Where is that in which we hoped?"

Blessed Augustine answers, "Your hope has not yet reached its fulfillment, for the egg is not yet the chick."

IV

There is a story about a certain poor man who, looking into his bag, realized that it was full of pieces of bread collected from many people, so he said, "Now I do not doubt that all will be well." We are very much like this poor man. We only allow ourselves to trust God when our granaries are full enough to last us many years. St John, the Patriarch of Alexandria (seventh century), was not such a man. He lost a tremendous amount of money when a storm at sea destroyed thirteen ships filled with wheat belonging to the Church. And yet, he placed all his trust in God alone, and in Him alone did he find great joy. Half of Alexandria seems to have lost something in this storm, and so all the sailors and surviving passengers hurried to Alexandria as the safest haven. St John sent each of them a letter immediately, consoling them with these words: "The Lord gave, and the Lord has taken away. As it seemed good to the Lord, so also it came to pass. Blessed be the name of the Lord" (Job 1:21). Be patient, my children, and fear nothing!

On the next day, many important citizens came to visit and grieve with him. But he, anticipating them, blamed himself entirely. He said,

> God prevented me from committing a great sin. I would have been exalted in mind, becoming proud that I have so much money to give in alms to the poor. I would begin to have a high opinion of myself, considering myself generous. Therefore the loving Father justly punished His vain son, lest I puff myself up. God mercifully admonishes us by wounding us a little, so that we wake up and quickly turn back to Him. But He is the same God Who existed at the time of Job, equally all-powerful and equally merciful, and He will not abandon us.

With these words, the patriarch consoled those who had come to console him. Soon afterward, the Lord God repaid the Patriarch's losses with interest, and he continued to give generous alms to the poor. To have doubt or weak faith in similar situations is the same as to say that God is miserly or forgetful, but such thoughts belong to godless reprobates, and we should reject them.

St Amatus[88] the desert dweller was, in his time, a living mirror reflecting the providence of God for all who refused to accept it. Amatus, after laboring for thirty years in a monastery, left for the deep desert, where he lived on a rock in great asceticism. One of the brothers of the monastery brought him some bread and a cup of water once every three days, and this was his only source of nourishment. Such asceticism did not please the devil, and he sent a raven to knock over the cup of water and to take the bread in his beak and fly away. Thus, the saint was deprived of three days' worth of food. How did this virtuous man react? Did he curse the raven or utter a foolish complaint against God's providence? Did he upbraid the devil's snares?

He did nothing of the sort. Only *we* would act thus in similar circumstances. Instead, he raised his hand and mind to heaven and began to pray, "I thank You, my Lord God, that it pleased You to arrange an even longer fast for me by Your holy will. I know that this will be very useful for me in the future, for nothing happens without Your providence. Without it, not even a single leaf can fall from a tree." Meanwhile, we sinners think that the destruction of a home by fire, the sinking of ships, the loss of our lands, and personal insults only occur when providence is asleep or looking away. Simply put, we do not believe in God's providence.

Even the pagans understood this simple truth better than we do, for the wisest of them knew that everything in the world does not depend on human will or on blind chance. For example, Seneca said, "We must endure everything bravely, never thinking that there is no first principle of justice that determines all events." Truly, everything happens by God's command and by His just providence. So why are we so often angry that we even curse God?

V

Countless examples and images inspire contemplation of God's providence. A certain pious traveler was nine miles away from a city, but he was weakened by heat, hunger, and thirst. Unable to reach the city, he fell down with a groan under a pear tree. While he lay there, he began to pray, and as he continued to pray, he saw that there was a single fruit on the top of the tree, too high up for him to reach. At that very moment, another man walked past the tree and approached the prostrate traveler. Having learned of the reason for the man's weakness and exhaustion, he gave him a piece of his own bread to strengthen him.

This is a true account, and thousands of similar examples and stories are told, and we see many such things with our own eyes. In spite of this, we have so little faith in God's providence that when our stores and granaries are not filled to the brim with all manner of riches, we despair. Only when our bag is full, when our wallet is packed with money, then we have hope in God. How blind we are! Hope in something we see is not hope at all, for if you see it, why are you hoping for it? But when we hope for that which we do not see, then we hope in perseverance (see Romans 8:24–25). True trust in God is this: when we find ourselves in great need, we do not despair, but instead we defeat all our misfortunes with patience, for the more we endure our sufferings patiently, the more we prepare glory and crowns for ourselves.

Blessed Theodoret wrote that a certain holy man had two barrels. One was full of wheat, the other full of oil. Though he gave both out generously to the poor, he could never empty either barrel. The all-merciful God, Who holds the universe in His hand, also has two barrels, as it were. One is full of food and all of life's necessities; the other is equally full, even overflowing, with spiritual gifts and His providence. Both barrels remain perpetually full.

We must turn to these two treasure houses of God when we are burdened by the greatest deprivations. We must strive to cultivate this one habit: trust in God and give yourself completely to His holy will. The ancients had a memorable saying: "If we did as we must, God would do everything we asked of him." Blessed Jerome said, "Let man be what he must, and that very hour God Who fillest all things will send him everything."

 CHAPTER 30

God's Providence for the Righteous

God gave a consoling promise to those who would do His will: "the one who assails you is as one who assails the apple of His [My] eye" (Zechariah 2:12). Here is proof of this: remember how greatly God preserved His chosen Psalmist even as a young man. He saved him from countless misfortunes, preserving him whole and unharmed. King David himself witnessed this, saying,

> Lord, Thou hast examined me and known me; Thou hast known my down-sitting, and mine up-rising. Thou hast understood my thoughts from afar off. Thou hast searched into my path and my lot, and all my ways hast Thou foreseen. For there is no guile in my tongue; Lo, O Lord, Thou hast known all things, the last and the first; Thou hast made me and hast laid Thy hand upon me. (Psalm 138:1–5)

I

King Saul constantly persecuted David, seeking to deprive him of health and life. But all his efforts were futile, for David's benefactor was God Himself. When David hid in the desert of Maon, Saul hurried there with many soldiers. They surrounded David like a crown, closing off all escape routes. Everyone thought that David was reduced to the condition of a cornered animal surrounded by nets and dogs. Everyone was sure that David's situation was hopeless. Saul himself, on the verge of victory, truly seemed to be the Lion of Judah, his quarry already in his jaws. But it was all in vain. God protected David, for unexpectedly a messenger arrived with news of a Philistine invasion. An angel also appeared to Saul, saying, "Hurry, rush to save your country, for invaders have already entered your lands. Do not delay to attack your enemies and cast them out of the land."[89]

This event, arranged by God, saved the life and freedom of David. The evil intentions of his enemies were destroyed by God's miraculous providence. It is not incredible that God protected David as the apple of His own eye, for David constantly did the will of God, and even when he sinned through human weakness, he always hurried to absolve his sin through heartfelt repentance.

But here is another amazing occurrence: David, already a king, fled from his own rebellious son, Absalom. A certain Shimei, a relative of Saul, began to curse David violently, even casting stones at him: "Come out! Come out! You bloodthirsty man, you unlawful man! The Lord brought upon you all the blood of the house of Saul because you reign in his place. And the Lord now gives the kingdom into the hand of Absalom your son. And now you are caught in your own evil because you are a bloodthirsty man!" (2 Kingdoms 16:7–8). What a frightening image of hatred! Shimei feared neither the Law of God nor the law of man. He had no respect for his own king. What a terrible thing this is!

But this is not the end of the story. David, the meek king of a many people, already brought low by indescribable sorrow and having lost all his riches and honor, walks in bare feet and covers his head and face in shame in order to hide from curious eyes his grief and tears. Such a man Shimei attacked and showered with stones and vile words like sharp nails. This picture vividly shows the great long-suffering and meekness of David, by which he always committed himself fully to the will of God. And so, he accepted Shimei's curses as sent from God. Abishai, the brother of Joab, said in indignation, "Why is this dead dog cursing my lord the king? I will go over and take off his head!" (2 Kingdoms 16:9). But the pious king, thrice chosen by God for the kingship, though rebuked by his angry subject, whom he had offended neither by word nor by deed, not only did not become angry or seek revenge but became the protector of his own persecutor. He said, "Leave him alone and let him curse, because the Lord told him to curse David. Who then shall say, 'Why have you done so?'" (2 Kingdoms 16:10).

Like David, every one of us must look at personal attacks and insults from angry people as sins of self-will that God uses as tools to make the innocent wise and to correct the sinful. All this is like a whip for us when we sin against God, or a bridle, to lead us away from future sin. Therefore, every person who is unfairly slandered or offended should say together with David: "Lord, I do not want to repay this evil done to me; I do not want revenge." "As the Lord lives, the Lord shall strike him, or his day may come to die, or he may go out to battle and be added to his fathers" (1 Kingdoms 26:10). This is how we must raise up our courageous mind to see the providence of God. And if our enemies rise up against us with shrewd plots, we should not fear them. The righteous are completely safe in God's hands, for He said, even to the ancients: "the one who assails you is as one who assails the apple of His [My] eye" (Zechariah 2:12).

II

Let us remember the wondrous Joseph, the first man in Egypt after Pharaoh. Let us remember how he endured troubles and misadventures until the moment that he rose to the highest dignity and power in the land. His first calamity was brotherly envy; it was the reason for his brothers' hatred of him, which was so great that they sold him like a slave, and he was taken to Egypt.[90] In Egypt, his master's wife lusted for him, and her attentions became even more dangerous for him than the hatred of his brothers. For when the beautiful youth, who loved moral purity and chastity, paid no attention to the enticing invitations of his mistress, she slandered him before her husband. Joseph was then imprisoned and remained there for three years.[91]

Truly, his road to glory was not quick, but rather he ascended to a place of authority by a difficult road of sorrows and misfortunes. All this occurred by the incomprehensible providence of God, of which Joseph himself assures us, saying much later to his brothers, "It was not you who sent me here, but God … Do not be afraid, for I belong to God. But as for you, you meant evil against me; but God meant it for good, in order to bring it about as it is this day, to save many people alive" (Genesis 45:8, 50:19–20).

St John Chrysostom expounds on the virtues of Joseph:

It is not enough merely to listen piously to this story, but we must also act as Joseph did. If we do, we will console and calm those who did evil to us without blaming them for it, and we will be able to endure everything patiently and cheerfully. The wise Provider, our God, turns the misfortunes of His friends into joyful events and often an offense can lead to great well-being. Many fell, and through their fall have become better people. The providence of God, in order to make our good intentions a reality, uses not only positive events but also sins. Have you heard of Joseph's fate? Abandon the hatred of his brothers, cast aside envy, destroy the evil counsel that led them to attempt murder. In a word, destroy everything that would have prevented the preservation of the entire nation of Egypt during famine, for if Pharaoh had not had a prophetic dream, there would not have been a mystical interpretation of the dream, and there would not have been any collection of resources for seven years, and Egypt would have perished, as well as the countries surrounding it.

Do you desire to understand the inscrutable mystery of Christ's redemption of the human race? If you had removed the avarice from Judas Iscariot's heart, or the envy from the hearts of the Jews, the salvation of the world, the passion and death of Christ, would not have occurred. If you destroy all demons, immediately pious, ascetic labors will greatly lessen, spiritual triumphs and their subsequent rewards will cease. If you get rid of all persecutors, where will we find the martyrs? These are the laws of God's providence: good comes not only from virtues, but also through evil men and even through the devils themselves.

The sale of Joseph by his brothers was truly arranged by God, but the act itself, inspired by hatred, was due to their sinful, evil will. St Gregory the Great said, "This is how God's power catches the wise in their wickedness. Joseph was sold so that his brothers would not have to bow down to him [that is, they envied his privileged status with their father]; but he became worthy of honor and deference precisely because he was sold."

The same occurred with Moses. Pharaoh condemned him to death, but the daughter of Pharaoh, by God's will, took him into her house. It was as if God told Pharaoh, "I will force you, Pharaoh, to raise in your own home the one who will labor to save all those whom you now cruelly persecute. He will avenge My people."

"This is a new miracle," said St Augustine, "for the daughter of a murderer of men commits deeds of great mercy. 'There is no wisdom, there is no courage, there is no counsel for the ungodly'" (Proverbs 21:29).

III

Let us give another example of God's providence in the life of St Chariton (third century A.D.) (September 28). As St Chariton went to Jerusalem, he was assailed by bandits who, finding nothing of value on his person, tied him up and threw him into their cave. When the robbers left to continue the plunder,

St Chariton immediately turned with his entire heart and soul to God, glorifying God's providence. Contemplating this unexpected attack, he thanked the merciful Heavenly Father for everything and committed himself completely to His will. As he prayed, he saw that a poisonous snake appeared out of a crevice and slithered to a bowl of milk and drank from it. Instead of being grateful, the snake injected some of its poison into the milk. The robbers, having returned to their cave tired and thirsty, immediately began to drink the milk. They drank so fully that they no longer wanted to eat or drink anything else. After a short period of time, they began to feel terrible pain and nausea, and soon they all fell down on the ground, dead.

In this manner, St Chariton became the inheritor and sole master of all the treasures of these robbers. And it was not in vain: having been saved by God's power, St Chariton built in that very place the famous coenobitic monastery that would later bear his name. And he still gave away half of the money to the poor and to other churches and monasteries, transforming the lair of thieves into a temple of God, their ill-gotten gains into virtue.

IV

A certain holy Abba, believing wholeheartedly in the providence of God and constantly committing himself and all his actions to it, gave away all he had to the poor. One time, he ordered that two loaves be given to two poor men standing at the gates of his monastery. But the man at the gate did not listen to the abbot's command, thinking that there was not enough bread to feed the brothers. The Abba decided that this was an opportunity to turn evil actions to the good. After the end of liturgy, when the signal was given to assemble at the refectory, the Abba asked, "From where did we receive these breads?" The man at the gate said, "I saved a few for our own needs." The Abba's demeanor became very strict, and he ordered that all bread be collected into a basket and immediately given away to the poor. Turning to the brothers, he said, "To prevent the spread of disobedience and lack of trust among us, fasting and hunger will be our teachers in trusting God. This good man (indicating the monk at the gate) desired that all the brotherhood put their trust in the generosity of the all-good God. The best medicine for evil avarice is fasting."

St Dorotheos told of a certain holy elder who, during the course of several days, could not eat because of a bad stomach. His cell attendant, hoping to firm up his elder's stomach, decided to prepare something a little more pleasant and filling than usual. He had intended to use honey but he chose the wrong container and used oil that was left over from previous meals and had gone very bad. Thus, despite his best intentions, he added not honey, but death itself, and prepared for his elder a meal that a starving dog would not eat. The sick elder barely tasted it and immediately recognized his servant's mistake, but he remained silent and forced himself to eat. When his stomach refused any more food, he put down the spoon, saying not a word about the quality of the food. But his cell attendant kept asking him to eat more, telling him that he had worked with great eagerness to improve his health. The good elder not only did not utter an angry word, but he did not even become angry in his thoughts. He merely said that he was full and could eat no more.

Then the cell attendant decided to try the food himself. No sooner had the food touched his mouth than he fell at the feet of his master and bitterly said, "I have killed you, reverent father! Why did you cover my error by your silence?"

"Do not fret, my son," said the elder. "If it pleased God for me to eat something sweet, then you would have brought me something sweet."

Abba Dorotheos then notes that the old man spoke truth, for if God willed the sick old man to eat something delicious, He would not have allowed the mistake of the cell attendant, or it would have been very easy for God to turn the old oil into fresh honey. A trusting soul, like this old man, never assumes evil intentions or is suspicious of others. Instead, he always admits that everything happens by God's providence and will.

V

I ask you, dear reader, to understand and memorize the following words of Blessed Jerome: "Everything in the world is directed by divine providence, and it often happens that punishment becomes the best medicine." Here, no doubt, we are amazed that providence allows every object to act in its determined time for the accomplishment of its intended goal, for it is natural for God's providence to connect and harmonize all things, in both small and great matters. Even Epictetus, that great pagan philosopher, said, "Do not ask for events in the world to follow your desires; however, if you are wise, you will desire for everything to be as it will be." This teaching is nearly from the mouth of God, a Christian instruction from a pagan wise man.

St Basil the Great agrees: "Inasmuch as events do not transpire as we would wish them to, let us in all things desire for events to occur as they will [that is, by the direction of the Most High]." St Nilus also agrees: "Do not pray for things to happen as you wish; it is better to pray as Christ Himself taught you to pray:

'Thy will be done on earth as it is in heaven.'" Do not contradict the Creator and Provider. Be favorably disposed to His arrangements, and submit yourself to His will, according to the commandment: Love the Lord your God with all your heart and soul, and love your neighbor as yourself (see Mark 12:29–33).

According to the teachings of all the Holy Fathers, and especially St John Chrysostom, no one can harm us (morally) except ourselves. Every disease is harmful for the body, but unexpected events are not. Lameness in the legs is a disease, but the inability to make decisions is not. If you reason well, you will understand that no misfortune—that is, nothing caused by other people—can harm you or obstruct your spiritual growth. Here are some examples: St James the desert dweller answered the devil who threatened him with physical harm, "If God allows you to, then beat me. Why are you waiting? I will eagerly accept wounds from Him Who in His good will allows me to be beaten. But if you are not allowed, then you can do nothing to me, though you try to attack me a thousand times."

The Greek Empress Irene, after a palace coup that deprived her of the royal throne, prayed to God with the following words, "I thank You, Lord, that You raised me, a foreigner and an unworthy orphan, to the throne of kings; but since You also allowed me to be deprived of it, I consider this to be the consequence of my sins; let Your will be done in me! In all times of plenty and times of want, blessed be the name of the Lord!"

It is absolutely true that no one can harm us except ourselves. Therefore, these words of Blessed Augustine are very apt: "Believe in the Lord God without any doubt, and entrust yourself entirely to Him, or as much as you are able. Then He will not reject you, He will not cease to raise you up to Himself, and he will never allow any evil to befall you, even if you are poor and ignoble." Every person should memorize this teaching and also firmly keep in mind the following principle: nothing contrary to our wishes can ever occur without the will or permission of God. Neither the devil nor any human being can harm us if God does not allow it. We must firmly believe that even if the heaviest calamities attack us by God's disposition, they are still sent by our merciful Father for our benefit, either to make us wiser or to correct our errors and sins. Consequently, no one can harm us except ourselves.

Judith, the pious Hebrew widow who strictly preserved her chastity before God, said, "Besides all this, let us be thankful to the Lord our God, who is testing us just as He did our fathers ... For He has not tested us with the fire, even as He did them, to search out their hearts. Nor has He punished us. Rather, the Lord scourges those drawing near to Him as a warning [that is, He teaches with love]" (Judith 8:25, 27).

The will of the Lord is so exalted, pure, and just that it does not desire, and cannot desire, anything other than what will benefit us, and not merely that, but it desires what is best and most blessed for us. And why would God not desire this? He is all-good; He is all-powerful. Therefore, there is no power greater than He; there is no power other than what proceeds from Him. We are surrounded on all sides and protected by His goodwill and providence. "For Thou wilt bless the righteous, O Lord, for with the shield of Thy favorable kindness hast Thou crowned us" (Psalm 5:13). Let no one ever become angry that this or that misfortune has grieved him; let it be known to him: that which grieves him is a means of preserving and maintaining the very world. God accomplishes human history through our misfortunes and troubles.

A demonic host in the wilderness surrounded St Anthony the Great. The demons took the forms of wild animals: lions, wolves, serpents, scorpions, bears, and so on, and every beast seemed furious to the extreme, roaring and threatening to attack the saint and tear him apart. However, the saint, foreseeing the cunning of the devil and laughing at the powerlessness of the demonic host, said,

> You poor and insignificant creatures. In order to frighten me, you assume the forms of beasts. But if you had any power over me, then a single one of you could destroy me completely. But since the Lord overwhelmed your strength entirely, you are angry because of your impotence. Therefore, you attack me not with power, but with phantasms, gathering as a great host of beasts, hoping to defeat me merely with terror.

He continued bravely, "If you can harm me in any way, then the Lord has given you that authority. Here I am. Approach; tear me apart. Eat me! But if you do not have that authority from God, then why do you waste your energy?"

Thus, brothers, let us trust only in God and His providence, for "the Lord is my shepherd; therefore can I lack nothing" (Psalm 22:1).

 CHAPTER 31

God's Providence for Friends and Enemies

There is an ancient fable about God's providence. Near a spring, a boy was playing, running among the flowers. Then he was tired and sat down near the river and fell asleep. In his dream he saw Fortuna, giver of gifts, and she said to the boy,

> Poor boy, you sat in a place where you could easily fall into the water while sleeping and drown. Stand up and go farther away, so nothing happens to you, for if something were to happen to you, everyone would blame me. They will not say that it was you who fell asleep, but I. They will blame me for not preventing the tragedy.

This is a mythological confirmation of the existence of divine providence. All Christians know David spoke about God in this Psalm: "Behold, He that keepeth Israel shall neither slumber nor sleep" (Psalm 120:4). God has such clear sight (so to speak) that nothing can be hidden from Him. He has such sharp hearing that nothing remains unheard, for He knows and hears every thought. He has hands and shoulders so great and all-encompassing that no one can escape them. The ancient philosophers reached this knowledge only by their reason; however, we know this not only by our reason, for we also read of it in the books of Scripture.

I

Jesus ben Sirach speaks extensively about divine providence: "The works of all flesh are before Him, and nothing can be hidden from His eyes. From age to age He looks upon them, and nothing is marvelous to

Him. No one can say, 'What is this? Why is that?' For all things were created for their uses" (Sirach 39:19–21). God sees the past, the present, and the future, examining it and foreseeing it in a blink of an eye, so to speak. Everything is before His eyes, from Adam to Antichrist, all human generations, all of creation. Never can the providence of God change. "All things are the works of the Lord, for they are exceedingly good. And every command shall be in His appointed time. No one can say, 'What is this? Why is that?' for every question will be answered in His appointed time" (Sirach 39:16).

Therefore, Blessed Augustine said, "To acknowledge the existence of God, but not to confess that He foresees all that will happen is obviously madness." Truly, providence "stretches out from one end of the earth to the other" (Wisdom of Solomon 8:1). Both the highest seraphim and the smallest ant equally receive God's unflagging care. Even in the Old Testament, Moses and Aaron declared, "At evening you shall know the Lord brought you out of the land of Egypt. In the morning you shall see the Lord's glory, for He hears your complaints against God" (Exodus 16:6–7). Truly, in the day of our death, we will know God's wondrous providence in full, for the steps of man begin with God. How then will a sinful man know his path? (see Proverbs 20:19).

Often God, wisely providing for us, leads us along difficult, barely passable roads, but He well knows by what road He will lead us into the heavenly gardens of paradise. Why must we raise our grumbling wails against the most wise and trustworthy pathfinder of our life? Why do we say, "Where are You leading us? Have we not lost our way long ago?" if the road we walk on is determined by God to lead us to heaven? Do not sorrow, my friend! God speaks to us mystically, "Believe only in Me. I will lead you well and you will not grieve in the least when you finish your journey." God's providence accompanies each person in life, from the day of his birth to the day of his passage into eternal life, if only we remain faithful to God's direction, clearly given by our Saviour in His holy Gospels. It is enough for us that this is the only trustworthy path. What does it matter if it seems difficult and painful to us?

II

Speaking of God's providence, we cannot fail to remember the story of King Saul. During that time, there was no other man so kind and courageous as Saul, but he did not remain worthy to the end of his life and subsequently God rejected him. Having been sent by his father to find a lost donkey, Saul found a kingdom. Let us examine the providence of God for this man. God said to the Prophet Samuel, "Tomorrow about this time I will send you a man from the land of Benjamin, and you shall anoint him commander over my people Israel" (1 Kingdoms 9:16). God sent Saul to Samuel in the following way: Saul's father lost his donkeys and he sent his son to find them. Saul, taking one of his servants, went to find them. They passed the mountains of Ephraim and the land of Shalisha, but they found no donkeys. They went through the land of Shallim, and found nothing. They went through the lands of Benjamin, but only when they came to the land of Zuph did Saul decide to abandon the search. But his servant told him of Samuel: "Look now, in this city there is a man of God, and he is an honorable man. All that he says surely comes to pass. So now let us go there; perhaps he can tell us the way we should go" (1 Kingdoms 9:6).

But before Saul met Samuel, the Lord revealed to His prophet that the one who would come to him was Saul, the man whom Samuel must anoint with oil to the kingship over Israel. Everything occurred as though nothing unusual had happened, since the events were guided by divine providence. Saul found the donkeys and also acquired a kingdom, something he never dreamed of. How unutterably profound are God's judgments! What a great mystery! How different are the judgments of God from the thoughts of men! Saul never thought of the crown and scepter, but by God's will he was raised to the throne.

It was not by chance that the donkeys ran away. It was not by chance that Saul was sent to find them. It was not by chance that he could not find them for a long time, nor was it by chance that Saul's servant counseled him to seek Samuel the oracle. All this occurred by God's foresight and mysterious urging to those who follow His will, all in order to establish a king for Israel.

At the same time, a question arises. Why was it pleasing to God to anoint a man like Saul to the kingship, when God knew he would fall into great sin and end his life tragically? Instead of a straight answer, I will offer another question. Why did God create His angels in grace, if He knew in advance that some of them would oppose Him and become eternally rejected by Him for their sin, burning forever in the fires of Gehenna? Why did God place Adam in paradise, when He knew that Adam would remain there only for a short time before being cast out? Why did Christ include Judas Iscariot in the number of the twelve, if He knew in advance that he would become a traitor? Why did Christ send His disciples ahead of Him to Samaria, if He knew that they would not be welcome there? What reason is there for such apparent changes in God's dispositions? You can find thousands of such apparent contradictions.

Blessed Jerome, answering similar questions, answered,

> Do you wish to know the reason for God's apparent change of heart? Here it is: God judges not future deeds, but present ones, and He judges no one

based on His foresight, even if He knows that a good man will subsequently turn into an evil and wicked one. Moreover, in His mercy, God always places a man in a position that he deserves in the present moment, and so gives every person the power, in case of his fall, to turn back to the true path by repentance. Adam did not sin because God foresaw it; rather, God foresaw it because Adam had the capacity, by his free will, to fall into sin.

St Ambrose of Milan said,

Adam did not sin because he received the commandment, nor did Judas sin because he was chosen as one of the twelve. God did not lay on them the inevitability of their future sin. Both of them, if they had strictly kept to their duties, could have held themselves back from the sin. They who God knows will become virtuous often begin as great sinners; while they who He knows will become evil often begin as good men. This means that if you think you stand now, you must be doubly vigilant not to fall later. Even the holy Apostle Paul fell, so you must be careful. Judas fell in order to warn you about your possible fall.

"This is a great instruction for us," said St Euthymius,

that no labor of asceticism or diligence of ours can preserve us whole without the help of God; but even God's help brings no benefit unless our will cooperates with it. Examples of this are Peter and Judas. We must avoid extremes in anything. We must not be too lazy, trusting God to take care of everything for us. Neither should we think that by ourselves, without God's help and His good will, we can do anything good. For God Himself does not do everything for us, to prevent us from falling into laziness, nor does He let us succeed entirely on our own, lest we become puffed up in vanity. Instead, God removes us from everything that may harm us, and inspires and helps us to seek those things that are useful to our salvation.

III

Again I offer the example of Saul, for truly great was God's providence in him. For though he tried numerous times to kill David with the evil sword of the

Philistines, he found himself surrounded by them and rejected by God. He even turned to dark magic in opposition to God's commandment. The witch of Endor called forth the soul of the dead Prophet Samuel (in his living form), who foretold Saul's imminent and inevitable death. Saul, no longer having the courage to avoid or endure his fate, fell on his own sword (see the details of these events in 1 Kingdoms chapters 18–31).

Punishment is inevitable for those who transgress against God's Law. Saul condemned himself to death only by trying to avoid the mockery of his enemies, dishonor, vilification, and shame. But he could not avoid them even so, for the Philistines chopped off his head and threw his body away to be devoured by the birds and the beasts, while his head they paraded with mockery and ridicule through all of Palestine.[92] O God! No one can hide from Your foresight. No one will avoid Your just judgment. The same Saul did not fulfill God's command to destroy the Amalekites and through this called down on himself terrible misfortunes, even death itself. "The weight of a scale is righteousness before the Lord, for His works are righteous standards" (Proverbs 16:7).

Divine providence is inextricable from divine wisdom. Usually, punishment does not immediately follow a transgression. On the other hand, no sin remains fully unpunished. If God did not punish any sins, people would believe that there would be no rewards or punishments after death. Therefore God, by punishing only some, reveals the depths of His providence. When He does not immediately punish a sin, that means that He reserves the punishment for the eternal life after death, unless the sinner repents in time. For this same reason, He delivers some righteous men from troubles and persecutions, while others He delivers into the hands of the godless to be tortured and killed. All the same, God accomplishes everything wisely and with definite intention. Thus, He preserved His three youths in the Babylonian furnace from harm, but the seven Maccabean brothers He delivered to Antiochus for torture and death.[93] Both situations were wise and foreordained by God's providence.

IV

All difficult events in our lives occur by divine providence. God transforms life's calamities to our favor and benefit. He even allows us to fall into sin in order to ultimately lead us to the heights of His divine and mysterious plans for our salvation. For to accomplish good deeds and to also allow evil ones is a quality exclusively belonging to divine providence. Truly, God would never have allowed evil if He were not Himself so mighty in goodness that He could not transform every evil deed into something positive.

Tell me, honestly, when was there a more terrible event in human history than the crime of Adam and the killing of Christ the Saviour, the New Adam? However, this ancestral sin brought God Himself down from heaven to earth to assume our human nature and body. The death of Christ opened heaven to us and returned to us all that we had lost in Adam. The Most High God is the wisest Artist, turning every evil action into a reason to create even better results, as though He were a goldsmith preparing purest gold from a mass of ore. "All things work together for good to those who love God" (Romans 8:28). The fall of Peter gave countless people a true example of genuine repentance.[94] The doubt of Thomas confirmed many in the truth of Christ's resurrection.[95]

From this we come to understand the great words of the Gospel: "I reap where I have not sown" (Matthew 25:26). God did not sow our sins, but from them He still gathers a great harvest of virtues. Truly God can pull honey from a rock and oil from a stone. From the worst crimes He creates the greatest wonders. In the same way, God's providence always works in our favor and always seeks our benefit; so much so, that even the smallest physical pain does not go by without improving us. Consequently, let every one of us, during physical pain or illness, remember that this sickness occurred either by our lack of vigilance, or by the hatred of man, or by something else, but in no case did it occur without God's providence. God determined that this illness is what is most appropriate for our weakness. Its beginning and its end depend solely on God's providence.

Similarly, the effectiveness of medicine also depends on God's providence. God inspires the physician and indicates the proper means for healing the sick, but only if He wills the person to improve. If not, then God's providence acts as a deterrent to the physician's help, for "good and bad, life and death, poverty, and wealth—these are from the Lord" (Sirach 11:14). She should strive to think likewise in any other troubles that we encounter in life, for they are all foreseen by God's providence. Is your enemy disparaging and cursing you? Know that all his curses and hateful words were placed before the ages on the scales of God's providence—the number of words has been long fore-counted, and your enemy is not allowed to speak any more than what God wills. So why do you argue with him and become angry in vain?

All other troubles have been measured, weighed, and foreordained by God. Therefore, submit to God's providence, saying with the Psalmist, "I became dumb, and opened not my mouth" (Psalm 38:10). Your will be done, O my God, for by Your providence and permission all this has been arranged. And since You willed all this, I would be a reprobate and a lawbreaker if I became angry with You. Thus, I submit to Your holy will, O my God, and with gratitude I accept and patiently endure everything You send me.

Clement of Alexandria said,

Everything that we have said already concerning God's will is known to the one who is faithful to God and who confesses that everything in the world is directed to the good. Therefore, with an untroubled heart, let us bravely endure everything that occurs to us in life. Truly it is not human reason, which often errs, but God's goodwill that directs everything to the best possible ends. God accomplishes His intentions sometimes with the most insignificant of means without any hindrance. "Remember the former things of old, for I am God, and there is no other besides Me, declaring beforehand the latter events before they come to pass and are accomplished together. I say, all my counsel shall stand, and I will do whatever I will to do." (Isaiah 46:9–10)

V

The previous discussion of divine providence, if reread daily, inspires profound peace in the soul. Then the human will easily inclines itself to the will of God and submits to it with joy and calmness. For whoever entrusts himself in all things to the providence of God always remains free from grief and temptation. "His people will dwell in a city of peace, and will dwell in confidence, and they will rest with riches" (Isaiah 32:18).

A certain God-inspired elder said, "Man will not have peace in his heart until he does not separate himself from everything, saying, 'God and I are alone in the entire world.'" Blessed Augustine said, "O my God! You have as much care for all people as You do for a single person." St Gregory the Great said, "Since God cares for every person as well as everyone in general, so His providence covers all, as though He only cared for one person." So, dear reader, God cares and provides for you individually, as though He had no other responsibilities in the world. The number of God's people does not divide His providence or weaken its power. For Him, the care of one person is the same as the care of countless millions. In the same way as God once cared only for Noah and his family—or for Adam in paradise—so now God's providence and care extends to all people in the world equally.

Let everyone call out to the Protector and trustworthy Provider as to the beloved: "My beloved is mine, and I am his" (Song of Songs 2:16). I revere God and keep all His commandments as though there were nothing else in the world to hold my attention and thoughts. Equally does my salvation belong in God's care and trust to such a degree that it truly seems that He has no other beloved than myself. He belongs to me completely, and I belong to Him. He is the Lord Who directs me, and I am an obedient servant ready to fulfill all the commands of my Lord, for He ordered that it be so, saying, "Think about Me, and I will always keep you in My thoughts as well; thus will I remember My promises to you and have constant care for you."[96] Truly God in His mercy and generous gifts is all-encompassing. By His providence He protects and saves everyone in general and every person individually. "The eyes of the Lord are in every place; they keep watch over both the evil and the good" (Proverbs 15:3). "The ways of man are before the eyes of God, and He keeps close watch on all his paths" (Proverbs 5:21).

O, if only we would cheerfully plunge ourselves into the unfathomable depth of His Fatherly providence! Then, every person would be able to say with unconquerable conviction, "The Lord is my protector, and I will not be left in poverty or danger. The Lord will protect me and will make easy all my ways" (compare with Psalm 22:1–2). If we strive for calmness of soul, if we desire to trust in God, if we want to live by the will of God, then it is imperative of us to always keep the providence of God before our eyes. The more completely we trust in God's providence, the more eagerly will we do His will.

CHAPTER 32

Concerning Widespread Doubt or Weak Faith in God

Christ spoke of nothing to His disciples as often as He spoke of weak faith or unbelief. He warned everyone against unbelief not only in words, but in actions that proved the power of faith and the powerlessness of weak faith or doubt in God's providence or in His ability to save people from dangers. There was only one reason for Christ's miracles—the calming of the storm at sea, the feeding of the five and four thousand, and others—to vividly confirm the ever-present help of God to the faithful and to those who hope in the One God in Holy Trinity. What was the significance of Peter's sinking into the waves as he walked on them? Christ Himself taught us by so many signs that doubt has no place in His followers' hearts, and so He chastened Peter for his lack of faith and his doubt. It was as if Christ were saying, "Are you so foolish, Peter, that you cannot understand the first and most important of My teachings?"[97]

Weak faith is found in different forms. Some people do not have enough faith in God because He does not always punish His enemies and allows them to remain in their sins. Others doubt that God will hear their prayers, especially when their conscience either rebukes them or terrifies them, suggesting that God will not forgive their sins. A third group fears that God will deprive them of all they need for life and sustenance. All these forms of doubts, obviously attractive in their delusion, turn many people away from God and plunge them into perdition. The less we recognize the evil of weak faith, the more dangerous it is for us. The source of weak faith is our excessive trust in ourselves. We often think more of ourselves than of God, even going so far as to imagine that everything will simply cease with death. We will examine how dangerous such unbelief is in these next sections.

I

Solomon rebukes such self-sufficiency, saying, "Trust in God with all your heart, and do not exalt your own wisdom ... Do not rely on your own discernment, but fear God, and turn away form every evil" (Proverbs 3:5, 7). The general message of his Proverbs can be summarized thus: "Do not glory in your own wisdom, for the first sign of madness is to consider yourself wise." But how many people are willing to consider their own wisdom as nothing? Who does not boast of his own strength, goodness, beauty, wisdom, or riches? But all this is to our detriment: "The thoughts of the righteous are judgments, but the ungodly devise deceits" (Proverbs 12:5). God, desiring to root out of us the sin of excessive self-reliance, sometimes punishes us severely for it.

Remember the arrogance of Goliath, who thought that he could beat the entire army of Israel merely with his imposing presence and his boasting tongue. Seeing the boy David challenging him, armed with a shepherd's staff and a purse, he said, "Am I as a dog, that you come against me with a staff and stones? Come to me, and I will give your flesh to the birds of heaven and the beasts of the field" (1 Kingdoms 17:22, 23).

Holofernes, who also thought highly of himself, was not even counted worthy by God to receive his death at the hands of a man, but his proud arrogance was trampled underfoot and defeated by a woman. Nebuchadnezzar, the king of Babylon, walked among his temples and said, "Is not this the great Babylon which I built as a home for my kingdom, by my mighty power for the honor of my glory?" (Daniel 4:30) O Nebuchadnezzar! Stop! Hold your tongue! Until this moment you have eaten thousands of platters of the best, most luxurious food, but soon you will see before your face another, unusual sustenance, which will inspire thoughts of abject humility. You will eat food more proper for oxen, until you learn how to speak and think of yourself in a more human way. Your morning bath will be the cold dew; your fine raiment will be replaced by long, matted hair like a lion's mane. Instead of buffed fingernails, you will grow claws like talons.

Nebuchadnezzar had hardly finished speaking these words of self-praise than he heard a voice from heaven, saying,

> King Nebuchadnezzar, your kingdom has passed from you, and they shall drive you from men. Your dwelling shall be with the wild animals, and they shall make you eat grass like an ox. Seven years shall bring this change upon you, until you know that the Most High rules over the kingdom of men, and will give it to whomever He will. (Daniel 4:31–32)

Immediately, all this happened to Nebuchadnezzar. For excessive trust in himself, a man became no better than cattle. But hear now how Nebuchadnezzar became a man again, having learned to put his trust in God, and not in himself.

Nebuchadnezzar said,

> At the end of the time, I, Nebuchadnezzar, lifted my eyes to heaven, and my understanding returned to me. Then I blessed the Most High and praised and glorified Him who lives forever; for His authority is an eternal authority, and His kingdom is from generation to generation. All the inhabitants of the earth are counted as nothing, and He does according to His will with the army of heaven and with the habitation of earth. No one can resist His hand or say to Him, "What are You doing?" (Daniel 4:34–35)

Arrogance is a terrible evil; it even toppled the holy Apostle Peter. Holy Peter! Why are you weeping so bitterly only at the cry of a rooster? You should have wept before, when the Lord told everyone of His Passion, when He announced His terrible death at the Mystical Supper. Then tears would have been timely. But arrogance banished your tears, and instead of them you made the foolish promise: "Even if all were made to stumble because of You, I will never be made to stumble" (Matthew 26:33). Is that so? Only a few hours later, this promise, given in arrogance, was not only not fulfilled but was destroyed utterly. St Basil the Great said, "No one is more often defeated than the person who trusts in himself excessively. On the contrary, whoever has little trust in himself never begins a single labor without first calling down God's help."

St Ambrose of Milan complained to Blessed Augustine's mother that Augustine was too arrogant and put too much stock in his own reason and wisdom. Truly, Augustine did not become free of this sin until he felt in himself how much damage it was causing. He admitted this later, saying to God in confession, "It seemed to me, Lord, that I could be self-sufficient; I did not suspect that You, my Lord, directed me and mystically guided me. But when You, my God, departed from me only a small distance, immediately I fell into despair, and became convinced of my need for You."

In summary, it is very dangerous, even calamitous, to trust your own mind, wisdom, talents, or strength, for they fall over even at the slightest wind. "Thus says the Lord: 'Let not the wise man boast in his wisdom, nor let the mighty man boast in his might, nor let the rich man boast in his riches'" (Jeremiah 9:22).

II

Not only should we not trust in ourselves, but we should not trust in other people either. "Cursed is the man who puts his hope in man, and who will strengthen the flesh of his arm in him, and withdraws in his heart from the Lord" (Jeremiah 17:1). For worthless and fickle is such trust in another human being who cannot save you or even himself.

In order to catch their prey, elephant poachers partially saw through the trees that elephants lean against when they rest at night. The tree remains standing, but it hangs by a thread, and the lightest touch can push it over. The elephant, as is its habit, leans on the tree, but immediately falls down with it, and because it put its full weight on the tree, the force of the fall crushes its internal organs, and the elephant dies.[98]

Many people, like these elephants, also choose to lean against trees. This man tries with all his might to impress a prince; that one flatters a rich master, offering his services at the least provocation, seeking his love and mercy. We also find some who try to attract the hearts of others through rich gifts and even bribes, or any number of other means. Poor people! You delude yourselves, and all this only leads to your own downfall. These trees against which you so like to lean have long been cut down by God's invisible scythe, and despite your hope and desire they will fall down unexpectedly. Together with them, all your hopes will be dashed. Blessed Augustine, warning against such delusion, said, "Many have highly valued friendship with the great of this world; but they fell and took their friends down with them into the same abyss."

The Prophet Jonah built himself a cover from a gourd, and sat in its shadow with great pleasure, but the short-lived plant had two enemies: the heat of the sun and the worm. And so, the gourd perished in a single day, and together with the gourd, Jonah's shade also disappeared, and he was left to the heat of the sun.[99]

If you examine the works of this world carefully, you will see that the world is filled with shade-giving trees that flourish and protect those who stand underneath, but only for a short time. Soon they will fall from many worms eating away at them—envy, slander, legal proceedings, dishonor, and death. All these things eat away and destroy these trees that provide such shabby hope for men.

A servant puts all his trust in his good master, but suddenly his master dies and the servant remains without a benefactor. Another chooses for himself a strong and rich man to be his protector, but soon even he will die, or his riches and authority will diminish, and immediately the shade of the gourd disappears. The sons of strong people hope to be covered by the shade of their fathers' honor, authority, or dignity, but suddenly God takes away this shade, and the poor men who hid under it are burnt by the sun.

Remember the story of Haman, the strong man at the court of King Artaxerxes, who persecuted the Jews.[100] Remember the many other powerful people who entrusted their lives not to the Most High, but to their own chosen benefactors, and through this misplaced trust, they perished.

III

We are all God's creation. Therefore, we must strengthen ourselves by God's grace, mercy, and might. David, taught well by his many misfortunes, instructs us by experience: "O put not your trust in princes, in the sons of men, in whom there is no salvation. His spirit shall go forth, and he shall return again to his earth; in that day all his thoughts shall perish. Blessed is he that hath the God of Jacob for his helper, whose hope is in the Lord his God" (Psalm 145:3–5). The scriptures call hope in man a "shadow." What is more inconstant and delusive than a shadow? Trust in man is the same. "Many serve in the presence of leaders, but righteousness comes to a man from the Lord" (Proverbs 29:27).

When Jacob returned to the land of Canaan from Mesopotamia, his brother Esau and four hundred of his men came to meet him. Jacob feared that Esau came against him in war, and he prayed to God for salvation. God was close to him and blessed him, promising His aid (though He left him with a limp).[101] You may ask, "Is this help or providence? Did God help Jacob by damaging his body?" Truly God concealed His help even in leaving Jacob with a limp, for now Jacob—and by extension, we ourselves—will learn not to trust in our own strength or the strength of other people, but only to establish our hope in the might, dominion, and goodness of the One God. For God sometimes takes the strength away from the mighty by His will; but to the weak, lame, blind He invisibly grants His help.

Gideon, that glorious commander, entered the fray against the Midianites with only 300 men after sending away twenty-two thousand soldiers back home, for God had commanded him to do this. God declared to him also the reason for this, saying, "Lest otherwise Israel boast against Me, saying, 'This my own hand, it saved me'" (Judges 7:2).

The son of Hadad, the King of Syria, berated Ahab, King of Israel, as a weak and worthless leader and threatened to destroy all of Israel. However, his threats came to naught. Though the son of Hadad had thirty-two kings as allies—many mounted warriors, infantry, and weapons—he was beaten in the first battle. The second time he gathered one hundred thousand Syrian infantry against Israel, but they were decimated in a single day. The rest ran away into the city of Aphek, where a wall collapsed on twenty-seven thousand people, killing them all.[102] This is a striking example of what happens when someone trusts not in God, but in himself and his own power.

Here is another example of arrogance and trust in other people. King Asa began his reign well and was pleasing to God, for which the Lord rewarded him with a glorious victory over the King of Ethiopia, who had attacked Israel with an army of a million.[103] But, alas! Even this pious king was brought down by trust in human strength, as the Prophet Hanani said to his face, "Because you relied on the king of Syria and did not rely on the Lord your God, therefore the army of the king of Syria escaped from your hand" (2 Chronicles 16:7). Much evil came about as a result of this.

Blessed Augustine, commenting on verse seven of Psalm 30 ("Thou hast hated them that hold of superstitious vanities"), said,

> Disdaining all that is worthless, you trust in the Lord God alone, for if you will put your trust in riches, you will be deluded. If you trust might, power, and human glory, then you embrace futility. In all these cases, when you die, all your previous hopes will avail you nothing, while if you still remain alive, they may still perish and you will remain with nothing. Every time you fail to believe in God, you will be hounded by despair, hatred, and coldness to all that is good and useful. Wherever there is unbelief, there is great fear of eternal perdition, unending worries, and confusion. In other words, every person who trusts in himself or in another man builds his home on the sand. The person who is established in faith in God builds his life on rock, and will never be destroyed.

IV

There is nothing so unpleasant to God as our weak faith, which was strictly punished even in those whom He loves. Moses, a man loved by God, sinned twice through unbelief, and for this alone he died before his time, unworthy of reaching the Promised Land, only seeing it from a distance from Mount Moab. This was Moses's first sin of unbelief. During the wandering in the desert, the people began to complain about their lack of normal food, saying, "Who will give us meat in the desert?" Moses spoke to God, saying,

> The people I am among are six hundred thousand men on foot; yet You are saying, "I will give them meat, so they may eat for a whole month." Shall sheep and oxen be slaughtered for them, to provide enough for them? Or shall all the fish of the sea be gathered together for them, to provide enough for them? (Numbers 11:21–22)

O Moses! Seek the source of this perceived impossibility in your own doubt, not in God's providence. "Is the Lord's hand unable to provide for them?" (Numbers 11:23) After this, Moses should have learned from his mistake and treated the providence of God with more respect. But he forgot about the quail that God rained from the heavens, and again fell into the same unbelief. When the Israelites were in the Desert of Sin, there was no drinkable water in the area. The Israelites complained at Moses and Aaron. God commanded them to gather the people at a cliff and say to them that the cliff face would be the source of their water. But Moses spoke rebuking words to the people instead: "Must we bring water for you out of this rock?" (Numbers 20:10). Then he struck the stone twice. The water indeed flowed forth, but immediately the voice of God came from heaven, informing Moses and Aaron of their punishment for their insufficient faith: "Because you did not believe me, to sanctify Me before the children of Israel, therefore you shall not bring this congregation into the land I am giving them" (Numbers 20:12).

When Moses was near death, God showed a fruitful land to him from a distance. At the same time, He rebuked Moses: "This is the land I swore to give Abraham, Isaac, and Jacob, saying, 'I will give it to your seed.' I show it to your eyes, but you shall not go in there" (Deuteronomy 34:4). How important it is for us to root out of our hearts this poison of unbelief—so abhorrent to God's honor—, which usually leads to heavy punishment. The Israelites often sinned by repeated unbelief, which even the greatest of miracles were not capable of correcting, for if the Jews did not touch with their hands or see with their eyes immediately, they regressed into their unbelief, saying, "Such a thing is impossible." This unbelief became so strong in them that they even uttered imprecations against God, as though He had forgotten them and despised them. Very often they said something like this: "Would we had died, smitten by the Lord in the land of Egypt, when we sat by the pots of meat and ate bread to the full" (Exodus 16:3). "Would we had died in the land of Egypt or in this desert. Why did the Lord bring us to this land to fall in war? Our wives and children shall be plundered. It is better for us to return to Egypt" (Numbers 14:2–3). As though all places are not the same when it comes to dying!

Perhaps someone is confused by this and asks, "These were God's chosen people! He did not give them wine; he did not even give them water! Why did God do this?" The answer is simple—this was the only way to root out their unbelief. Why did He afflict those same people with the serpents that not only wounded them but even killed many? This was allowed because of their unbelief. Why did God not forbid the killing of twenty thousand or thirty thousand at once? Only for the sake of their unbelief, because God could not uproot the unbelief from this obstinate people by any other means except greater punishment. For unbelief constantly reappeared within them.

God spoke of them both with anger and with pity: "How long will these people provoke Me? How long will they not believe Me with all the signs I performed among them? I will strike them with death and destroy them, and I will make you and your father's house into a great and more numerous nation than this one" (Numbers 14:11–12). Moses then began to beg for his people. He fell on the ground and prayed, but God's decision was the following:

Say to them, "As I live, says the Lord, surely in the manner you spoke in My hearing, so I will I do to you: our bodies shall fall in this desert, and all your census, who were numbered from twenty years old and above, as many as murmured against Me; and you shall not enter the Land upon which I stretched out My hand that you might settle upon it, except for Caleb the son of Jephunneh and Joshua the son of Nun; but your children, whom you said would be plunder, I will bring them into the land, and they shall inherit the land from which you apostatized." (Numbers 14:28–30)

In a word, only those who did not show unbelief entered the Promised Land. Thus weak faith was punished. However, even after this, during the crossing over the river Jordan, the Jews one again revealed their unbelief.

V

In the first book of Kingdoms, after the Amalekites destroyed the city of Ziklag, they took women and children of all ages into captivity. The people were brought to despair by this calamity, even ready to stone David for his failure to save the town. But no matter how great their lack of faith or trust in God, David showed his greatness and constant trust in the Lord his God. Strengthened by his undoubting hope, he pursued the enemy with only four hundred men. Finding them encamped and celebrating with food and drink in excess, David attacked them and harassed them from the morning to the evening, destroying them utterly by the next morning. Thus David returned everything and everyone taken in Ziklag by the Amalekites, from the least to the greatest, including plunder and the wives, sons, and daughters of the inhabitants of Ziklag. In addition, he brought back a great supply of booty from the enemy. In the process, he did not lose a single man. This is how God justifies those who trust in Him (1 Kingdoms 30).

During the great famine in Samaria, Elisha foretold that tomorrow at this time "a measure of fine flower will be sold for a shekel, and for a shekel, two measures of barley. So the officer on whose hand the king relied retorted to Elisha and said, 'Look, even if the Lord in heaven will make a downpour of rain, this event shall not happen.' And Elisha said, 'Behold, you shall see this with your own eyes, but you shall not eat of it'" (4 Kingdoms 7:1–2). Elisha's prophesy occurred just as he predicted—the army of Syria fled at night from Samaria, frightened by God, and left behind its entire supply train. Because of this, bread became extremely cheap, and the people hurried to buy in bulk. At the same time, the doubting officer was there to witness all this, and he was crushed by the throng of people rushing to buy the cheap bread. Truly, "the reasoning of mortals is cowardly, and our intents are unsafe" (Wisdom of Solomon 9:14).

God is almighty. He knows the present, past, and future completely and in exact detail. He knows the order of His deeds, and He has exact knowledge of all things created by His hands. Everything revealed to us in the world seems as if it is being uncovered sequentially, like a light gradually illuminating the shadows. However, what seems to us to be accidental, He foresaw before the ages. Divine providence cannot change in its all-wise dispositions. These dispositions are the deepest and most inscrutably mystery. However, many see the countless crimes and lawlessness that remain unpunished by God's longsuffering. They also see how the chosen of God are corrected and tested by many sorrows, and so they fall into the bottomless abyss of unbelief, because they think that God pays no attention to the deeds of mankind. The Preacher said, "Vanity is in all things: one event happens to the righteous man and the ungodly man, to the good man and the evil man, to the pure man and the impure man, to the man who sacrifices and the man who does not sacrifice. As is the good man, so is the man who sins; as is he who takes an oath, so is he who fears an oath" (Ecclesiastes 9:2).

All these things seem to us without a reasonable cause occurring by accident. But when we think like this, we are no different from a madman who looks at a watch and, not knowing anything about the internal mechanism, thinks that the hands move on their own, by accident, and not because of the clockwork mechanism. A mechanic, on the other hand, understands the mechanism very well. In the same way, God's providence is not understandable to us and remains hidden from us because we are fools, but it contains within itself an all-encompassing rational order that justly rules the cosmos. We see the external order of cosmic and local phenomena and events, but the wondrous, wise providence of God, which brings into movement the mechanism of the cosmos and maintains and tunes its workings, is hidden from us.

Thus many, seeing the prosperity of the evil and the misfortunes of the good, insist that God's providence does not exist, and everything depends exclusively on the will and reason of man, or it occurs by blind chance or fortune[104]. However, those who believe in the most-high wisdom of God and in His providence think quite differently. St Gregory the Theologian said, "I truly know that God is the highest cause, Who knows in complete fullness the reasons for our intentions and actions."

This unerring clock of God's providence accurately depicts all the milliseconds, seconds, and minutes of every person's actions. King Belshazzar, during a lavish feast, saw a hand writing something illegible on the wall, and his demeanor suddenly changed from joyful to frightened. What did you see, O king? Why are you afraid? Whose hand is it? If the writing is illegible to you, why do you freeze in fear?

The frightened king asked all the wise men of Babylon to explain the written words, but no one could interpret them. All they saw were letters, like the hands on a clock face, but no one knew why they moved the way they do. Then the Prophet Daniel came and explained to the king both the words and their meaning, saying,

> You lifted yourself up against the Lord God of heaven and brought the vessels of His house before you. You, your nobles, your concubines, and your wives drank wine from them and praised the gods of gold, silver, copper, iron, wood, and stones, which do not see or hear or know. But you have not glorified the God who holds your breath in His hand and knows all your ways. Therefore the finger of the hand was sent by Him, and He ordered this writing. So this is the writing He ordered: Mene, Tekel, Upharsin. Now this is the interpretation of each word. Mene: God has measured your kingdom and finished it. Tekel: He weighed

you on the scales, but you were found lacking. Upharsin: Your kingdom has been divided and given to the Medes and Persians. (Daniel 5:23–28)

How did Daniel know all this? He read it in the unerring clock of God's divine providence. That same night, Belshazzar was killed.

VI

From the preceding example, it should be obvious that the deeds of every person, whether successful or not, are indicated to the smallest detail in the chronometer of divine providence, and this chronometer cannot err even the slightest bit, for it is perfectly tuned. "For assuredly, I say to you, till heaven and earth pass away, one jot or one tittle will by no means pass from the law [that is, God's will] till all is fulfilled" (Matthew 5:18). If we believe the time on a clock (knowing that it was built by a good engineer), then what sort of madness or obstinacy is it to rebuke, or even disparage, the chronometer of the great divine economy ruling the world? That clock is unerring, and all events in history are arranged by it in the best possible manner.

The wise man prays thus to the Lord: "Your providence, O Father, governs its [a ship's] course, because You have given it a path in the sea and a safe track in the waves, showing that You can save from every danger, and that even without skill one may embark upon the sea" (Wisdom of Solomon 14:3–4). Therefore, one must always trust only in God's providence. When we see that virtuous people are humiliated, mocked, and abused—while the evil live calmly and successfully—we sometimes think of providence as either sleeping or excessively lenient. Even saints were disturbed by such thoughts sometimes, but their doubts always served for our instruction and confirmation.

King David said concerning himself:

Nevertheless, my feet were almost moved; my steps had well-nigh slipped, for I was envious of the wicked, seeing the peace of sinners. For there is no fear in their death ... Their injustice swelleth out like fat ... They are not in the labor of other folk, neither are they plagued like other men. Then in vain have I cleansed my heart and washed mine hands in innocency? (Psalm 72:2–5, 13)

David thought to reveal the reason for such incongruity between rewards and merits, and so he continued, "And I sought to understand, but it was too hard for me, until I went into the sanctuary of God; then understood I their end" (Psalm 72:16–17). We will come to know all this later in the kingdom of heaven; now, in this life, there is no possibility of fully understanding the judgments of God.

The Prophet Jeremiah said with regret, "O Lord, You are righteous, that I may plead my case with You, to speak to You concerning judgments. Why does the way of the ungodly prosper, and all who deal treacherously flourish? You planted them, and they took root. They bear children and are fruitful. You are near in their mouth, but far from their mind" (Jeremiah 12:1–2). Habbakuk also asked the Lord why He does not look at the violence done against the righteous by the ungodly; the innocent sufferers are like voiceless fish. There is no just judgment. The law has lost its force, and injustice reigns over the land (compare with Habbakuk 1:1–4).

What is the reason for this seeming doubt in the justice of God's providence, which is expressed even by the prophets? The reason is this: we look at only one aspect of God's providence, while the other side of His justice is hidden from our eyes, because the narrow scope of our vision cannot see the entire view of the Lord's judgments. Only after the Second Coming will we understand God's justice concerning every person and the whole world. Therefore, Apostle Paul said, "Judge nothing before the time, until the Lord comes, who will both bring to light the hidden things of darkness and reveal the counsels of the hearts. Then each one's praise will come from God" (1 Corinthians 4:5).

We see and understood only the smallest part of God's providence, but His dispositions, decisions, actions, and ultimate intentions are not understandable to us. Even historical events, events of our own past, are difficult to assess accurately (if we know them at all!). As for the future, we know nothing. We make foolish judgments about God's providence and falsely criticize it. But when the Lord comes, His light will illumine the reasons for everything—why He allowed the fall of the angels and the first sin of our ancestors, or why He chose such an obstinate nation to be His chosen ones. Why does He allow some to be born Christians, and others not? Why does He deliver some from all afflictions and grief, while others He allows to live a life filled with sorrows and misfortunes? Only then will every person receive a proper reward for everything that he patiently endured here for Christ our Saviour.

VII

From the previous sections, our responsibility to align our actions and deeds with the will of God becomes obvious. However, when we learn the will of

God, we may have some questions. For example, someone who is sorrowful in his soul and confused in his thoughts might ask:

> The same thing happened to me that happened to Saul. When Saul asked the Lord how to react to the attack of the Philistines, the Lord did not answer him, either in dreams or by the high priest or through the prophets (1 Kingdoms 28:6). God does not tell me anything about the resolution of my problems. What should I do? Should I go to mediums? But that is forbidden by God.

The best answer to this can be found in the words of Jesus ben Sirach:

> My son, if you draw near to serve the Lord, prepare your soul for temptation. Set your heart right and be steadfast, and do not strive anxiously in distress. Cleave to Him and do not fall away, that you may be honored at the end of your life. Accept whatever is brought upon you, and in exchange for your humiliation, be patient; because gold is tested in fire and acceptable men in the furnace of abasement. Believe in Him, and He will help you; make your ways straight and hope in Him. (Sirach 2:1–6)

Think about it: it is hardly a labor at all to be brave when everything in life goes our way. A helmsman will never show his skill at directing the ship if he always sails in still waters and with a stiff wind. In order to test our heart's mettle, we must experience something contrary to its desires. Our entire life is filled with troubles and misfortunes, and rarely do we ever have a calm moment (even if we do, it rarely lasts long). If you react to misfortunes with anger, you will feel the greatest heaviness. But if you accept everything cheerfully, then you will always have peace of heart. Cry as much as you like, but you will still have to drink the cup of bitterness to the dregs, because the heavenly Physician gives you this cup for your own benefit.

If you are good, you will understand that sorrows are sent to you to correct you in your fallenness. However, if you are angry, your sorrow will be the same as penal servitude. Do not repeat the words Saul spoke to Samuel: "I am deeply distressed. The Philistines are making war against me, and God has departed from me and does not answer me anymore" (1 Kingdoms 28:15). God would not have departed from you, O king, if you had not first left Him. Let every person remember this—God leaves no one during any kind of difficulty, except when the person has already turned his back on God. If Saul had even a little wisdom, he would have spoken to the Lord with the words of the Byzantine Emperor Maurice (539–602 A.D.): "Lord, it is better if You punish me here, rather than there [in the eternal life]."

So, Christian, do not seek the help of soothsayers or mediums, the enemies of God, during your troubles, sorrows, or persecutions. Do not lose hope, but trust in God. Run to the Mother of God for help, fall down at the feet of the crucified Lord Jesus Christ, pray to His angels and to His friends, the saints. They are the only trustworthy haven and protection. Comfort yourself with the words of David and Job. "But I shall always hope in Thee, and will set myself to praise Thee more and more" (Psalm 70:14). "Though the Mighty One should lay His hand upon me, and already He has begun, I will speak and reason before Him. This will turn for me into salvation, for there shall be no deceit before Him" (Job 13:15–16). Many of us are greatly deluded when we turn to the help of other people. Often we do not abandon our delusion until, having labored for a long time in futility, we are left with no choice but to remember God. Therefore, all help that we seek from men first of all, before God, is often rendered useless by God's disposition, in order to wake us up from our delusion.

Why then does God allow many people, even in our time, to be spiritually destroyed by the cunning of mediums and soothsayers? It is not strange, because this lack of faith—so widespread in the world—deserves to be punished. Many people seek so-called faith healers instead of physicians for their ailments, preferring the devil's friend to a proper pharmacist. God justly punishes us with our own sin. Paulinus recalls that not a single magician could harm St Ambrose of Milan, because Ambrose had a firm and hopeful trust in God in all things. After the death of Empress Justina, who was an Arian, a certain magician named Innocent was brought in to be tortured, and during his tortures he screamed, saying that he felt more pain from Ambrose's guardian angel than from the torturers.

They asked, "Why does his angel punish you?"

He answered,

During the reign of Justina, I used my power to incite the people of Milan against Ambrose. I even climbed to the top of their church at midnight and brought sacrifices to the demons there, in order to provoke even greater hatred for Ambrose among the populace. But no matter how much I tried to attack him, I had no success. I even noticed that the people came to love their bishop even more, holding fast to the truth of Orthodoxy. Being in no state to commit any kind of evil, I sent the demons to Ambrose's house to kill him, but the demons told me that not only could they not approach the bishop, but they could not even approach the gates of his house, because fire came from the doors and burned them.

Do you see how God protects and preserves those who lay their complete trust on Him? Truly, the more we trust and are bold before Him, the more He increases His goodness and generosity to us. But alas! How few of us commit our hearts entirely to God! Examine the habits and customs of people, and everywhere you will see that unbelief prevails and constantly returns and even increases, resulting in many pointless and false fears. Often people fear that their harvest will be destroyed by snow or driving rain or drought or lightning strikes. Sometimes they fear they will not have enough food. Sometimes they fear that when disease or unexpected calamities strike, they will not have enough money saved up. Sometimes they despair at the mere rumor of impending war. Sometimes their despair at losing a loved one is so great that they even attempt to take their own life. Finally, they anticipate some difficulties or inconveniences, and immediately they doubt the success of their enterprise, believing only that which they see at this moment.

All this occurs only because they have an incorrect, doubtful understanding of God's goodness and His all-powerful might, and this leads to pathetic, unbelieving anxiety for perishable things. We care for them much more than we strive to acquire the eternal blessed life. A true trust in God with undoubting faith in Him is the key to all God's treasures, both necessary temporary goods and eternal heavenly blessedness. On the contrary, lack of trust in God is either the beginning of countless iniquities or the threat of a calamitous end for the reprobate.

CHAPTER 33

Knowledge of God's Providence Leads to Greater Trust in God, and This Trust Gives Birth to Agreement with God and His Holy Will

In the same way as the chain links of a gold necklace connect to each other perfectly, so the knowledge of divine providence is related to trust in God, and trust in God is intimately connected to fashioning the human will to the divine. Show me a man who is completely sure of God's providence, no matter what is going on in the world, no matter what happens to him personally, and I will show you clear proof that he has already entrusted himself and submitted to the will of God. In other words, such a man considers the will of God to be either in command or the limit of his own will, according to the Scriptures: "[For God has] made known to us the mystery of His will, according to His good pleasure which He purposed in Himself" (Ephesian 1:9) "that [we] may be filled with the knowledge of His will in all wisdom and spiritual understanding" (Colossians 1:9).

I

Noah was the first to receive from God the instruction and teaching concerning God's constant providence. God revealed to him in detail the reasons for the building of the ark. He told him exactly how it should measure in height, width, and length. He told Noah how he should bring all the different species of animals (both pure and impure) into the ark, indicating the number of each. He taught Noah how to properly arrange them within the ark and how to prepare food for them. He also told Noah the exact time he was to enter the ark with his own family. The Lord God willed that the entire human race, except for Noah's family, be drowned in the waters.[105]

Thus Noah came to understand God's wondrous providence for all creatures; this knowledge created in him a desire to completely entrust his fate, as well as the fate of his family and the beasts, to God (though they would be stranded and floating in amid the coffins of all things that live upon the earth). Because he trusted God, it was easy for Noah to submit his own will completely to the will of God and to do everything that God commanded. This is why Noah is so highly praised: "Thus Noah did according to all the Lord God commanded him, so he did" (Genesis 6:22).

Here it is necessary to carefully elucidate the language of Scripture. Noah entered with his family into the ark and "the Lord God shut him in the ark" (Genesis 7:16). Why is it important the God locked them into the ark and, so to speak, took away the key? Would it not have been better to give the key to Noah, so that Noah himself could open the ark when the floodwaters receded? But God willed it otherwise, so that everyone in the ark would know Who was their true Master and Saviour. Knowing this, they would put all their trust in Him alone.

In the same way Joseph, second-in-command in Egypt, was instructed through amazing misadventures to know and to trust in God's providence. When he understood that this providence encompasses everyone and everything, he learned also to trust God in all situations. For this reason alone God allowed Pharaoh's cupbearer—whom Joseph asked to remember him before Pharaoh when he would be freed from their shared prison—to forget about Joseph entirely, only to remember him after two years had passed. God allowed this strange lapse in memory, because through it Joseph learned not to trust in human aid and love, but to trust only in the mercy of God, and to thank God alone for his liberation from prison (see Genesis 40–41).

St John Chrysostom said,

Think about the fact that after the return of the cupbearer, two years had passed. For it seemed good to God to wait for a better time, so that Joseph would be freed from prison with even greater honor and glory. If the cupbearer remembered Joseph before Pharaoh's dream, Joseph would have been immediately freed, but Joseph's virtue would not have become obvious and glorified by all. But now the almighty and all-wise God, knowing, as the perfect Artist, how much time gold must remain in the fire to be purified, allowed the cupbearer to forget for two years, until the time came for Pharaoh's oracular dream, when necessity itself forced him to remember Joseph as a talented interpreter of dreams. Thus was Joseph's virtue glorified in all Pharaoh's kingdom.

Here is the reason for the great reverence that Joseph held for God's will, the reason for his boundless gratitude to God. He ascribed all of his life's misfortunes not to the hatred of his brothers but to the will of God, for through him God wanted to prevent the deaths of his father, his brothers, and many other people in the coming terrible famine. Joseph said as much himself: "you meant evil against me; but God meant it for good, in order to bring it about as it is this day, to save many people alive" (Genesis 50:20).

How zealously did Noah and Joseph strive to fulfill the will of God! We see the same submission to His will in all the holy chosen ones of God. All of them are worthy of these words: "They first gave themselves to the Lord, and then to us by the will of God" (2 Corinthians 8:5).

II

St Polycarp of Smyrna (69–155 A.D.), whom the pagan authorities pursued many times, was informed of God's providence concerning him and thus was able to escape persecution for a long time. Later, even though he had the time and opportunity to escape a martyr's death, he accepted death for Christ willingly, saying that the time had come to stop running and may the Lord's will be done. He, and many other martyrs, truly defeated the fierce hatred of the godless persecutors, even though it seemed impossible to win them to Christ's side by either kind words or intelligent reasoning. Blessed Augustine gave the following advice concerning victory over those who oppose Christ God: "Let not our own will hold us back on this path of life, nor let the cruelty of others terrify us, for the evil world will be defeated in any case, whether it speaks kindly to us or rages at us."

Everyone who ardently believes in God's providence for the world—and who truly sees the workings of this unsleeping eye in the history of the world—will disregard all slander, rebukes, dishonor, or vilification, accepting them as the noise of the enemy, as rocks and arrows cast from a great distance, which fall to the earth without harming anyone.

Here is another example of such firm trust in God. A certain chaste, modest young woman, who had developed many Christian virtues, lived quietly and was content with spiritual pleasures. One time an unknown woman dressed as a beggar visited her, commanding her to ask anything of the All-Pure Theotokos, and she would receive it. The young woman humbly answered that all she wished was for everything to happen to her as God willed. Her only consolation was the will of God.

The Empress Eudoxia, the wife of Arcadius, the Roman Emperor (fourth century), was unworthy of praise for many reasons.[106] However, in one thing she acted honorably. When her son became grievously ill, she invited the Archbishop of Cyprus, Epiphanios, to pray for the healing of his body. The bishop promised to do it, but under one condition. The heretic Dioscorus had to be exiled from the city. The empress answered, "If God wills my son to live, he will live; if He Who gave my son to me desires to take Him back, then let His will be done." Such a submission will be firm and enduring if it is founded on the knowledge of God's providence.

III

All the saints of God tried to understand the workings of God's providence in all things, for this knowledge brings about undoubting trust in God. From trust they labored to achieve the sweetest submission of their will to God's will and to strengthen themselves in this accord day by day. Finally, they strove to make their will submit to God's not by compulsion but as a free union, because only in this did they find the greatest consolation and blessings. The saints of God achieved such blessedness even in this earthly life.

Nothing can be repugnant to the person who understands that everything that happens by God's will occurs also by his own, since the union with God's will is so complete. Therefore, the Holy Fathers had a praiseworthy custom to ascribe everything to God's providence and His holy will, no matter what occurred in the world, no matter what the immediate causes of these events.

Joseph's brothers were cruel and simple men. However, they deserve praise for being honest with money. When the money they used to buy wheat from Egypt appeared in their packs on the way back, they were horrified and said, "What is this God has done to us?" (Genesis 42:28). These words need to be examined thoroughly. What did God do to them? Who among us would not instead have said, "This is an obvious attempt by the Egyptians to entrap us. They want to destroy us, and so they arranged this apparent thievery!" But no, they did not consider that the money could have accidentally been placed in their packs or placed there as alms by a merciful Egyptian, seeing their poverty. They did not think that this was the action of a shrewd Egyptian businessman who wanted to encourage them to return to Egypt to buy more grain. No, they openly said, "What is this God has done to us?" They understood that no matter what the immediate cause of the return of this money—entrapment, mistake, or alms—God made it happen to punish them for selling Joseph. For without the will of the Lord, not a single particle of dust will fall from a mountain, not a single hair will fall from your head, not a single leaf will fall from a tree, not a single bird will tumble from the sky.

Oftentimes, when we do ourselves harm, we blame the instrument that hurt us—the stick that we handled badly or the pen with which we wrote something incorrect—without thinking about the Hand that directs our hand. God's hand arranged everything. In order to better understand that in all events God is the ultimate organizer, ruling and completing all things, let us offer the words of Christ Himself and His saints.

IV

Jesus Christ, during His preaching to the people concerning the providence of God for the salvation of the world, was enraptured by the sweet flame of love for His Heavenly Father and exclaimed in ecstasy, "I thank You, Father, Lord of heaven and earth, that You have hidden these things from the wise and prudent and have revealed them to babes. Even so, Father, for so it seemed good in Your sight" (Matthew 11:25–26). This, O My Father, is how well You arranged all things. No one living can find anything to rebuke or condemn in Your arrangement of the world, for so it seemed good in Your sight.

This is how sweetly Christ teaches us not to place limits on God's authority, not to test the judgments of God, not to condemn the revelation and commandments of God. Instead, we must be content with this alone: "for so it seemed good in Your sight." Why it seemed good, Christ does not say, for God's reasons cannot be defined or tested by men. Instead of many thousands of reasons, one is enough for us: "It pleased God thus." The will of divine providence is the greatest unchangeable law by which all occurs in the moral and physical world. Therefore, we are obliged to submit definitively to this law as to God's will, which cares for the good of His faithful. Whether you will suffer or be delivered from sufferings, you should emulate Christ your Saviour, crying aloud together with Him, "Even so, Father, for so it seemed good in Your sight."

Repeat these words both in want and in prosperity, both in waking and in sleep, both in health and in illness. And when you die, say this: "Lord, I do not want to oppose You in anything. You know this, Lord, and so let it be as You will, as You chastise, as You allow. Let Your holy, wise, true, and righteous will be done in me today and for all time." One of the ancient Fathers of the Church had the custom of praying in these words: "Son of God! Son of God! In whatever way You know and desire, save me, Son of God!"

A Christian should pray, with his heart, and fulfill all by God's commandments. Here is another prayer:

> O All-good Jesus! You so loved me that You gave Yourself up to the anger of the torturers for the sake of my salvation, allowing Yourself to be crucified on the Cross. What sort of a trial will it be for me if I, a sinner, give myself to Your Fatherly hands, and not the hands of the torturers? I know without a doubt that everything happens in my life for my own benefit. Do with me, O Lord, everything that is pleasing in Your sight, for everything is Yours and there is no man who can oppose Your will, "As it seemed good to the Lord, so also it came to pass. Blessed be the name of the Lord." (Job 1:21)

This is how the Old Testament righteous men [and women] prayed. Tobit, prayerfully turning to God, said, "Now do with me as is best before You" (Tobit 3:6). Judith commanded us to pray, saying, "Let us call upon Him to help us, and if it pleases Him He will hear our voice" (Judith 8:17).

V

The Apostle Paul said, "He who is joined to the Lord is one spirit with Him" (1 Corinthians 6:17). This does not mean that we become one in nature with Him, but it does refer to the union of the human will with the divine. You say, "If God wishes for my parents to die, how can I possibly desire to see their passing from this world? Or if God wants to deprive me or them of the heavenly kingdom, must I want the same thing?"

Listen! God sends death to your father and mother not only in order to cease the flow of their life and to preserve the laws of nature, and these things you should certainly desire to see upheld. Try to understand likewise God's desiring to remove you from the eternal blessedness and send you to hell. He wishes this not because He wishes evil on you, but in order to punish evil and preserve His justice. Therefore, it is proper for you to desire the evil in your own self to be punished. It is useful to remember the words of a certain teacher on this subject:

> If you will be ready every hour to follow the will of God and submit to it in all things, then you will receive forgiveness of your sins and you will become worthy of such grace that not only will you not fear

the fires of hell, but you will not even fear the aerial tollhouses. This offering of your own self to the will of God is equal to, and sometimes replaces, repentance, penances, and almsgiving.

Why should we oppose the will of God when all of nature bows to it? Is man alone so great that he should refuse to obey God's will? Such refusal completely destroys man's honor and dignity, and so, let it never be! God approves and arranges the end of everything. Let us then also fulfill God's dispensation concerning our own life by examining His providence and submitting our own will to His divine will. This is the calling of our moral freedom. But, alas! We are very weak and we bitterly complain and moan at the least physical discomfort.

True are the words of Seneca: "How can a man who never accepts God's will with a good and grateful heart become obedient to God? Such a person complains at God's rule over the world, becomes a loquacious interpreter of his own misfortunes, and collapses under the smallest weight of affliction and unpleasantness." When God allows any sorrow that terrifies the weak powers of our soul, we must emulate Christ all the more in His submission to the will of His Father: "Not my will, but Yours, be done" (Luke 22:42). Here is true self-rejection; here is true commitment of self-will to the will of God; here is obedience that sets aside the need to make the correct choice and prevents our corrupt will from disagreeing with the will of God.

A Short Biography of the author of The Sunflower, St John Maximovich, Archbishop of Chernigov and Metropolitan of Tobolsk

St John Maximovich was bishop of Chernigov after St Theodosius of Uglich; he was the son of a Polish nobleman named Maxim Vasil'kovskii (named after his home town of Vasil'kovo). Maxim liked to call himself *pecherskii* (of the caves), acknowledging that he was able to support himself financially by renting land and a mill from the Kiev Caves Lavra. Six of his sons served as ensigns, captains, and scribes in the Cossack army, but the eldest (John Maximovich) followed a different path.

St John's father and ancestors came from the city of Uman' (Kiev region). His father eventually moved to the city of Nezhin, situated near the land he rented from the Lavra, and here the future saint was born in the middle of seventeenth century. According to the words of His Eminence Eugene, Metropolitan of Kiev, the future saint was educated in the Kiev Theological Academy and later remained there to teach. Here he was also tonsured a monk by Hegumen Gisel' of the Lavra with the name John, after which he was given the responsibility of preaching to the academicians. Soon afterward, he was put in charge of the Lavra's finances. In 1678, when Turkey threatened to attack Ukraine, Hieromonk John Maximovich was sent as an emissary to Moscow to beg the Tsar to help the monks of the Lavra in case of an attack by the Turks on Kiev. He also asked the Tsar to grant them a monastery as a shelter in case they had to leave Kiev. The Tsar, having sent a strong army, assigned the Svenskii Monastery (three *versts*[107] from Briansk) for their use, naming Hieromonk John as the monastery's abbot.

Archbishop Theodosius of Uglich wanted his future replacement to the See of Chernigov to first become abbot of the Eletsk Monastery. He was on good terms with Fr John, then the abbot of the Svenskii Monastery, while in Kiev; therefore, after conferring with the civil authorities, Archbishop Theodosius invited Fr John (in 1695) to join him, elevating him to the rank of archimandrite and assigning him to be the abbot of the Eletsk Monastery. Archbishop Theodosius, having matured in the spiritual life through long ascetic labors, died on February 5, 1696. The humble archimandrite of the Eletsk Monastery, Fr John, zealously fulfilled the will and instructions of his archbishop until his last breath. Archbishop Theodosius of Chernigov was buried on the right side of the Church of Sts Boris and Gleb in a crypt specially prepared by Fr John. Soon afterward, on November 24, the Rada of Ukraine (a legislative body) gathered in the home of the archbishop in order to choose his successor. Representatives were present from the Kiev Metropolia and the Hetman of Ukraine. Despite various differences of opinion and grievances, the white and black clergy[108] assembled were unanimous in their choice of Fr John as Archbishop Theodosius's successor. An official petition was sent to Moscow along with Fr John. The Hetman wrote a personal letter to the Tsar and the patriarch, begging them to consecrate Fr John. Fr John was elevated to the rank of bishop on January 10, 1697. The Tsar also confirmed the diocese's continued land holdings.

Bishop John was a model archpastor. His life, according to Metropolitan Philaret of Moscow, shone with exalted virtues, especially humility and prayer. This was clearly visible in his many writings. The language Bishop John used contained many words and expressions taken from Latin, Polish, and local dialects. He wrote syllabic verses in a style typical of South Russians of that time. Despite this, their content makes them worthy of careful reading, since they are full of genuine piety and instructive and pithy wisdom. The best monument to his love for spiritual learning was the Chernigov Seminary that he established first as a collegium (i.e., a high school) that educated not only the sons of priests but also nobles, Cossacks, and merchants. Living an exemplary virtuous life, Archbishop John wrote spiritual literature with unflagging energy, all in the style of his time.

Here is a list of his published works:

1. *A Mirror of Moral Instruction* (Chernigov, 1703 and 1707)
2. *An Alphabet of Saints* (verses, Chernigov, 1705)
3. *O Theotokos Virgin* (verses, Chernigov, 1705)

4. *An Interpretation of the Fiftieth Psalm* (sent in 1708, along with the two previously mentioned writings and a personal letter, to the Tsar)
5. *Thoughts on the Lord's Prayer* (verses, Chernigov, 1709)
6. *The Eight Beatitudes of the Gospel* (verses, Chernigov, 1709)
7. *The Royal Path of the Cross* (Chernigov, 1709)
8. *Mindfulness of God* (Chernigov, 1710–11)
9. *The Sunflower* (Chernigov, 1714)

We cannot omit two other events in the life of Archbishop John of Chernigov that impressed on him the utter necessity of giving up his will entirely to God's. As a result of the first, the crypt of Archbishop Theodosius was opened, and as a result of the second, his own honor and life were saved from a slanderous accusation of treason against his Tsar and his country.

The first event was a protracted and serious illness that left him completely wasted away. Finally, he prayed to his predecessor Archbishop Theodosius, who immediately appeared to the sick bishop to reveal God's mercy. He miraculously healed him, saying, "Do not sorrow, brother, the Lord has heard your prayers and gives you health. Rise from your bed and prepare yourself to serve a liturgy of thanksgiving tomorrow morning. Let this be a sign for you!" Archbishop John, having awoken from this miraculous dream, stood up from his bed and called his cell attendant.

"Go to the abbot and tell him that today I will serve a liturgy. Let everything be made ready," he said.

All were amazed, thinking that Vladika John was feverishly hallucinating, until the sight of their physically and mentally healthy prelate convinced them. As a result of this miracle, Archbishop John ordered that the crypt of Blessed Theodosius be opened. He had his icon painted and wrote a poem of thanksgiving on the icon itself:

Theodosius, you gift of God, from Uglich called,
By God you were gifted an Archbishop to Chernigov
In your long life you saw little evil
And soon you were found worthy of the bridal chamber of heaven.
On earth you appeared to all as an angel in the flesh,
And you are raised to the heights like a second Paul.
Your incorrupt relics are a witness—
Let him who doubts but see!—in the tomb is the proof.
In the one thousand six hundred ninety sixth year

You reposed after a holy life,
In this life you placed me in Eletsk
To be abbot, from that life you left me this cathedral,
This same John to be Archbishop.
And now you exult in the seraphic flock,
O High Priest of God, O Holy Theodosius!
As I ascend your throne, all say: who is this man?
Truly I am not a worthy monk,
But by your prayers I will become one.

The second event was an implication, as a result of slander and hatred, in the betrayal of Hetman Mazepa against Tsar Peter I.

Mazepa, angry at those who did not act according to his orders, decided to relay false accusations against the innocent hierarch to Peter I, and by the tsar's unjust reprisal, to incite discontent with his reign. Mazepa instructed the Cossack Parkhomenko to publicly declare that he was his emissary and, held letters to Archbishop John and to several local military leaders, and that the letter to the archbishop was given to him by his own clerics. When the Cossack was captured, he continued to repeat the same story even in the presence of those who were accused (i.e., the archbishop and the military leaders), but Peter I drew the truth out of him, and their innocence was established.

Tsar Peter the Great, desiring an ever-greater spread of the Holy Faith among the pagan nations of Siberia, could find no more capable archpastor than Archbishop John, and in March 1712, an imperial ukase transferred Archbishop John from the diocese of Chernigov to the Metropolia of Siberia. However, the aged metropolitan only served his Siberian flock for three years, reposing in the Lord on June 10, 1715. He was buried in the Tobolsk Cathedral of the Divine Wisdom.

NOTES

Discerning the Will of God and Conforming to It

1. Blessed Jerome (ca. 347–420), best known for his translation of the Bible into Latin, the Vulgate.
2. *The City of God*, Book IV, Ch 18.
3. This is a reference to the siege of Jerusalem in 70 A.D. by the Roman General and future emperor Titus, recorded in Flavius Josephus's "The Jewish Wars," Book 5, Ch 12.4: "However, when Titus, in going his rounds along those valleys, saw them full of dead bodies, and the thick putrefaction running about them, he gave a groan; and, spreading out his hands to heaven, called God to witness that this was not his doing; and such was the sad case of the city itself."
4. Blessed Lupus of Troyes, a fifth-century Bishop of Troyes in modern-day France. He saved his city from destruction by a barbarian army.
5. See Jeremiah 34.
6. Lived 540–604 A.D.; Pope of Rome from 590 to 604 A.D.
7. See Job 1:21.

Why Does God Allow Evil?

8. See Genesis 36–47 and 1 Kingdoms 19–24·
9. See Daniel 6:1–25.
10. See Matthew 26:57–68; Mark 14:55–65; Luke 22:66–71; John 18:19–24.
11. See Genesis 39–41; Daniel 6; Luke 23:39–43; Luke 24:50–53 and Mark 16:19–20.

How to Recognize God's Will in His Inscrutable Judgments

12. See Genesis 40.
13. Athanasius: Select Works and Letters, Life of Antony, §59. Of the two brethren, and how one perished of thirst. https://www.ccel.org/ccel/schaff/npnf204.xvi.ii.xxiii.html
14. Saying 2 in Sayings of St Anthony the Great.
15. Genesis 19:1–25.

How to Determine God's Will in All Events and Actions

16. See Matthew 19:16–30; Mark 10:17–31; Luke 18:18–30.
17. See Matthew 1:18–25.
18. See Matthew 2:12.
19. See Genesis 18:1–8; Genesis 16:7–14.

How God's Will Is Revealed in Jesus Christ, and How We Can Conform Ourselves to It

20. These are two different people and the author seems uncertain as from which the teaching he is recollecting originates. Cassiodorus was born about 50 years after the repose of St John Cassian in 435 A.D.
21. Genesis 3:19.

How Can Human Will Become Pleasing and Worthy of Union with God's Will?

22. King of Persia from 465 to 425 B.C.
23. A pagan, stoic philosopher who lived from 55 to 135 A.D.

How Human Will Can Conform to Divine Will in Various Everyday Circumstances

24. Lived ca. 340–450 A.D. He was a monk in Egypt and a spiritual guide for many monks.
25. Lived ca. 360–435 A.D. He was a monk and theologian known for writings and his influence on monasticism.
26. Lived ca. 125–180 A.D. He was a satirist and rhetorician.
27. Lived ca. 4 B.C.–65 A.D.

Which Signs Indicate That Our Will Agrees with God's Will?

28. Died ca. 375 A.D. He was a disciple of St Anthony the Great.

Is It Possible to Avoid Sorrow Entirely?

29. Lived 65 to 8 B.C. He was a lyric poet in the time of Augustus.
30. Live 470 to 399 B.C. He was a classical Greek philosopher, one of the founders of Western philosophy. After being found guild of impiety and corrupting the youth of Athens, he was sentenced to death by Hemlock poison.

Fashioning One's Will to God's Is a Pleasing Sacrifice to God

31. See 1 Kingdoms 1:8–28.
32. Tradition teaches that Sts Joachim and Anna took the Mother of God to the Temple when she was three and left her there to reside in the Temple.
33. Also known as St Gregory Nazianzen, ca. 329–290 A.D.
34. Lived ca. 450–404 B.C. He was an Athenian statesman and general; he was a student of Socrates. While Aeschines was a poor man his gift of himself made his real wealth surpass that of Socrates' other student Alcibiades.
35. St Epictetus (not to be confused with the pagan Epictetus mentioned elsewhere in this text) was a wonderworker and brought many to Christ, including St Astion. They were martyred in 290 A.D.
36. Lived 295–392 A.D. He was a Desert Father and disciple of St Anthony the Great.

37. Lived 292–384 A.D. He was a Desert Father and founder of cenobitic monasticism.
38. See Exodus 13:21–22.

Conforming the Human Will with the Will of God Is the Greatest Good in Life

39. This is not a direct quotation from the Gospel of Luke, but rather a creative retelling and adaptation of it by the author.
40. Lived ca. 524–460 B.C. He was an Athenian politician and naval strategist, who was influential in the defeat of the Persians in 480 B.C.
41. Brocard, a Catholic monk of the twentieth century, was in the first group of hermits at Mt Carmel.
42. ca. 575–641 A.D.; emperor of the Byzantine Empire from 610 to 641.

The Agreement of the Human Will with the Divine Is Truly Heaven on Earth, the Only Genuine Blessedness in Life

43. ca. 480–542, known for the "Rule of St Benedict," precepts for monks.

What Prevents Us from Living According to God's Will

44. A Flemish Benedictine monk and writer.
45. See Matthew 2:13–15.

The Dangers of Irrational, Unrestrained, and Deeply Rooted Self-Will

46. A gallows with a projecting arm at the top, from which the bodies were left suspended after execution.
47. See 3 Kingdoms 17:6.
48. See Matthew 27:51.
49. Trebellius Pollio wrote part of *Historia Augusta*, a collection of the lives of Roman emperors. He wrote during the reign of St Constantine. Marcus Aurelius Marius reigned in 269 A.D.
50. See http://www.newadvent.org/fathers/1801101.htm. Note that Psalm 100 in the Septuagint Greek Old Testament is Psalm 101 in the Hebrew text.
51. Cassian, John. 1985. *John Cassian: Conferences*. New York: Paulist Press. Conference 14.7.
52. ca. 155–240 A.D. He was a prolific early Christian author, an apologist, and a critic of Gnosticism.
53. Of Patience, Chapter 14.
54. This seems to be loosely drawn from the chapter of Tertullian cited in the previous note.
55. Acts 12:23.

How Our Will Can Become Obedient to the Will of God in All Things, Even in That Which We Do Not Desire

56. See Matthew 26:36–39; Mark 14:32–36; Luke 22:39–42.

Factors That Incline Us to Disobey God

57. ca. 427–347 B.C. Greek philosopher, student of Socrates, and teacher of Aristotle.
58. See 4 Kingdoms 25:27–30, LXX.

We Must Be Ready to Reject Ourselves and Submit Our Will to God Both during Times of Trouble and in the Hour of Our Death

59. A Vandal king who reigned from 428 to 477 A.D.
60. See 2 Chronicles 16:12–13.
61. See 4 Kingdoms 20:1–11, LXX.

The Agreement between Human and Divine Will Cannot Occur without Complete Trust in God

62. Sir Thomas More (1478–1535) opposed King Henry VIII's separation from the Catholic Church. Because he refused to take the Oath of Supremacy, acknowledging the monarch as the Supreme Head of the Church of England, More was convicted of treason and beheaded.
63. See also Matthew 14:31–21; Mark 6:30–44; Luke 9:10–17.

The Essence of Trust in God

64. For the account concerning Jehoshaphat, see 3 Kingdoms 22:41–47.

How the Saints Trusted God

65. See Judges 7.
66. See Jeremiah 41.
67. A play on the famous Latin expression attributed to Julius Caesar "veni, vidi, vici," which translates "I came, I saw, I conquered."
68. See Daniel 3:19–90.
69. The original text cites this section as Tobit 2:15–18, but this is clearly incorrect.

The Many and Diverse Gifts That God Gives to Those Who Trust in Him

70. See Exodus 14.
71. Eusebius (260/265–339/340 A.D.) was bishop of Caesarea in 314 A.D. and was a biblical scholar. His *Ecclesiastical History* recounts the development of the Church from the first to fourth centuries.
72. This seems to be St John's summation of Job's speeches rather than an exact citation.

Trust in God Weakens and Dies without Acknowledgment of His Providence

73. This appears to be a reference to Maximilian, the Holy Roman Emperor (1508–1519).
74. See Exodus 16.
75. See 4 Kingdoms 13:20–21, LXX.
76. See Exodus 2:5–10.
77. See 3 Kingdoms 22:34–35, LXX; 2 Chronicles 18:33.
78. According to Ammianus Marcellinus, *Res Gestae*, 25.3.6, Julian was pierced by a spear in battle with the Persians on June 26, 363 A.D. He died of this wound. There are several different accounts of his wounding including an arrow and a knife.
79. See John 4:4–26.
80. An Egyptian Desert Father, d. 466 A.D.
81. See Genesis 28:10–22.

How Greatly God Provides for All Our Needs in Life

82. St Mark the Ascetic lived in the fifth century. Three of his surviving discourses can be found in vol. 1 of the *Philokalia*.
83. See 3 Kingdoms 17:1–7, LXX.
84. See 3 Kingdoms 17:8–16, LXX.
85. See 3 Kingdoms 19: 5–8, LXX.
86. A female deer.
87. Once an independent kingdom Brittany comprises the peninsula in the northwest corner of France.
88. A seventh-century monastic in France.

God's Providence for the Righteous

89. See 1 Kingdoms 23:23–27, LXX.
90. See Genesis 37:11–28.
91. See Genesis 39.

God's Providence for Friends and Enemies

92. See 1 Chronicles 10:8–9.
93. See Daniel 3; 2 Maccabees 7.
94. See Matthew 26:69–75; Mark 14:54, 66–72; Luke 22:54–62; John 18:15–18, 25–27.
95. See John 20:24–29.
96. Perhaps drawn from Psalm 39:6.

Concerning Widespread Doubt or Weak Faith in God

97. See Matthew 14:22–33.
98. This anecdote is based on the incorrect supposition that elephants cannot bend their legs and, therefore, cannot lie down. This description of elephants can be found in several sources from the Late Roman empire and medieval times, including the *Physiologus* and works by Pliny the Elder and St Ambrose.
99. See Jonah 4:6–8.
100. Haman's plot to kill the Jews is foiled by Queen Esther, and "Haman was hung on the gallows he had prepared for Mordecai" (Esther 7:10).
101. See Genesis 32:6–32.
102. See 3 Kingdoms 21:16–30, LXX.
103. See 2 Chronicles 14.
104. For the ancient Latins fortune was personified as the Goddess Fortuna, known as Tyche to the pagan Greeks.

Knowledge of God's Providence Leads to Greater Trust in God, and This Trust Gives Birth to Agreement with God and His Holy Will

105. See Genesis 6:9–7:16.
106. She instigated the exile of St John Chrysostom from Constantinople.

A Short Biography of the author of The Sunflower, St John Maximovich, Archbishop of Chernigov and Metropolitan of Tobolsk

107. A *verst* is about 1.1 km (0.66 mile).

108. White clergy refers to parish, or secular, priests; black clergy to monk-priests.

SUBJECT INDEX

SCRIPTURE INDEX

The Old Testament

The New Testament